ACADEMIC MUSINGS
THE LEGACY OF THE EURO-MÉDITERRANÉE

A Festschrift in Celebration of
the Reverend Doctor Thomas H. Curran

EDITED BY

Peter Bryson

Susan Dodd

Neil Robertson

ISBN: 978-1-988908-16-8
First published by Underhill Books in 2019.

Underhill Books
4183 Murray Harbour Road
RR#3 Belfast PE C0A 1A0

Cover Images:
The Rape of Europa, Valentin Serov, 1910.
The Evening, Caspar David Friedrich, 1820-21.

Time present and time past
Are both perhaps present in time future,
And time future contained in time past.
—T.S. Eliot

If by metaphysics we mean those truths of the pure reason which always transcend, and not seldom appear to contradict, the understanding, or (in the words of the great Apostle) spiritual verities which can only be spiritually discerned—and this is the true and legitimate meaning of metaphysics, [*metà tà physikà*]—then I affirm, that this very controversy … in which both are partially right in what they affirm, and both wholly wrong in what they deny, is a proof that without metaphysics there can be no light of faith.

—Samuel Taylor Coleridge

There are only two tragedies in life: one is not getting what one wants, and the other is getting it.

—Oscar Wilde

ACKNOWLEDGEMENTS

Approaching Tom Curran's current and former colleagues, students, friends, and family to participate in this project has resulted in a cornucopia of offerings. We hope Tom and other readers will be both surprised and delighted by this "rich and strange" collection. The editors of this volume would like to thank the many contributors for their thoughtful—in every sense of that word—offerings.

This volume began its journey as a splendid idea in the mind and heart of Kara Holm. She has supported its production (and its distracted editors) throughout.

We also offer deeps thanks to Dr. Victoria Goddard of Underhill Books for her work and vision, essential to bringing this project to bookish reality.

Readers will be interested to know that some contributions could not be contained in a printed volume. We thank Elisabeth Stones and Garth MacPhee for their musical gift, which readers can find at www.tomcurranfyp.com, along with other content.

It is important to recognize that no single volume could possibly contain all of the Reverend Doctor's interests and influences. One of the most marked qualities of Tom's engagement with the world is his enthusiasm and openness for ideas, people and experiences.

We are all grateful to the people who have supported and inspired Tom throughout his life: his parents Rosi and Stanley, his beloved late wife Jane, their children Martin (Emma), Veronica (Thomas) and Rozzi, his brother Patrick and sister-in-law Lucille, current and former Colleagues and students, and his many friends. Tom often speaks of gratitude so we close these acknowledgements with Tom's own words to this year's graduates from King's.

> [We] owe it to ourselves, not to others, to be grateful for what we have received, and of which we aren't the authors. If we are lucky, we are guardians of something that has been given to us. Obviously, I think of mothers and fathers. Obviously, I think of siblings who have enriched our lives. Obviously I think of children we may have known. Obviously, I think of the teacher who taught me grammar and the English language so I could express myself. And obviously I think of this College which has meant so much to so many of us—an institution, into which we are embedded and matriculated, not its authors but its guardians.
>
> —Tom Curran, October 7, 2018

—The Editors

Contents

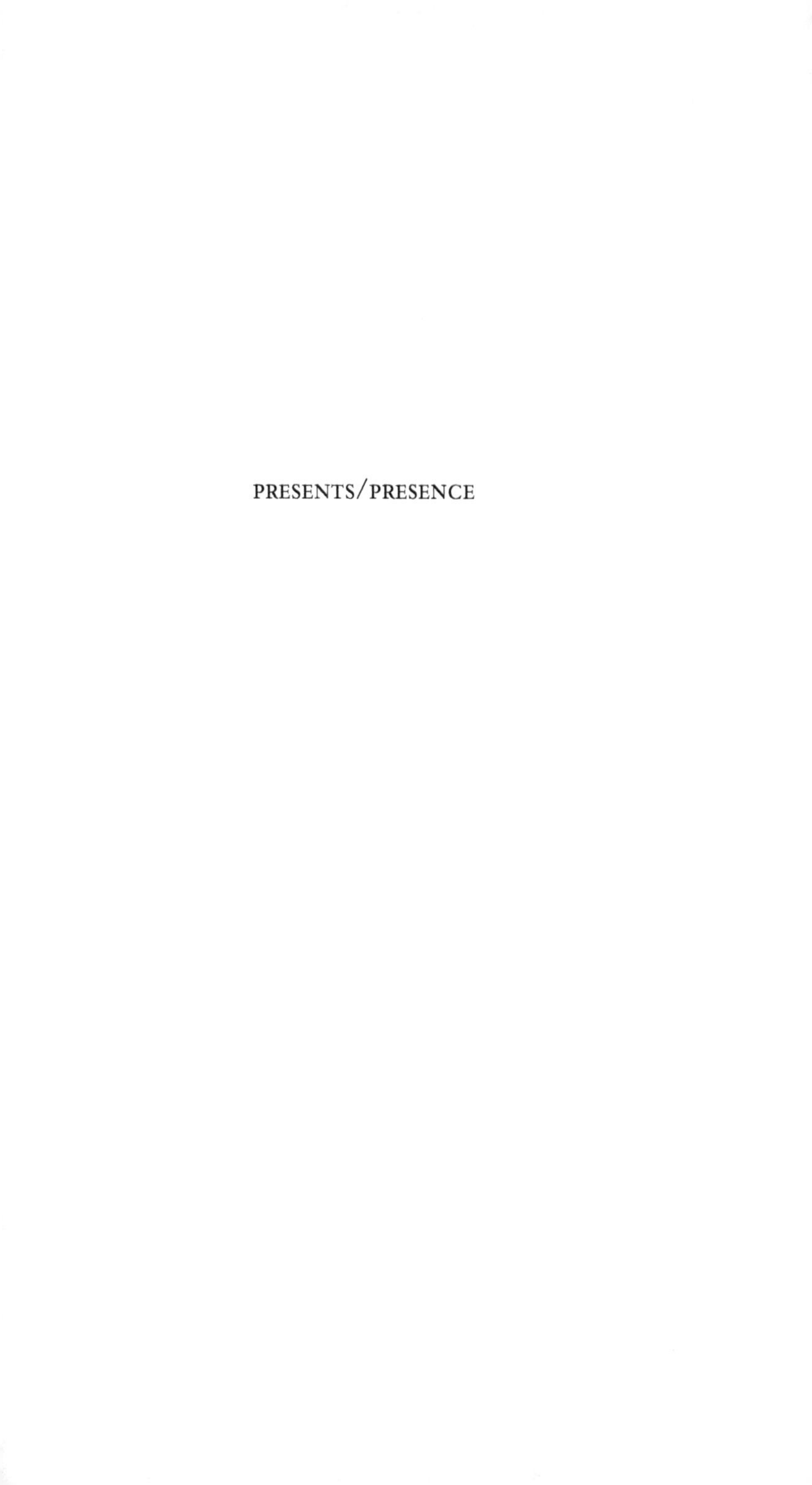

PRESENTS/PRESENCE

WILLIAM LAHEY

Top Ten

May 18, 2019

Being the President of King's, I should be able to do better than produce a "top 10 list" when asked to share a few thoughts in honour of the esteemed Rev. Dr. Thomas Curran on the occasion of his 70th birthday. But a top ten list is what I have come up with, hoping it conveys a little of my admiration, appreciation and affection for Tom.

I am grateful for the life I lead living and working at King's. A primary reason is that I can now say Tom Curran is a friend. Here are some of what make me grateful for that friendship:

1. How he made Kathryn and I feel welcomed, when my suitability for the role of President was for everyone, myself included, unproven and probably doubtful to many.

2. The assistance and encouragement he has generously given to help me be a useful President for King's, while I learned from within the deep end how to be a useful President for King's … as someone who never quite got the knack of swimming.

3. Keeping me optimistic about King's and its future—by epitomizing and embodying so much of what makes King's a truly distinctive university … and by always complimenting me on my optimism, which reminds me to stay optimistic.

4. The education he has provided to me to make up for some of the gaps in my own on many things, including Dante, Nietzsche, theatre and movies, some of which I do not now have to see given how much I know about them from listening to Tom.

5. He gives sermons every Sunday that make me want to listen to more of his sermons, including because they teach me so much about Dante, Nietzsche, theatre and movies! I haven't felt this way about sermons in many years. His allow me to (sort of) keep up with FYP when I can't make it to the lectures—and to understand its grand architecture better than I would otherwise. They give me insights to think upon for the rest of each Sunday and beyond.

6. He likes action movies, NFL football and maintains a very clever blog on which he displays capacious knowledge of contemporary culture, all of which seem surprising and out-of-character until you learn these and other things about Tom that you find surprising and out-of-character.

7. He is "relatable" for his students not by being "relatable" but being authentically different from what they otherwise have the opportunity to experience. In this and in so many other ways, he calls on them to become their better selves and, from what I can tell, they answer the call.

8. He is the keeper of the flame for the distinctive King's

sense of occasion and ceremony, including at meetings of Convocation, for grand functions in Prince Hall, and at Encaenia, whether or not the President or others are doing their part to live up to the expectations of the occasion.

9. He loves good food, fine wine, generous company and edifying conversation. His curiosity about the world and what is happening in and to the world is without limit, as is his ability to be more up-to-date on everything than anyone. He is fun—and funny—to be with.

10. He honours his father and his mother—and parents in general, especially mothers. He is devoted to his children. He sometimes almost cries when he is moved by a line in scripture or in the course of preaching or giving a lecture. He gets visibly upset at the things that upset him, all (or most) of which are things that should upset us all.

Thank you for the opportunity to contribute to this collection of tributes to Tom.

Happy birthday Tom.
Your friend and admirer,
—Bill

PETER BRYSON

The Reverend Dr. Thomas H. Curran: A Clerk in Holy Orders

With characteristically unnecessary modesty, Tom tells us how he became so described when his son, Martin, was born:

> When my son was born, Midsummer's Day, now almost exactly twelve years ago, I went to the Registrar in Durham, England […] to provide the necessary details for his birth certificate.[1]

As Tom puts it, he was an Anglican priest without a living, and therefore the "unrighteous" steward. How could he be known?

> Dilettante? Knight-Errant? Mendicant-Scholar? Former College Dean? Future College Chaplain? Nothing seemed to do my new son any credit […][2]

Tom explains that the Registrar relieved his temporary occupational embarrassment by suggesting "Clerk in Holy Orders." And so it was. And this is as it should be, because for Tom his various vocations find appropriate expression in priestly office. The professorial Tom would know that which the clerical Tom believes and celebrates. This priest/professor embraces the Hegelian description of Christian revelation as speculative in the philosophic sense of attaining unity with its opposite.[3]

Relying on the *Lectures on the Philosophy of Religion* Tom repeats the Hegelian affirmation that "in worship, the individual is raised to the thought of God, and is brought into union with God."[4]

But cracks appear between form and content: "[...] the Christian cleric must always become suspicious. What will remain of the Christian truth if it is disembodied from its sensuous trapping?"[5] Tom points out that the Christianity of Hegel's time is self-destructive. Transformation of religion into romantic feeling or historical erudition is the ultimate surrender to the spirit of modernity.

In contrast to Hegel's contemporary, Schleiermacher, Tom tells us that Hegel did not try and separate speculation from piety or describe the practical future of the Christian religion. The Hegelian philosophy has no practical aims. Hegelian speculation may be transformative, but not predictive. Tom concludes by quoting from the *Phenomenology of Spirit*:

> The life of the Spirit is not the life that shrinks from death and keeps itself untouched by devastation, but rather the life that endures it and maintains itself in it.[6]

For Tom, the Hegelian endurance becomes a spiritual insight as Christian suffering. In his article on the Book of Job, Tom laments the resignation (or is it abdication?) of Benedict XVI on February 28, 2013. He contrasts this unfavourably with Princess Elizabeth's affirmation of duty on her 21st birthday when she famously assured us, "I declare before you all that my whole life, whether it be long or short, shall be devoted to your service ..."[7] Tom sees Benedict's resignation as too closely resembling the repudiation of Pope Celestine V in 1294 whom Dante places in the Vestibule of Hell in the third Canto of the *Inferno*. This Great Refusal, Tom tells us, is sometimes associated with Esau or Pontius Pilate (not exactly stellar company). This failure of will is the opposite of the wisdom that comes with suffering described in the Book of Job. And while Tom appreciates that Benedict XVI's ill health and increasing incapacity made him unsuited for the "Office of Chairman of the Board and the CEO of Latin Catholic Church Limited," he maintains the Dantesque criticism of the Great Refusal, reminding us of Nautes' advice to Aeneas in Book Five of the Comedy:

> Whatever fortune may be ours, we must at all times rise above it by enduring it.[8]

Tom concludes:

> Even if he had been lying paralyzed in his bed and unable to fulfill his executive and bureaucratic duties as the Vatican's Head of State, he would still, in my opinion, have been fulfilling his office as the Vicar of Christ. That is one of the issues that makes the reading of the Book of Job worthwhile.[9]

By now it must be obvious that Tom is no ordinary priest. He cannot offer us homiletic advice without invoking philosophical and poetic assistance. Nor can he describe philosophy without resort to Christianity: it is the speculative form of a Christian unity of opposites. His relation to both must be both thought and felt.

Tom enlists his love of music in the cause. Music gives institutional stability to the English Church and its offspring. In an Epiphany homily earlier this year, Tom reports:

> … that the Christian religion, especially in the form it's been practiced in the Church of England is alive and well. This is due in my view largely to the musical tradition of the country since the musicians insist on retaining all aspects of Christianity—ancient, medieval, reformed and modern—in order to have the complete panoply of what it is to be Christian in all ages through all forms of music.

Tom then connects this historical musical sustenance of the Church to her fundamental message and purpose, using a Trinitarian analogy from St. Augustine:

> … memory is the score, "the will" is perfected through … rehearsals and the performance is the "understanding" or Word of God.

Tom concludes by quoting Wigglesworth:

> Both religious buildings and concert halls provide us with an opportunity to enter an enclosed space, in order to discover an infinite one.

Tom describes this as the gift of Epiphany. Few homilists could gather so many rich images and ideas to unite the appetitive and rational in our souls with the universal gift of Epiphany.

Media Man

The University of King's College web posting reveals this "Tomistic" confession:

> Tom is always interested in exploring how modern popular culture and practices can be informed (and reformulated) by reference to the great philosophical and literary tradition that we have inherited from the ancient Greeks.

Tom's latest project is "Fake or Facsimile," found at www.recherché.com. *Recherché*'s webpage elaborates: "Tom Curran's Outtakes, Knock-offs & Do-overs: the Legacy of the Euro-Méditerranée." Notice the legacy of "Euro-Méditerranée." That is telling. The geographic reach has didactic purpose, embracing Ancient, Medieval and Modern; Pagan, Christian and Islam; and sacred and secular; the cultural heritage is thereby implied—and as Tom tells us—appropriated or misappropriated accordingly.

On the *Recherché* webpage a wide array of topics appears ranging from recent posts on Goethe's *Werther*, Dante's *Inferno* to the question of the relationship between handbags and art. Or is it real handbags and real art? One is not sure which.

In part 13 of *Fake or Facsimile* we encounter Parisian semi-couture—the Louis Vuitton (LV) Spring Collection. LV's creative director, Marc Jacobs, rejects the notion that he was producing highly derivative fashion styles. These are subjects and arguments beyond the usual fare of classical, medieval or enlightenment scholars.

With *Bladerunner 2049* we are on firmer ground. Here a post-modern Tom grounds the remake of the Ridley Scott original in the tradition of Shelley's *Frankenstein*: the "monstrous" human and the humanized "monster."

The original protagonist is Bladerunner Rick Deckard, who is in the ironical position of "terminating" "replicants"—humanoid robots—whose principal sin is trying to live like us. Their designer's motto reflects the unattainable contradiction: "more human than human." Tom hardly need remind us of the poignancy of the original film's ending when Deckard is rescued from a fatal fall by the replicant he is trying to kill and whose closest associates he has already "terminated"; a reprise of an earlier scene in which the replicant Rachael shoots one of her own to save Deckard from imminent death. Deckard then flees the perpetually inclement urban decay of Los Angeles with Rachael, to a wild and sunny north. A new Eden?

Tom has always exhibited a disconcerting interest in contemporary "culture." A reasonable proof is Tom's summary:

> Modernism defies precise definition, but significant elements of the genre are fragmentation, dislocation, discontinuity, *ennui*, and perspectivism.[10]

Tom cites Nietzsche, Eliot's *The Waste Land*, Joyce's *Ulysses*, the Cubism of Picasso and Braque as illustrative of these elements. For Nietzsche, there is only a perspective: Eliot is a "grab bag of half-formed and half-remembered quotations." Cubism presents a variety of differing perspectives simultaneously on a two dimensional surface. Tom then rescues us from the nascent dissolution and incipient anarchy of these allusions:

> Modernism has something of very great value to teach us in our attempt to take hold of the divine providence in this Twenty-first Century. Unless we re-establish some connection with the thinking of ancient classical and Christian antiquity … all we shall have left is [quoting Eliot] "the immense panorama of futility and anarchy that is contemporary history"…[11]

Tom then explains that this is really what Eliot and Joyce were doing. For Joyce the mythic connects us to the past; for him Homer's Odyssey was iconic; for Eliot, the Romantic vision of the Holy Grail played that part. Tom exhorts that this deconstructive regeneration has been the history of "the classic" and the Christian religion. He concludes with Eliot by quoting the third priest in *Murder in the Cathedral*: "Even now, in sordid particulars / The eternal design may appear."[12]

Tom observes that the modern must include the ancient; contemporary and classical must be reconciled; high and low culture must have a common message. That explains not only the width and depth of Tom's cultural allusions—but also his fascination with film which arguably plays the role of "low culture." Tom never tires of connecting films with the wider and older iterations of what appear in them. Whether the medium can ultimately sustain the message, can be left to others.

And here we see Tom as a fully modern man; because all these things reflect his interests of reconciling the apparently disparate present and past, thought and feeling, optimistic belief and obstinate despair. The dialectical reconciliation sought is the life we have; not simply what was or impossibly in what may be.

Total Tom

Tom doesn't like to gamble. So he goes to Las Vegas. Not to gamble. Las Vegas is the perfect "fake or facsimile" exemplar. One can stay in Caesar's Palace and view the Casa di Livia; visit Venice; dine French; enjoy a Turkish steam bath; and watch Cirque du Soleil or listen to Celine Dion. And there are no students; at least, not Tom's.

Tom teaches in the Foundation Year Programme. While no fan of the unrelenting revisionist impetus to transform the Programme into the contemporary post-modern, Tom wisely recognizes that he must take the students as he finds them.

Tom is dedicated to his students, painstakingly re-reading and commenting on their musings—worthy or otherwise. Tom wants them to learn and cares that they thrive. And they know it. Student reviews of Tom's teaching invariably repeat a common theme that Tom is the most "caring" professor they have had. This care animates Tom's philosophic purpose. He wants to engage students in the post-modern where he finds them and introduce them to the dialectical reconciliation of past and present by which they may more fully find themselves.

Tom's service to others is informed by his devotion to family. Tom's mother still lives in Hamburg where his British father first discovered his "Rosi" more than 70 years ago. Tom and his brother Patrick both eventually found Halifax where Tom met Jane whom he married soon after. They imparted their common love of German literature to their three children, Martin, Veronica and Rozzi, who all inherited their parents' cultural interests. In 2011, Martin married fellow classicist, Emma, in the King's chapel. Strong familial bonds and a shared faith helped sustain them following Jane's untimely death. All still make regular pilgrimages to see their *materfamilias* in Hamburg. More recently, Tom has welcomed grandson Henry and fiancée Kara to his growing family.

Tom's friends are equally beneficiaries of his generosity of spirit. Concern for others requires imagination about what is appropriate to them. Who hasn't been given a book, an article, or a small gift to further an interest or one's pursuit of it? Who hasn't been asked for a quiet drink or a pastoral coffee when needed? In that reciprocity of friendship, Tom will also turn for support to those able to give it. His service includes facilitating your service. All of this is not simply personal or pedagogical; theological or philosophical. Ultimately these are acts of piety. And there you have him—scholar-priest-professor-family man—and dear friend. Total Tom.

—Peter Bryson, Trinity Term 2019

Endnotes

1. "The Priesthood of all Believers," in "*Take Thou Authority ...": The Theology of the Ordained Ministry in the Church Today* (Charlottetown: St. Peter Publications, 2000), p. 57.

2. *Ibid,* p. 57.

3. "A Priesthood of Speculation," in *Who do you say that I am? The Person and Mission of Jesus Christ* (Charlottetown: St. Peter Publications, 1998), p. 117.

4. *Ibid*, p. 119.

5. *Ibid*, p. 120.

6. *Ibid*, p. 125-126.

7. "Philosophical and Religious Comfort in the Land of Uz", in *The Biblical Job: Comfort, Righteousness and Holiness* (Charlottetown: St. Peter Publications, 2014), p. 15.

8. *Ibid*, p. 14.

9. *Ibid*, p. 15.

10. "Modernism and T. S. Eliot: The Fragments and Sordid Particulars" in *Providence: The Will of God in Human Affairs* (Charlottetown: St Peter Publications, 2004), p. 95.

11. *Ibid*, p. 97

12. *Ibid*, p. 104.

STEVE DOWDEN

Reading as Gift, or: Reading Itself

Ephemeral things are deeper than the eternal ones.

—Imre Kertész

Thoughtful—in both senses of the word—Tom Curran has always been a great giver of books and cds. He likes to share his reading and listening. Over the years I have been the recipient of many such gifts. It seems obvious that now would be a good opportunity to say a few words about all this reading—and in so doing also about the pleasures of reading itself. The phrase is not neutral: Roland Barthes famously championed "writing itself" as a practice and writing as intransitive verb. Oddly, he never had much to say about "reading itself." All these Curran-gifted books are on a wide range of unforeseeable topics and in various genres. Consequently, I will single out just one of them as an exemplar of the experience of reading. It serves this purpose well because it is a book that would otherwise would never have occurred to me to read and would never have read but for the gift of it.

Some years ago, Tom Curran took a trip to Turkey, a place I have never been and, given the natural compression of time, I am progressively less and less likely ever to go to. He returned from his travels full of excitement about the place, enthusiastic especially about the Hagia Sofia, and he pressed on me—with assurances of its many pleasures as a fine read—an out-of-the-way book called *Portrait of a Turkish Family,* written by Irfan Orga. Originally published in 1950 by Gollancz, *Portrait* returned to print in the late 1980s, Eland Books having picked it up for republication. This appealingly out-of-the-way London publishing house specializes in travel writing, both new and forgotten.

The book is a family memoir of the early twentieth century. In 1908 Orga was born into a leisured, wealthy Turkish family in the Ottoman Empire's waning years. What the book is "about," naturally enough, is the family's way of life and then harsh fate in tumultuous times and those times themselves. But what of the book as a reading from the perspective of "reading itself"? You will recall it had been promised as a good read. *Portrait* can be read from the perspective of its view of the time, which is to say: for eye-witness information about history and its first-person account of what it was like to live in and through those times. The historian would sift and sort the information to separate out narrowly subjective impression from objective fact. In the current atmosphere of intellectual life, it would also be easy to imagine an ideologically skeptical view of the very attractive, sensual world of Muslim life in Orga's Turkey before the First World War.

For example, at the age of five, Irfan accompanies his grandmother and her servants for an opulent day at the Hamam: the Turkish Bath, a topos of orientalism. Only girls and women are allowed, and little Irfan, already five, is pressing the upper limit of male eligibility. In a few months' time he will be circumcised, sealing his entry into the strictly male world and closing off a sexual identity that is, as yet, still ambiguous and unformed, or at least not officially declared. The Hamam is an emphatically sensual place:

> When we arrived at the Hamam, the attendants came out to meet us, bowing very deeply to my grandmother but looking a little startled and uncertain when they caught sight of me beside her. They did not make any remark however and led the way to the disrobing room which had been prepared for us. [...] Nobody ever dreamed of taking a bath in under seven or eight hours. The young girls went to show off their pink-and-white bodies to the older women. Usually the mothers of eligible sons were in their minds for this purpose, for these would, it was to be hoped, take the first opportunity for detailing to their sons the finer points of So-and-so's naked body.[1]

These preening girls are not yet thirteen, the preferred age of marriage. However, it would be misleading to suggest Orfan dwells on erotic sensuality. He does not. Rather, the erotic is only one dimension of life's sensuality, which is the memoir's overriding emphasis, also in his prose style itself. He seeks out the vivid and memorable detail, especially those that are ephemeral—such as this now lost culture of the Hamam. In this is a clue to his appeal and his basic theme: it is the small, passing, perishable—even doomed —pleasures of life, which is why the stitch that binds the whole text together is his interest in food, cooking, and eating. Over the course of the book, he lavishes a great deal of attention especially on food and eating, as in this early passage concerning the food prepared by servants to be taken to and enjoyed at the Hamam:

> Poor Hacer ... would look apprehensively as my grandmother critically poked and sniffed at her cooling dolmas, and nine times out of ten she was ordered to prepare fresh ones as those already made were fit only for the Christians to eat. Feride was called in to superintend the making of *kadin-göbegi*, heavy, syrupy doughnuts which when properly

> made are light as air and heaven to eat. I was very fond of *kadin-göbegi* and purposely delayed in the kitchen looking for a chance to steal one of them as they were cooling in the rich syrup. (19)

Orga is not merely describing the world and offering information or taking positions. He is bringing it to life as words that are light as air and delightful to read. The direct appeal to the senses is characteristic of his prose too: light as air and heaven to eat. He would go on after the publication of this memoir to write books of Turkish cookery. But the point here is this: Orga's prose itself is as appetizing, as delicious as the food he portrays.

Is it mere aestheticism to think about the pleasures of reading itself in terms of something as unintellectual as, say, food? It may be aestheticism, but not "mere." Brecht—to name the most obvious example—was contemptuous of what he thought of literature that is culinary, that is, art as the object of thoughtless consumption, and it is easy to see his point. He advocated the critical moralism inherent in aesthetic distance, his *Verfremdungseffekt*. Food cannot be enjoyed and is not nourishing at a distance (and surely this can also be said of literature). Yet at least since Kant we also speak unselfconsciously of taste in art and literature with hardly a second thought to the metaphorical character of the term. No doubt Brecht, too, hoped to inculcate a taste for his critical theater in the public of his time, his distaste for the merely culinary notwithstanding.

Kafka and Baudelaire can offer prooftexts for the line of thought I am seeking to develop: defending a taste for the pleasures of reading. It is an aestheticism, too, but not one that is trivial. Here is a classic passage from Baudelaire's essay on Constantin Guy, "The Painter of Modern Life." His taste for ephemeral fashions is akin to the transient pleasure of good eating:

> Modernity is the transient, the fleeting, the contingent; it is one half of art, the other being the eternal and the immovable. There was a form of modernity for every painter of the past; the majority of the fine portraits that remain to us from former times are clothed in the dress of their own day. They are perfectly harmonious works because the dress, the hairstyle, and even the gesture, the expression and the smile (each age has its carriage, its expression and its smile) form a whole, full of vitality. You have no right to despise this transitory fleeting element, the metamorphoses of which are so frequent, nor to dispense with it. If you do, you inevitably fall into the emptiness of an abstract and indefinable beauty, like that of the One and only woman of the time before the Fall. If for the dress of the day, which is necessarily right, you substitute another, you are guilty of a piece of nonsense that only a fancy-dress ball imposed by fashion can excuse. Thus the goddesses, the nymphs, and sultanas of the eighteenth century are portraits in the spirit of their day.[2]

This passage is Baudelaire's famous adumbration of modernism. To be modern, he says, is to take note, relish, and understand the evanescent realities. This does not mean that the old masters were dead to the ephemeral. Think of the *memento mori* still-life paintings of the Flemish school or their lavish portraits of comestibles: hares and boars, fish, fowl, and fresh fruit. Perishables all—just like the worldly luxury they embody. These tableaux stood as reminders of the afterlife—eternal and immoveable—that lies before us. Baudelaire has in mind rather those modern artists who in the nineteenth century began more than ever before to take note of and celebrate the fullness of life evident even in trivial things, perhaps especially in trivial things, such as the small realities in Constantin Guy's drawings of everyday ephemera.

So goes the conventional reading of his famous passage, and rightly so. But I think there is more there to ponder. Let us consider Baudelaire's reflection in the light of Exodus 20:4.

> Thou shalt not make unto thee any graven image, or any likeness of any thing that is in heaven above, or that is in the earth beneath, or that [is] in the water under the earth.

This prohibition concerns first of all but not only the making of idols to displace God. But is also a warning not to make images of *anything*. It bears a family resemblance to the prohibition against using or even knowing God's true name. The reason for this ban is plain enough: images—pictures, words, sculptures, even names—all too easily become reifications that falsify, misrepresent, and even replace the divine fullness of being, because being is always in flux.

Baudelaire has nothing against the making of images per se, but he is alive to the warning that images threaten to become idols. As Ottilie writes in Goethe's *Elective Affinities*: "There is no better escape from the world than through art; there is no closer bond to the world than through art." Art should illumine and disclose the real, but it can also serve to fashion a false reality. Hence Baudelaire's distrust of the eternal and immutable as categories in art. They are prone to idolatry, given our fallen, time-bound, ephemeral lives. Hence his embrace of an art that offers us inconsequential glimpses of perishable moments in time. I use the word inconsequential advisedly. This art does not seek to immortalize the ephemeral—this would necessarily misrepresent it—but it seeks instead to reveal the ephemeral's true, temporal nature with a lightening flash of illumination that does not stay.

This attitude does not diminish the value of classic memorializations by image-makers such as, say, Théodore Géricault or Jacques-Louis David. But it does relativize their claim on capturing the fullness of reality. The categories "great" and "classic" art have idolatry built into them. The claim, lazy and boring, that Shakespeare is "universal" misses the more crucial experience in reading of the living detail, of savory particularity, of the unrepeatable scent or taste of the real. Constantin Guys' modest ambition—like the ambition of memoirist Irfan Orga—to capture the forgettable details of quotidian life is actually not so modest at all.

It is not modest for this reason: if it is true that we are made in the image of God, then we are infinite. Great art inevitably tends in the direction of reification and so also idolatry. Minor art, art that dwells lovingly on the insignificant detail—such as the remembered childhood pleasure in a heavy, syrupy doughnut—acknowledges the infinitely inexhaustible, ultimately unrepresentable nature of our truer life in the Heraclitean river of time.

Still, it might be objected that this sort of pleasurable reading must occur at the expense of critical reading, a phrase that has become a shibboleth of contemporary education. Let me offer one last parable of reading, this one a late, short narrative by Franz Kafka that highlights the tension between critique and pleasure:

> A philosopher always hung about wherever children were at play. And if he saw a boy with a top, he became watchful. No sooner had the top begun to spin than the philosopher pursued, in order to catch it. That the children made a racket and tried to keep him from the toy did not bother him, if he caught the top while it was still spinning he was happy but only for an instant, then he threw it to the ground and went away. For he believed that the knowledge of each detail, for instance of a spinning top, sufficed for the knowledge of the whole. As a result he did not trouble himself with grand problems, which to him seemed uneconomical. If the smallest detail were really known, then all was known, and so he busied himself only with the spinning top. And whenever preparations for spinning the top were underway he had hope that success was near, and when the top began to spin he pursued with bated breath as hope became certainty, but when he held the stupid chunk of wood in his hand he felt sick and the shouts of the children, which he had so far not

> noticed and now suddenly pierced his ears, drove him away,
> he went reeling like a top driven by a clumsy whip.

The philosopher wants knowledge and seeks to read the situation properly, which is to say critically: he stands outside the children's game as a detached observer. In his mind, the point of the game is to spin the top, so the essence of the game boils down to the top as it spins, which he wants to capture, isolate, and, like any good scientist or scholar, submit to analysis. But when he stops the top—reifies its action—it no longer is what it really is: a small, relational component of the larger play that had been occuring in time and space. The philosopher fails to understand that the essence of what he is observing is the pleasure of the time-bound game as a whole, something that is transient, fleeting, contingent.

So too with all these books that Tom Curran hands out so freely: the reading of them is a relational pleasure. This pleasure is not opposed to knowledge, though: reading is itself a species of knowledge that is closely related to the sensual pleasures of life that are a kind of knowing, such as eating or travel or a visit to the Hamam. Books can be instrumental, of course, but they need not be and, like Kafka's spinning top, are not so in their essence. This basic insight has been summarized nicely by Samuel Beckett who said, referring to the work of a novelist he admired: "his writing is not *about* something, *it is that something itself*."[3]

Notes

1. Irfan Orga, *Portrait of a Turkish Family* (London: Eland, 1993), 23-24.

2. Charles Baudelaire, "The Painter of Modern Life," *Selected Writings on Art and Literature*, trans. P. E. Charvet (London: Penguin Books, 1992), 403.

3. Samuel Beckett, "Dante … Bruno …Vico … Joyce," *Samuel Beckett: The Grove Centenary Edition* (New York: Grove Press, 2006), 4:503.

GEORGE COOPER

Felicitating the Rev'd Doctor Tom Curran

Rudyard Kipling was a King's student. I know some people are skeptical about this claim. Why, some don't even believe it. But I have proof.

A few weeks ago while rummaging around the Kipling Room in the basement of the Dal Library, I stumbled across the original version of Kipling's famous poem "If." His notes demonstrate my claim beyond doubt. They show that Ruddy (as he was known by his fellow students) took the Foundation Year Programme, and Tom Curran was his favourite Professor. Sadly, the later (and better known) version of his poem fell dramatically away from the literary elegance of the long lost original, but now for the first time I am able to present it to a thirsty public.

IF, by Ruddy Kipling

If you can walk with Dons and keep your humour,
Or teach at King's nor lose the common touch;
If puffed up President or Chancellor
Can't outward faze you while you inward grouch;
If you can cope with Kant and Alighieri
And treat those two imposing souls the same,
And pivot to *The Wasteland* oh so brightly
That FYPsters reading with you will stay sane;

If you can mesmerize a Convocation
And make them follow any precedent
That you alone can conjure, in a motion
To choose the best Hon. Docs. for King's advancement,
And steer Encaenia like beguiling Merlin
So all enraptured students and their parents
Embrace King's College as their seat of learnin'
Forever in their hearts and minds each moment;

If at Chapel Sunday after Sunday
You can preach a sermon on the Gospel
Yet manage every time to summon Dante
As our Guide to teach us hustle-bustle's
Not the Way, the Truth the Life, but rather
That the practical investigations
Of Aristotle's good life's not mere blather
But pours pure bliss on humans in their stations;

If you can wear a tweed of Harris daily
  Throughout December up to March's freezes—
And with it naught but vest and scarf most jaunty,
  Then keep on wearing both through June's hot breezes,
And bear a box top briefcase with no shame:
  "Man's inborn aim is serving, not mere flaunting,"
He seems to say. TOM CURRAN 'tis by name—
  A good and gentle man of wisdom daunting!

—George Cooper

WILL ENGLISH

As King's as the Wardy

Dr. Tom Curran is a fixture of King's. From his trademark facial hair to his kind demeanor Tom Curran is a true Kingsman.

Tom has always fully immersed himself in the life of King's. Tom and his late wife Jane would always go for drinks in the Wardroom. They would often be the only true adults there; but they would happily chat up students while drinking the "fancy beer." (And kindly buying drinks for poor students.) I always appreciated that Tom is extremely student-centric. I can easily see how he was the dean of residence at one point.

When Tom was my FYP tutor I was impressed by the time and effort he put into grading a paper. Every comment was footnoted in a methodical fashion. (The man used a pencil and a ruler.) The comments were thorough and really strove to help you grow as a writer. It was obvious to me—an 18-year-old who knew nothing—that Tom Curran was a passionate educator.

When I decided to write a thesis my final year and I was struggling to find an advisor Tom stepped up for me. The process was intimidating but with Tom's support I was able to cobble together a passable work. All along the way Tom advocated for me against a less enthusiastic panel.

Tom does not have much patience for school politics and that has probably held him back. But he has an immense sense of justice and will always speak up for what is right. Tom is an absolute treasure who helped me have an amazing university experience. For me Tom is as King's as the Quad … or the Wardy.

—Will English, BAH '07

JAMIE CARROLL

Lector, si monumentum requiris circunspice

I have had the privilege of knowing the Reverend Dr. Father Thomas Curran first as a lecturer and tutor in FYP, then as a customer of one my first entrepreneurial ventures, then briefly as a "colleague" (though even twenty years later that feels grossly inflated) and finally as a dear, lifelong friend.

Tom's openness and genuine curiosity about the people and things around him is infectious—the best of qualities for any molder of young minds. His was always the tutorial one made sure to attend—not sure one could say the same of all others.

Sir Christopher Wren's epitaph—inscribed on a plaque in St. Paul's Cathedral—reads:

LECTOR, SI MONUMENTUM REQUIRIS CIRCUMSPICE.

While this would obviously be true of Tom standing in the quad at King's—as he as much as anyone had made that place special over the years—I would argue it is true in midst of writers, thinkers, journalists, citizens across Canada and around the world who benefited from his advice, guidance and grace.

KARA HOLM

Receiving and Recognizing Gifts

Shortly after assuming my position as Advancement Director at the University of King's College in August of 2004, I was surprised to receive a gift from one of the tutors. The tutor was Tom Curran and the present was a plaque-mounted poster of the 2004-2005 Foundation Year Programme Handbook cover. It was of his own design and based on the Toronto subway "route map," replacing place names with the authors included in that year's reading list. I did not know Tom well at the time, but his gift was greatly appreciated as it made me feel welcome and gave me an insight into the Foundation Year Programme which is—in my opinion—the heart of King's. From the route-map image I understood FYP not as a destination reached by following a linear path, but as journey where multiple approaches and outcomes are possible. The route-map suggested the authors and ideas were in dialogue with one another—mirroring the approach of FYP. The image also revealed something of the personality of my new colleague.

During my time at King's, Tom was a frequent visitor to my office and we soon became good friends. I enjoyed—and continue to enjoy—his individuality and enthusiasm for a surprising range of topics. Tom's main reason for coming to the Advancement Office was to share his latest idea. A devoted tutor beloved by his students,[1] Tom was equally committed to:

1. Finding ways to demonstrate how the content of FYP—always said in full by Tom, Foundation Year Programme or F-Y-P, never "FYP"—could be shown to be relevant to a modern reader, and
2. Sharing his passion for the King's College community.

As Advancement Director, my priorities were to help alumni stay connected to the College, provide donors with an understanding of the mission of King's and what made it unique, and support recruitment efforts. Tom supported all of these objectives. Here is a short list of some of the work Tom initiated in service of King's.

★ Tom produced a column for the alumni magazine *Tidings* called "FYP Texts".

★ On campus he organized "The Popular Lecture" series on subjects such as *Dracula*, *Harry Potter,* and *The Golden Compass* that were attended by current students, alumni, prospective students, and members of the community.

★ He was one of the professors that came on the Faculty lecture tours, bringing the intellectual energy of King's across Canada.

★ Concerned about the sound system in Alumni Hall, he

---

1 Note this comment from the website RateMyProfessor.com (2017): "Dr. Curran is one of the most intelligent, caring instructors I have EVER had. This a man with deep and vast knowledge and a passion for sharing it, and he cares about his students. He'll notice if you're struggling, academically or otherwise, and will try to help in any way he can. *You are all ends in yourselves.* —Dr. Curran"

advocated for the need to correct this short-coming to enhance the student experience. As a result of his efforts, a donor was found to fund improvements.

It must be recognized that Tom can always be counted on to "show up" for events organized by his academic colleagues, students and administrators. Concerts, plays, lectures, receptions, dinners, discussion groups/clubs—no event is too small to escape his attention.

Despite his great industry and vast contributions, Tom has always been extremely modest. He wasn't pushing himself forward when he shared his ideas: the College community is the star of any Tom Curran production. From Tom I have learned the true meaning of the word "pious." His sense of duty, service, community, and gratitude drive him.

This *Festschrift* project is an opportunity for those who have benefitted from Tom's caring and generosity to reciprocate. The essays included in this volume form a route map of Tom's experience—including reflections from students and colleagues who have become friends over the years.

Through this recognition of Tom's work, we also anticipate Tom's future projects, inspired by the continued dialogue and engagement with his many friends and his interest in the world.

In truth the true gift I received back in 2004, was one Tom offers everyone he encounters: a welcome and connection to community, driven by his love of learning and zeal to share ideas.

Kara Holm
Halifax, May 26, 2019

FOUNDATION YEAR PROGRAMME

[ROUTE MAP]

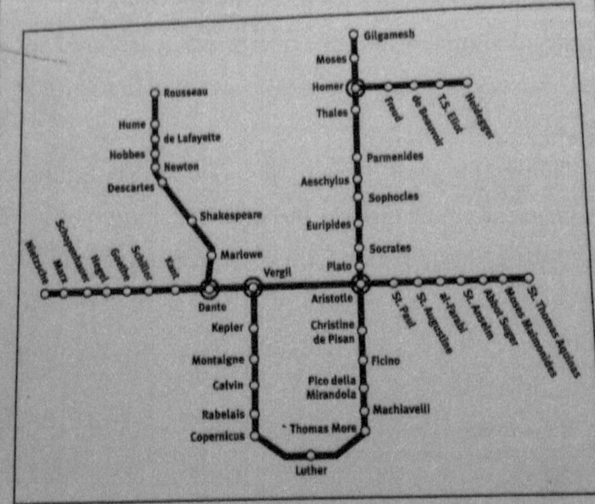

University of King's College

Foundation Year Programme Handbook 2004-2005

Sections 1, 2 & 3

CHRISTOPHER ELSON

Rapt Abductions: A Divagation for Thomas Curran

> There remains, certainly, the little princess who flaunts the bounds (too): no doubt mythologically, she is available to figure the freeing from provenance and dwelling. (Denis Guénoun, *Hypothèses sur l'Europe*)[1]

In 2018 I accidentally bought a painting.

This happy accident (I love the painting) came to mind immediately when considering my contribution to a *Festschrift* for Reverend Doctor Thomas Curran. The unintentional but fortuitous purchase struck me in fact as a very *Curranesque* gesture. Saying that, I place myself in smiling and admiring proximity to Tom, to his fruitful and erudite disarray, to his enthusiastic finds, his boundless gifts, his cubistic cultural cuttings, his *you musts*.

But it gets better and the story of the painting is much more than just a convenient anecdote at the threshold of this wandering text of friendship.[2] To begin making myself clearer: last year I *almost-unwittingly* purchased a *copy* of a great work of early

20th century art by the Russian painter Valentin Serov. A work which recapitulates and reinvents a central civilizational motif. A representation situated in a network of countless exchanges between and amongst myth and art, literature and thought, a refracted, beautiful visual essay in a heaving sea of *renvois*. A painting which I might in fact have seen twice before commissioning the copy (I can't be sure). A painting which experts tell us belongs to an unfinished quasi-series and which has an intriguingly similar near-twin. A painting which has crossed oceans to America and which is held right at the heart of Eurasia.

Following this inspiration and seeking to speak in the vicinity of the painting of course leaves far too much aside from our conversations of twenty years and more. But it does allow me to address a certain number of things that we share, think about and cherish. The specific point of intersection between my copy of the Russian painting and our decades old thinking-sharing-cherishing will be Tom's wonderful, unexpected website, *recherché.com* (how did he ever secure that domain name?!?). In particular, whatever I can say here will be oriented by two striking features of that site: (i.) the intriguing evocation of the "legacy of the Euro-Méditerranée," which gives its title to this whole celebratory collection, and (ii.), the preoccupation, front and centre in the extraordinary series *Fake or Facsimile*, with "the disciplined future preservation of the heritage that we so much admire."[3]

This naming of a legacy that belongs to Europe but must constantly reassess its bounds,[4] which is inherently and originarily a reflection on bounds,[5] allows for reflection on the origins and the destiny of such a geopolitical and geopoetical space and, preciously, centrally, for us to think of ourselves as displaced legatees and to think that displacement.[6] Furthermore, the urgent and entertaining reiteration in these online pages of a preoccupation with preservation and with heritage puts us on the terrain of a small-c conservative preoccupation with the sustainability of culture, doing so in very contemporary terms. Curran's *Fake or Facsimile*, it seems to me, cannot be thought of simply in terms of *the work of art in the age of mechanical reproduction* (Benjamin) or those of the *imaginary museum* (Malraux) to cite two illustrious and influential twentieth-century examples. Beyond questions of democratization, of authenticity and aura, or of simple conservation and accessibility, Tom's siting of and thinking on these matters aligns more closely, it seems to me, with acutely contemporary concerns for the *afterlife of culture* (Stephen Henighan), concerns with the menace of the *deluge of the cultural culture* (Michel Deguy), in brief, with the status and precarity of the work of art in our moment of *the apogee of cultural capitalism* (Martin Rueff). What kind of *recourse to the sources* (Eric Bédard) might allow for such a rethinking?[7] What does it mean to be alert legatees today?

To begin to answer those questions, I want to return to the story of the painting. In the fall of 2005 I had the great fortune to be in New York to hear Keith Jarrett at Carnegie Hall and was staying with friends in Hoboken, New Jersey.[8] At some point during the visit, finding myself alone in Manhattan (that is how I remember it), I decided to visit the Guggenheim museum which I knew was then hosting an exhibition of Russian art. It was to be my discovery of the Guggenheim and I was excited to see over 250 Russian masterworks, ranging from 14th century icons to early 21st century pieces. *Russia!* took me back as well to the unforgettable illustrated Foundation Year Programme lectures of Yuri Glazov in the early 1980s and indeed we could say that they really brought me there in 2005. The corkscrewing, cumulative disposition of the snail-shell museum's spaces allowed for some really remarkable looking at art.[9] Rising higher among the art works, moving upward and chronologically forward, I saw a painting that particularly held me.

The plastic qualities of the work come in first, before any recognition of cultural forms, any intellectualized cross-indexation, can occur. It is a seascape, but also, at first, more simply a canvas, not quite square, slightly broader than tall, a two dimensional field of grey blue with accents of garden pot ochre, fish-belly white, drowned nocturnal black, and furling, windy greys. It takes place for the eye, gradually, on two or three planes or more, at the intersection of sub-surface, wave-swell and glimpsed-horizon. It is a steep painting and the viewer approaches what it frames as if from below, as though seeing it from a periscope emerging from the face of a wave.[10] In the centre, there is a youthful woman, poised on the back of a bull. The painterly elements then congeal into a recognizable mythical dynamic: the foamy power of the bull's course, the mannered poise of the woman's precarious perch; the powerful beast turning its head gently, the princess holding to his lyre-horns, a hand on her hem.

Похищение Европы. "The Rape of Europa."[11] It was painted in 1910, not long before his death, by Valentin Alexandrovich Serov (1865-1911), one of the most brilliant and beloved painters of turn of the (20th) century Russia.[12] It is a beautiful example of his later work and, art historians point out, evidence of a striving for a grand new synthesis in his art which intensified following a life-changing trip to Greece in 1907 with his painter friend, Leon Bakst.[13] Macha Chlenova, one of the curators of the *Russia!* Exhibit, tells us that "this work shows the artist's growing interest in Henri Matisse's use of colour and the decorative stylization of Art Nouveau,"[14] and the cross-fertilization of styles and aspirations, evident here, indeed makes one wonder, with the specialists, where he might have gone if not for his early death (and of course, in abstraction from other world-historical facts on the horizon).

This painting was already oddly familiar to me. Was this because of its strong archetypal qualities? Because of having seen so many other depictions of abductions based on myths? Was I situating it in a tradition or fitting it into a sequence, evolutionary or otherwise, a kind of missing-link, aha!, inevitable? Or had I really seen it before? I did visit the Tretyakov Gallery on a remarkable trip to Moscow in 1994 and it seems very likely that I had seen it there among its strong holdings of Serov. (Returning to Halifax, I checked a volume purchased then at the museum but it did not feature the 1910 painting, rather a very different Greek-inspired piece. It was much later that I found the internet resources allowing me to localise my semi-forgotten experience.) Uncannily, or however one might prefer to put it, of all the works in that remarkable Russian treasure trove, it was this one that struck hardest and stuck longest.

This painting would in fact stay with me for years, occasionally surging up in an insistent, difficult to explain manner. Was it the humour, the divine joke that Ovid puts so pithily in his version of the abduction as "Love and majesty go together with difficulty"?[15] (But in Serov's painting, isn't that dilemma resolved, humanized, very precisely in the adventure of awed tenderness and desire that is depicted?) Had it somehow lodged both in my *imaginary museum* (available for quotation) and in my dreams (in its combinatory potentiality) because of its primal character and erotic energy? Or perhaps just precisely because of its onirism it had stayed at the intersection of conscious interests and unconscious drives, historically prefiguring in some ways the more radical openness to the subconscious that was to come in art and intimately set on a leading wave? Or, more theoretically, was it because its paraphrasable propositions about Europe, about the proper name, about culture and the risk and violent change at the heart of culture had somehow come to inform and improve my thinking about those matters ?[16]

One thing I had to admit to myself: like the Tyrean princess in Denis Guénoun's reading of the myth, the desire, the "greediness," the "passion" for the painting had carried me away. I felt its waves in the city. I wanted it, wanted to hold onto something of its rhythmic compositional elevation, its erotic élan, its situation in the space-time of myth, its ideational clarity.

And so, over ten years later, still thinking about this painting, I finally admitted to that longing. I found a used copy of the exhibition catalogue. I began to discover the web resources. And then I thought, I know someone who could make me a copy of the painting. I contacted the gifted Brooks Kind, a friend from undergraduate days, painter, classical guitarist, Russophile extraordinaire.[17] I asked him if he might be able to do a copy, asked if he would be interested. We exchanged a few emails in the fall of 2017 and I told him that I would recontact him after my sabbatical leave.

As it turned out, Brooks too had gotten carried away. He wrote me in the fall of 2018, inquiring gently if I might still be interested in a copy. I was interested, more than interested. Then he admitted to having already done the work, seizing a moment between his Nova Scotian and Albertan activities to engage actively with a painting that he found fascinating, compelling, through the analytical interpretation of a copy. There was no pressure to purchase it, but of course I did. *The Abduction* was at hand, attainable at last, I would say home at last if the imagery didn't question the notion of belonging so profoundly.

Turning now from these multiple and, at least for me, evocative transports and transpositions of the motif of Europe's abduction to the two points of intersection identified earlier, I will make some very compacted remarks by way of a wandering conclusion. They will address and link Tom's questions of the Euro-Mediterranean legacy and the intimately related point of the preservation and transmission of works. The two threads in my thinking, still in the vicinity of the painting and improved by it, threads which can only be lightly traced here, are the notions of the *improper proper* and of the *transport of relics* in a time of deluge.[18]

Two statements by two quite different thinkers anchor and suggest what a longer development might yield. First, Rémi Brague, from the back cover page of his influential book, *Europe, La voie romaine*: "What is proper to Europe? It is an appropriation of what is foreign to it."[19] Second, from perhaps the most important and decisive essay of the late 20th Century on the subject of culture, Jacques Derrida's *The Other Heading* (*L'Autre Cap*), written in the interval between the collapse of the Soviet bloc and the first Gulf War: "*What is proper to a culture is to not be identical to itself.* Not to not have an identity, but not to be able to identify itself, to be able to say 'me' or 'we'; to be able to take the form of a subject only in the non-identity to itself, or, if you prefer, only in the difference with itself [*avec soi*]. There is no culture or cultural identity without this difference with itself."[20] Brague uses a language of 'hygiene of the proper,' or what the English version of the text calls, the "improper proper." Derrida develops his 'opuscule' about culture and turn of the (21st) century Europe on the basis of 'axioms' like the one cited and it contains an astonishing closing orchestration of quasi-Kantian imperatives, with the important deconstructive nuance that they are founded upon an aporetic and double duty.

I have on several occasions attempted to bring together these two texts in graduate classes about contemporary culture. (In fact, Brague's chapter about the hygiene of the proper opens explicitly with a reference to Derrida.)[21] What is at stake, broadly and narrowly, is *belonging*, a word which perhaps both avoids certain pitfalls of a too-insistent use of *culture* or, especially, of *identity*, at one and the same time that it almost inevitably forces a polarization (rootedness vs. cosmopolitanism; globalists vs. localists; the nowheres vs. the somewheres; etc.), usually expressed in considerably less nuanced terms than the Derridean axiom quoted above, with its vibrant play of identity and alterity. Seeing through to the dual imperatives of *The Other Heading*, Derrida implores readers to attend to "the duty to respond to the call of European memory to recall what has been promised under the name Europe, to re-identify Europe—this duty is without common measure with all that is generally understood by the name duty, though it could be shown that all other duties perhaps presuppose it …"[22]

Denis Guénoun's rich and provocative reading of the founding myth of Europe can help us with this complexity, this apparent incommensurability, might help us to end where we began, under the name of Europe or re-identifying her, or at least can help us sight a familiar/unfamiliar shore, *the other shore of another heading*, perhaps, to quote Derrida.[23] And Serov's painting is never far from my mind in citing passages like this one:

> Europe is carried off toward anonymous foreignness and if the name of Europe designated anything for the Greeks, it is first of all, above all else, that: not the land situated across from them, and its proper name, but the movement of tearing-away and of abduction from the paternal lands, from Asia as a land (the being-earth of the earth), toward the strange and nameless place. The carrying-away, the ravishing—forced but delicious, worrying and desirable—carrying off in itself.[24]

Though Guénoun situates "the little princess" in a primary dynamic of tearing away from any provenance and belonging, as our liminary quotation asserts, it seems to me that the cumulative force of his European hypotheses (which do not derive only from the Greek moment), and indeed of his whole dramatic and philosophical oeuvre, might lie somewhat closer than these quotations would indicate to an invigorating undecidability about Europe and belonging, one that is in fact very close to the Derridean drawing together in *The Other Heading* of obligation under the paradox of paradox[25]: "One could multiply the examples of this double duty. It would be necessary above all to discern the unprecedented forms that it is taking today in Europe."[26]

Another figure whom I believe might be profitably interposed between Derrida and Brague to aid in grasping the double duty inherent in our present moment is that of François-Xavier Bellamy, a young philosopher whose books *Les Déshérités* and *Demeure, Pour échapper à l'ère du movement perpétuel* enunciate a very principled and coherent defence of a contemporary sense of belonging both to a grand, if not perhaps strictly universal, civilizational project and to a specific place.[27] He does so in the face of multiple current commonplaces, as, for example, the fundamental and irrefutable reality of constant change or *disruption*, or the desire to re-found upon disqualification and disinheriting (*deconstruction*, in the narrow, caricatural sense so often used by many who might find great usefulness in its approaches and who could benefit from its modesty). His work may be eminently open to critique on particulars, but it focuses on the dilemmas of culture today and takes the responsibility of decision opened up at the heart of duty.

To conclude, to close this loop of friendly speculation and spiralling references while drawing upon a sense of dutifulness which I believe will appeal to Tom, I will quote a text by Jacques Derrida's friend Michel Deguy, forthcoming in an issue of *Dalhousie French Studies* to which Tom has also contributed: "What entirely reinvented Renaissance could allow for the difference of transforming/conserving *the same* in the ark of another archive? I do not know."[28] I think that Tom Curran's resolute commitment to thinking, his hard work of transmission in the context of the Foundation Year Programme and King's College, and his inspired interventions like the series *Fake or Facsimile* all participate in the difficult, questioning, multi-faceted duty of today's intellectual, as implied in Deguy's statement. Thomas Curran seeks the 'ark of another archive' and in doing so shows himself an exemplary contemporary. For this, and for much else, I gratefully offer this divagation.

Endnotes

1. *"Reste la petite princesse, certes, qui franchit les bornes (aussi) : et sans doute mythologiquement, elle est disponible pour figurer l'affranchissement de la provenance et de la demeure"* (Guénoun, 48). This remarkable book by the French philosopher and *homme de théâtre* Denis Guénoun is a revised version of the thesis that he wrote in the 1990s under the direction of Philippe Lacoue-Labarthe and which had as its title then, '*Transferts du corps enlevé*', Transfers of the abducted body. This is a formulation to be kept in mind for what follows.

2. Tom, it will be much a matter of wandering, here and elsewhere in the neighbourhood of your *Fest.* (Dear Reader, some of these footnotes are in whole or in part apostrophes to Thomas, recalling common experiences, references, friends.) In calling my text a "divagation," I hear waves (*vagues*), want to hear them, but that is not borne out by the etymology. The noun in both English and French comes straightforwardly enough from the Latin *divagari* which has as its core signification, to wander. It should be underlined that one sense of divagation in French (we are far from Mallarmé here) is a legal term referring to the wandering of livestock beyond the bounds of their owner's property. This too might be kept in mind in what follows, where a certain errant faux-bovine looms large, as do questions of bounds and of the proper.

3. The first expression figures right in the masthead of the welcome page to the site, *Recherché Tom Curran's Out-Takes, Knock-Offs and Do-Overs: The Legacy of the Euro-Méditerranée.* The second direct quotation comes from Part 7 of the series *Fake or Facsimi-*

le, entitled "Fake Philanthropy," but formulations very much like it expressing the same fundamental concern are sprinkled *passim* throughout this enlightening and stimulating fifteen part (and counting?) excursion.

4. We might first note Tom's conjunction of Europe and the Mediterranean, "in the haven of a hyphen" (George Elliot Clarke); this is a decision about bounds that begs further explanation. On the one hand, Denis Guénoun, in his incisive rereading of the original ancient texts about *Europé* and their implications, notes that "Europe is ... certainly not the Mediterranean, just precisely it is opposed to it" (Guénoun, 45). This is an aspect of a general thrust that will lead him to found his "hypotheses" on Europe on the non-identifiable, inward, receding, improper character of Europe in its origins and origin stories, about which I will try to say a little bit more in conclusion. On the other hand, Robert Kaplan, the influential and controversial American geopolitical commentator, reminds us that no less an historiographer than Fernand Braudel emphasizes another reading of the history of the name (Brague would say the *space* and the *content*), in the *longue durée* rather than the origin, one that situates the bounds of Europe at the Sahara: "the French geographer Fernand Braudel intimated that Europe's real southern border was not Italy or Greece, but the Sahara Desert, where caravans of migrants now assemble for the journey north" (Kaplan, 5). In the shorthand of sharing that this piece encourages and requires, I would refer you, Tom, to an exciting pop culture achievement, the *Canal+* series, widely regarded as one of the best that French television has ever produced, entitled *Le Bureau des Légendes*, with its depiction of the interpenetration of Western European and North-African/Middle Eastern culture and politics through the dramatic lives of covert French intelligence agents (*les clandés*). On the high culture side, reading the late Tunisian professor, poet and essayist Abdelwahab Meddeb on his

gamble on civilization would be highly complementary. These are two representations of what the Braudelian sense of bounds might imply for us in 2019. (Speaking from my own experience, since that is the gamble, in part, of these notes, I can recall looking over the back wall of the late Canadian writer Scott Symons's stunning garden of succulents in Rasoir, Morocco, looking out over the arid transitional *cambrousse* falling away to the south, right to the horizon, and feeling an overwhelming, shuddering sense of otherness, of edginess, of *frontier*.)

5. I can do no more in the space available than refer readers again to the opening chapter of Guénoun's *Hypothèses* where he triangulates (the term is deeply pertinent) a wide range of ancient texts to set forth for us an understanding of Europe as pure/impure ravishment in the step beyond. Three quotations, based on Herodotus and others (sources which are synthesized quite differently by Robert Graves, for instance) will suffice: "Europe is an Asian" (p. 38) ;"Europe, born in Asia, is consanguineous with Africa" (40); "The tri-continentality of the world must have been thought as a triple terrestrial bound, beginning with the passage of the step (not beyond) (as one says *le Pas-de-Calais*)" (36). Tom, it seems to me that your Egyptophilia and your travels there and elsewhere in the eastern Mediterranean have put you in a better position than me to grasp the implications of this insight.

6. I ask myself how we might apply the insights of the myth read through the painting, and their respective displacements, to our own new world situation of settler or immigrant culture, *Euro-American* (Jan to Patocka) in its character? One thinks of George Grant in *Technology and Empire* noting that in the Rockies we feel the presence of the gods but they are 'not our gods' or of Northrop Frye's reflections on the very specific coming to Canadian shores that approaching Newfoundland and the Gulf of St. Lawrence means. Much more geopoetical and geopolitical work needs to

be done on these bounds. This is very likely a part of the work of Reconciliation as well. A recent, imaginative book by a non-philosopher, Victor Suthren, entitled *The Island of Canada*, helps point us in this direction.

7. The piling up of references here is in keeping with the overflowing character of the divagation, my chosen quasi-genre. The Canadian hispanist, the French *dichter-denker*, the University of Geneva comparatist, and the conservative Québécois historian are all thinkers whose work vitally informs this reflection. *Recourse to the sources* is of course an inadequate rendering of Bédard's punning title, *Recours aux Sources*, in that it does not aurally suggest in English the common French expression, *retour aux sources*, with its notion of return. In various ways all of the aforementioned contemporaries would passionately agree with Michel Deguy that things are presently, radically, *sans retour*, without possible return. Recourse is another matter.

8. Tom, you know that it was Stephen Blackwood and Aaron Orzech who orchestrated the Carnegie concert convergence. And you know that it was later released as a double CD, another in the line of Jarrett's completely improvised concerts like the Köln Concert or the La Scala concert. Jazz piano has always been part of our conversation. And you may remember that it was two economists, Kings alumnus Richard Howard and his partner Gabriela King, who hosted me in Hoboken. Richard with whom we once spent a memorable New Year's Eve at the late, lamented South Street cellar *ristorante*, Tomavino's.

9. Tom, I know you appreciate geopolitical thrillers in film or popular literature. I think you have probably seen the vividly violent Guggenheim gunfight scene in *The International* (dir. Tom Tyker, 2009) starring Naomi Watts and Clive Owen. The Interpol officer played by Clive Owen has part of his ear shot off there. A sequence for cinephiles' anthologies.

10. Tom, you know that I am the son of a submariner.

11. If I had more space, I'd like to consider the title at greater length. The sense of 'rape' as an abduction rather than an actualized, immediate crime of sexual violence ("To carry off [a person esp. a woman] by force," *OED*) is largely lost in English. In an era when terms like *rape culture* inflect campus debate, this cannot help but be a nervous-making word. I tend to prefer 'abduction' anyway and would add the qualifier 'rapt' to abduction in this particular case, where a reciprocity is strongly underlined in the source texts and in many of the works they have inspired. It also seems the more pertinent, dare I say more European, choice for Europa when we consider the English word 'rape' alongside the alternatives of other neighbouring languages. In French and in Spanish the noun is 'Rapt', *le rapt* or *el rapt* (though in French, some paintings of this and related episodes use the term "*enlèvement*"). I connect this, among other things, to the version of the abduction recounted by Moschus (1st Century BCE) in the Loeb translation by Edmonds, "Then did the *rapt Europa* [my italics] turn her about and stretch forth her hands and call upon her dear companions; but nay, they might not come at her, and the sea-shore reached, 'twas till forward, forward till he was faring over the wide waves with hooves as unharmed of the waters as the fins of any dolphin." (I take these translations from the extracts on the website, www.theoi.com.)

12. See the varied online resources dedicated to the painter indicated in my Sitography.

13. The rather awkwardly translated text on the Tretyakov's website points to the importance of the Greek sojourn. "[*The Rape of Europa*] is produced under the impression of the artist's trip to Greece. Serov turned to monuments of Crete-Mycenaean culture, introducing into the picture's imagery a vessel in the shape of a bull head from the smaller palace in Knossos on the island of Crete, fresco paintings from the Knossos palace with the motif of flying

fish and other monuments of the archaic period. Serov draws a comparison between the academic image of antiquity and archaic Antiquity." I would speak here of a retranslation, an *exportation*, very much another kind of abduction. A ravished and ravishing *carrying-off-to-Russia* of the Greek motif of the Abduction of Europa. The abduction of an abduction.

14. Chlenova *et alii*, p. 46.

15. The edition of *The Metamorphoses* I have at hand is a 19th century French translation by G.T. Villenave, it gives this for Book II, l. 846: "*Amour et majesté vont difficilement ensemble.*"

16. If I were to continue any longer in this 'auto-bio-poïetical' vein, I would have to address how the painting de- and re-composed in my memories, how it metamorphosed and persisted in a changing re-presentation.

17. Brooks Kind works out of Halifax and the Alberta foothills. His website will give a sense of his creative output. Mine is not the first copy in his portfolio, a certain Halifax television executive, a contemporary of ours in Dalhousie Philosophy classes in the 1980s, has a fine Poussin copy, *Et in Arcadia Ego*, hanging in his Jubilee House.

18. Tom, in 2014 you very kindly and helpfully read the manuscript of my translation of *A Man of Little Faith* by Michel Deguy, a book where the concept of relics in a time of cultural effacement begins to get elaborated. "Where are the *precious relics*? In language. The religious is that which remains when we've forgotten everything else. Palin-ody or literature, general translation (and translation's treason) of ancient into modern meaning, that coming into the game in "relief" of the gods or of their loss (active loss: the question is how to lose them), such is the future of "culture," the duty of civilization" (74). There are resonances here with the diplopia and other forms of double vision and double-mindedness which you discuss in your essay "Deguy's Poetry and Philosophy:

Each only *Half of Two*," forthcoming in *Dalhousie French Studies*, no. 114, "Michael Deguy: *Honoris Causa*."

19. "*Le propre de l'Europe? C'est une appropriation de ce qui lui est étranger.*" Tom, I know you have read this work in its English translation, *Eccentric Culture*, where eccentric is understood in its primary sense of non-concentric circles.

20. Derrida, 9-10.

21. In the more recent work and public engagements of Rémi Brague, one finds a tension between this theory of ex-centric culture, of European secondarity, emphasizing a prudent, hygienic belonging, and his growing anxiety about the becoming of Europe, particularly the European Union. Reading a document like *The Paris Statement*, which begins, "We belong to Europe and Europe belongs to us," signed by Brague and well-known intellectuals of a conservative bent from ten countries, including Roger Scruton, one may find the nuances of extended work like *Europe, La voie romaine* worryingly distant. But here as elsewhere in these telegraphic and jerky concluding moves, I find myself pulled in at least two ways.

22. Derrida, 76.

23. Ibid.

24. Guénoun, 41.

25. This notion too calls out for patient commentary. Summarizing brutally, the paradox of the paradox in the closing orchestrations of Derrida's *Other Heading* is derived from Derrida's reading of Paul Valéry and his intensification of Valéry's insight that France's *particularity* is its commitment to the *universal*. All of the implications of double duty for the European intellectual that are drawn out at the end of the essay depend upon that.

26. Derrida, 80.

27. The 33 year old Bellamy has juggled the teaching of philosophy for the *classes préparatoires aux grandes écoles* (now at Lycée

Blomet in Paris) with political activity. Once the adjunct mayor of Versailles for youth and culture, he is currently the *tête de liste*, the leader of the list of candidates for the party *Les Républicains* in the European elections of May 2019. From a series of comprehensive articles and interviews produced during the campaign, I take away the slogan, "We have a future to save," and this quotation: "We are attached to the transmission to our children, just as well of culture and civility as of a world that is still breathable, livable." Not surprisingly, Bellamy's book *Demeure* (which we could well translate as dwelling) makes a significant place for questions of poetic habitability in the Hölderlinian tradition so strongly relayed in France by generations of poets and poeticians. *Voll Verdienst, doch dichterisch wohnet der Mensch auf dieser Erde.* Tom, you will recall that the link between the transmission of works of culture and a successful ecology is one that I attempted to make in my recent reception speech when I was inducted into the *Ordre des Palmes académiques*. Interestingly, there is a whole quirky family of intellectual eco-conservatives (many of them Catholics inspired by Pope Francis's second encyclical, *Laudato si*) congealing around the review, *Limite*. I am grateful to Dalhousie's Canada Research Chair in European Studies, Dr. Jerry White, for bringing the existence of this journal to my attention.

28. To appear in *Dalhousie French Studies* no. 114, "Michel Deguy *Honoris Causa*." This number gathers the papers of participants in the Study Day at the University of King's College held in conjunction with Deguy's receiving an honorary doctorate in May, 2016. It includes some unpublished texts and translations by the French poet-philosopher (1930-), including "Antiquity," from which this quotation is taken.

Bibliography

Bédard, Eric. *Recours aux sources. Essais sur notre rapport au passé*. Montréal: Boréal, 2011.

Bellamy, François-Xavier. *Demeure. Pour échapper à l'ère du mouvement perpétuel*. Paris: Grasset, 2018.

— *Les Déshérités ou l'urgence de transmettre*. Paris: Editions J'ai lu, 2016.

Brague, Rémi. *Europe, La voie romaine*. Paris: Gallimard, coll. Folio Essais, 1992.

Braudel, Fernand. *The Mediterranean and the Mediterranean World in the Age of Philip II*, trans. Sian Reynolds. New York: Harper and Row 1972 reprint.

Chlenova, Masha, Chubenskaya, Valentinya *et alii*. *Catalogue of the Exhibition RUSSIA!* New York: Guggenheim Museum, 2006.

Deguy, Michel. *A Man of Little Faith* (Trans., edited, with an introduction by Christopher Elson). Albany: State University of New York Press, 2014.

Derrida, Jacques. *The Other Heading* (Trans. by Pascale-Anne Brault and Michael Naas, with an introduction by Michael Naas). Bloomington and Indianapolis: Indiana University Press, 1991. (Original French text published 1991 with Editions de Minuit)

Graves, Robert. *The Greek Myths*. London: Pelican Books 1955, 1960.

The Greek Bucolic Poets. Translated by Edmonds, J. M. Loeb Classical Library Volume 28. Cambridge, Mass.: Harvard University Press, 1912.

Guénoun, Denis. *Hypothèses sur l'Europe*. Paris: Editions Circé, 2000.

Henighan, Stephen. *A Report on the Afterlife of Culture*. Ottawa: Biblioasis, 2008.

Kaloyanov, Venelin. *Valentin Serov: Selected Paintings*. Lexington, Kentucky: First Edition (self publication), 2017.

Kaplan, Robert D. *The Return of Marco Polo's World*. New York: Random House, 2018.

Meddeb, Abdelwahab. *Pari de civilisation*. Paris: Seuil, 2009.

Ovid. *Les Métamorphoses*. (Trans. G. T. Villenave, coll. La Bibliothèque illustrée). Paris: 1983.

Rueff, Martin. *Différence et Identité: Situation d'un poète lyrique à l'apogée du capitalisme culturel*. Paris: Hermann coll. Le Bel aujourd'hui, 2009.

Suthren, Victor. *The Island of Canada*. Toronto: Thomas Allen Publishers, 2009.

La Galerie Tretyakov. (collectif) Moscow: Les Editions de l'Aurore, 1979.

Sitography

François-Xavier Bellamy. European Election campaign articles and interviews. http://www.lefigaro.fr/elections/europeennes/francois-xavier-bellamy-nous-avons-un-avenir-a-sauver-20190520

Le Bureau des Légendes. Trailer: https://www.youtube.com/watch?v=Fxx6DXmkmNI Seasons 1-4 available (with English subtitles) on Apple TV.

Denis Guénoun. http://denisguenoun.org

Guggenheim *Russia!* Exhibition. https://www.guggenheim.org/exhibition/russia

Brooks Kind, artist. http://brookskind.com

Limite. A journal with an eco-conservative perspective. http://revuelimite.fr

Moschus, Greek Bucolic poet. https://www.theoi.com/Text/Moschus.html

Paris Statement. Brague, Scruton, et alii. https://thetrueeurope.eu/a-europe-we-can-believe-in/

Russian Virtual Museum.

Serov Biography: http://rusmuseumvrm.ru/reference/classifier/author/serov_valentin_aleksandrovich/index.php?lang=en

Gallery of Serov Images:

http://www.virtualrm.spb.ru/ru/resources/galleries/serov

Serov and Russian Style. Four Versions of the Rape of Europa: https://russian-style.tumblr.com/post/82916443909/four-versions-of-the-rape-of-europa-by-valentin

SIMON KOW

Messing About in Books: *Intertextual Visions in* THE WIND IN THE WILLOWS

> "Believe me, my young friend, there is *nothing*—absolutely nothing—half so much worth doing as simply messing about in boats."
>
> —Grahame, *The Wind in the Willows*, 13; emphasis in original)

Introduction

Like any classic of children's literature, Kenneth Grahame's 1908 novel *The Wind in the Willows* is susceptible to various interpretative approaches. Grahame's tales of four friends—the Mole, the Water Rat, the Toad, and the Badger—who live along or near the River Bank can of course be simply savoured as the delightful adventures of anthropomorphised animals in a pastoral, Edwardian setting resembling the Thames Valley. For students of the liberal arts, however, *The Wind in the Willows* also offers fascinating intersections with great books in ancient and modern times: what I have characterised as "intertexual visions." Grahame was a clerk at the Bank of England, but had received his education at Oxford

University and was active in the New Shakespere [*sic*] Society and the Early English Text Society (Gauger, xx-xxi). Although much of the novel's plot originated in bedtime stories conceived by Grahame and related to his six year-old son Alastair in a series of 1907 letters to "My Dearest Mouse" (Gauger, xxvii), it is nonetheless rich in literary allusions.

Just as the characters in the novel are between man and animal, so the novel's themes occupy the spectrum between children's and adult literature. I shall dip my toes, as it were, into three intertextual visions in the novel: just as the Water Rat waxes idyllic about "messing about in boats" on the River, so the liberally educated reader can mess about in the books to which *The Wind in the Willows* refers, either explicitly or implicitly. I ask, then, for your forbearance and patience as I drift down a few literary tributaries and rivulets in the spirit of an idle boater and dilettante.

Into the Light: Mole End and Plato's Cave

> "Something up above was calling him imperiously, and he made for the steep little tunnel [like the exits] … owned by animals whose residences are nearer the sun and air."
>
> (Grahame, 1)

The Wind in the Willows begins with the Mole, annoyed with spring-cleaning his little home, Mole End. Hearing an unexplained call from above, he laboriously climbs out of his abode, "muttering to himself, 'Up we go! Up we go!' till at last, pop! his snout came out into the sunlight …" (Grahame, 1). Elatedly, he surges past grumbling rabbits (jeering "Onion-sauce! Onion-sauce!"—dressing for baked rabbit) and passes through meadows until reaching the river, making the acquaintance of and lunching with the boating Water Rat and being introduced to an entirely new life of friendship, society, and adventure. The novel is a *bildungsroman*, at least for the Mole, in terms of the development and growth of his character.

The Mole's ascent also echoes, perhaps unintentionally, the allegory of the cave in Plato's *Republic*. In the *Republic*, Socrates presents the image of prisoners in a cave who watch shadows (cast by a fire) of people carrying objects and speaking to each other; they assume that the shadows themselves are making the sounds. One of them is set free, turned around, forced to look at the fire, and told that what he is now seeing has more reality. He is then dragged up the slope leading from the cave and pulled into the sunlight. After an initial bedazzlement, he is eventually habituated to seeing things in the light of the sun. He realises the false perceptions of his fellow prisoners. If he goes back down into the cave, he has to adjust to the darkness, while his fellow prisoners would deny his greater knowledge of appearances. Such a person resembles the philosopher, who attains knowledge of the good but is scorned by his fellows in society (Plato, 514a-517e).

Grahame's Mole behaves more like a child than a rational philosopher, but he becomes a lover of wisdom. While Plato's prisoners are comparatively fortunate to be able to enjoy non-stop video streaming in the form of shadow puppet-plays, as opposed to the labour of housework, the Mole like the freed prisoner escapes convention and experiences a new sun-basked life. The fact that he does his own spring-cleaning, with no servant or spouse, suggests his relatively humble social status as opposed to his new well-to-do friends: the hedonistic Water Rat, the country squire Badger, the aristocratic adventurer Otter, and of course the wealthy playboy Mr. Toad. Unlike the freed prisoner in Plato's allegory who is forced to undergo the (at least initially) painful process of education from shadowy images to the sun, the Mole experiences not so much the Good as the good life: messing about in boats, overflowing picnic baskets (as the Rat epically catalogues it, "coldtonguecoldhamcoldbeefpickledgherkinssaladfrenchrollscresssandwichespottedmeatgingerbeerlemonadesodawater——" (Grahame, 17)), and gipsy caravan trips, not to mention a distinctly superior station to the working-class stoats and weasels.[1]

The wisdom the Mole gains is not upper-class hedonism but rather the value of *home*. By escaping the confines of his burrow, the Mole gains in sophistication. But during a cold mid-December stroll through a small village with the Rat, the Mole was suddenly struck by a "summons":

> It was one of these mysterious fairy calls from out the void that suddenly reached Mole in the darkness, making him tingle through and through with its very familiar appeal, even while yet he could not clearly remember what it was ... the home had been happy with him ... and was missing him, and wanted him back, and was telling him so, through his nose, sorrowfully, reproachfully, but with no bitterness or anger; only with plaintive reminder that it was there, and wanted him. (Grahame, 111-12)

Although the Mole's home may be small and shabby compared to the Rat's riverside abode, Mr. Badger's ancient burrow, and especially Toad Hall, it is *his* and calls to him. This may be a distinctly English or British sentiment—one might compare it with Edmund Burke or Adam Smith on the need for local attachments—but it also reminds one of Plato's freed prisoner who goes back down into the cave, as if out of a sense of civic duty despite his differences with his chained fellows. Just as the forcibly educated jailbird knows the Good and brings his enlightened perspective underground, so the Mole only learns the value of his home after leaving

1 For a clever and entertaining retelling of *The Wind in the Willows* from the perspective of a working-class ferret, see Jan Needle's delightful *Wild Wood* (London: Methuen, 1981).

it. In contrast to the restless Toad who loses his home because of his thrill-seeking, Mole regains and truly cherishes his home in the course of becoming a wiser animal. The Toad, as we shall see below, will only learn his lesson after great suffering.

The Curious Incident of the Rat in the Night-Time

Having heard so much about the mysterious Badger, the Mole decides one evening to venture outdoors alone while his friend Rat has dozed off and seek out the Badger's burrow in the middle of the Wild Wood. As he enters the Wild Wood, he senses the malicious faces of the woodland creatures surrounding him, accompanied by whistling and pattering. The Mole, now thoroughly frightened and lost in the Wild Wood, seeks refuge in a tree hollow; "he knew it at last, in all its fullness, that dread thing which other little dwellers in field and hedgerow had encountered here, and known as their darkest moment—that thing which the Rat had vainly tried to shield him from—the Terror of the Wild Wood!" (Grahame, 67).

In this terrifying predicament, the Mole can only be saved by the world's first and greatest consulting detective—or at least a rodent facsimile of the latter. Mole's Virgil through the Wild Wood is none other than his friend the Water Rat, who rises to the occasion of the Mole's disappearance to embody the hero of Sir Arthur Conan Doyle's famous detective stories, Mr. Sherlock Holmes. While Mole's realisation of the value of home may be a higher wisdom, the powers of the rational intellect are in full display in the Rat's rescue of Mole from the Terror of the Wild Wood. Awakening from his slumber to find his friend absent, he observes that the Mole's cap and galoshes are missing, and retraces the Mole's footprints (or should that be hind-pawprints?) in the mud, "running along straight and purposeful, leading direct to the

Wild Wood" (Grahame, p. 69). Like Conan Doyle's detective, often compared to a bloodhound, the Rat tracks down his friend, armed with "a brace of pistols" and "a stout cudgel" (Grahame, p. 69).

There may be more at work here than mere homage or parody of English literature's most famous detective and his friend Dr. Watson. Conan Doyle's fictional creation provided excitement but also a kind of comfort to his Victorian readers: life may seem chaotic and terrifying, but Sherlock Holmes is an agent of justice who sorts things out with his unfailing mental abilities. Malicious murderers, rascally ruffians, and even spectral hounds may abound, but reason will prevail once the denizen of 221B Baker Street has been consulted. Likewise, the Rat can quell the terrors besetting the lost Mole—particularly the threat of violence from the lower-class rabble which inhabits the Wild Wood, and which, we learn later, even overturns the social order by occupying Toad Hall. As with Conan Doyle's ultra-rational Victorian superman, the Mole's friend is an Edwardian super-rat who—at least in Mole's eyes—condescends to set things right, especially when deducing that the Mole has tripped himself on the Badger's door-scraper (so that they have literally fallen upon their destination):

> Rat! ... you're a wonder! A real wonder, that's what you are. I see it all now! You argued it out, step by step, in that wise head of yours … at once your majestic mind said to itself, "Door-scraper!" … Did you stop there? No. Some people would have been quite satisfied; but not you. Your intellect went on working. … You're so clever, I believe you could find anything you liked. … Well, I've read about that sort of thing in books, but I've never come across it before in real life. You ought to go where you'll be properly appreciated. You're simply wasted here, among us fellows. (Grahame, 76)

Of course, Grahame is gently satirising the Victorian fantasy of the super-human intellect, but he surely shares with Conan Doyle the desire to see English gentlemen uphold traditional values against chaos, most fully reflected in the adventures of Toad.

The Wanderings of Toad-ysseus

The most explicit intertextual references in *The Wind in the Willows* are to *The Odyssey* of Homer. The vain, pompous, and reckless playboy Toad may seem a far cry from the battle-weary Greek hero wandering the wine-dark sea on his return home from the Trojan War. Those very contrasts, however, only serve to heighten the humour of depicting Toad as an amphibian Odysseus with warts and far too much inherited wealth for his own good. The number of chapters in *The Wind in the Willows* (12) is precisely half the number of the books in *The Odyssey*, while the final, climactic chapter of Grahame's novel is entitled "The Return of Ulysses." The Toad, like Odysseus, undergoes great suffering—though mostly of his own doing. The caprice of the gods, especially Odysseus's mortal enemy Poseidon, is transformed into the cause-and-effect of *nouveau-riche* folly. While Odysseus has recognisable human failings and only the occasional hubris, the well-intentioned Toad is rather a menace to society, particularly behind the wheel of an automobile.

When we—through the Mole—first meet the Toad, he is presented as likeable, dreamy, and impulsive. He is caught up, however, in the clutches of that shiniest and deadliest of technological inventions, which continue to transform the earth's landscapes ever since the rural Arcadia of Grahame's world was liable to be torn up and paved over: the motor-car. In Chapter 2, a promisingly bucolic caravan trip is literally wrecked by the super-fast, noisy demon of modernity. The Toad, however, falls under its spell amidst the ruins of his caravan: "Toad sat straight down in the middle of the dusty road, his legs stretched out before him, and stared fixedly in the direction of the disappearing motor-car. He breathed short, his face wore a placid satisfied expression, and at intervals he faintly murmured 'Poop-poop!'" (Grahame, 52).

The "Poop-poop!" of the motor-car is, for the Toad, an irresistible siren-song. After being forcibly confined by his friends for his reckless driving, car crashes, and brushes with the law, he sneaks out of Toad Hall, lunches at an inn, and overhears the most alluring of sounds:

> He was about half-way through his meal when an only too familiar sound, approaching down the street, made him start and fall a-trembling all over. The poop-poop! drew nearer and nearer, the car could be heard to turn into the inn-yard and come to a stop, and Toad had to hold on to the leg of the table to conceal his over-mastering emotion. (Grahame, 157)

Parodying Odysseus, who upon approaching the sirens commands his crew "to tie me up, tight as a splint, / erect along the mast, lashed to the mast, / and if I shout and beg to be untied, / take more turns of the rope to muffle me" (Homer, XII.195-98), the Toad must grab his table-leg upon hearing the motor-car—albeit futilely. While Odysseus is the sole survivor among his doomed crew, the solitary Toad—in defiance of social convention and good form—lets "the old passion" seize and master him, "body and soul" (Grahame, 157,) as he steals the car for a joy-ride. Similarly, after he escapes from prison ignobly disguised as a laundress, the Toad is rescued by sympathetic gentlemen in a motor-car (in fact, the same fellows whose car he stole). He requests to move to the front seat to catch his breath, and feels the master passion just before he re-takes the wheel: "He sat up, looked about him, and tried to beat down the tremors, the yearnings, the old cravings that rose up and beset him and took possession of him entirely" (Grahame, 258).

Between these vehicular throes of ecstasy, the Toad—like Odysseus—visits the Underworld, though he doesn't seem to learn anything from it. His escapades as "the Terror of the Highway" (Grahame, 143) come to an abrupt end in a court of law, where he is sentenced to twenty years as "a helpless prisoner in the remotest dungeon of the best-guarded keep of the stoutest castle in all the length and breadth of Merry England" (Grahame, 162). When Grahame continues narrating the Toad's adventures—after the Mole's and Rat's mystical, neo-pagan encounter with the Piper at the Gates of Dawn (resembling a Miyazaki film but obscure reading for children)—we find the Toad "immured in a dank and noisome dungeon ... he flung himself at full length on the floor, and shed bitter tears, and abandoned himself to dark despair," echoing the equally unconventional and reckless Oscar Wilde of *De Profundis*, written after he was sentenced to hard labour in Reading Prison (Grahame, 184-85 & note 1). The Toad does not encounter the shades of such legendary figures as Achilles and Tiresias, but he is blessed by the Athena-like figure of the jailer's daughter, who enables his escape by disguising him as an elderly washerwoman—just as Athena disguised Odysseus as an old soldier when returning home.

The hardest lessons the Toad learns, however, magnify upon the wisdom gained by the Mole, and before him, Odysseus: the value of home. Congratulating himself on his clever escape from jail (rather than crediting the jailer's daughter) and after a madcap romp through the countryside, the Toad's swagger is thwarted by the news that the Wild Wooders have taken over Toad Hall. Like Odysseus, who must defeat his wife's suitors who have long occupied his home in Ithaca, the Toad reclaims his estate—neglected and then unjustly seized by the envious rabble. But it is only under the guidance of his friends the Badger, the Rat, and the Mole, that the Toad can, through subterfuge and shock-and-awe tactics with pistols and truncheons, effect the restoration of the traditional order. The stoats and weasels are subjected to a bruising lesson, the

Toad realises how integral his (fellow upper-class) friends are to his fortunes, and most of all the Toad learns humility and gratitude. Although the Toad's deeds hardly measure up to Odysseus's epic heroism, his puffed-up ego (appropriate to a toad) is deflated after undergoing his own trials and tribulations.

Conclusion

Knowledge of the possible and actual sources behind *The Wind in the Willows* is not essential for the reader's enjoyment, but it certainly enhances one's appreciation for Grahame's text in its intellectual and historical contexts. Similar to other pre-First World War writers, Grahame draws upon classical and modern literature to depict characters between animal and human, and who are caught between England's rural, social traditions and the disruptive, fragmentary forces of modernisation and industrialisation. The Mole emerges from the cave of convention to experience a new world, but it requires the Sherlockian rationalism of the Rat to fend off the dangers of the Wild Wood, and it requires the united forces of the River Bankers to undo the harm caused by the Odyssean Toad's motor-madness and to restore the rightful social order to Toad Hall and its environs. *The Wind in the Willows* expresses an English conservatism both gently humorous and quietly profound.

Works Cited

Gauger, Annie. "Preface" to *The Annotated* Wind in the Willows. New York: W.W. Norton & Company, 2009. xix-xxix.

Grahame, Kenneth. *The Annotated* Wind in the Willows. Edited by Annie Gauger. New York: W.W. Norton & Company, 2009.

Homer. *The Odyssey*. Translated by Robert Fitzgerald. New York: Farrar, Straus and Giroux, 1998.

Plato. *Republic*. Translated by G.M.A. Grube. 2nd Edition. Indianapolis: Hackett Publishing, 1992.

ELIZABETH EDWARDS

Perilous Gifts and Hospitality
A small scholarly flower for Tom Curran's FLORILEGIUM

Medieval romance is replete with examples of hospitality; literature reflects back some of the ideals of hospitality in courtly society, and some of the social reality of entertaining the guest. Of course, hospitality is one of the central practices from antiquity on—one might suppose, globally—from Zeus as the god of hospitality in the *Odyssey* and the Biblical commandment at Leviticus 19.34, and the Benedictine Rule's requirement, hospitality is sacred. As an act of generosity and good will, hospitality holds a parallel place with the gift, in what Marcel Mauss calls 'total prestation,' the structure of the exchange of services and obligations that primally constitute the social. Both are instances of generosity and fellow feeling that are also in fact obligatory and obligating. The modest aim of this essay is to show two small instances of the perils of the gift inside the practice of hospitality in medieval literature.

For the gift, and hospitality, can be dangerous. The dangers inherent in hospitality are not an aberration of the welcome, but are structurally constituted as part of the dynamic; I will characterize three of these dangers as disarmament, duty and duplicity. The guest is disarmed both literally and psychologically—the errant knight leaves his sword and accepts the more comfortable clothing offered by the host, and in accepting hospitality he is obliged to trust his host, as his host is obliged to trust the guest. The mutuality of the relation is shown by the languages (French, Italian) that have one word for host and guest. This trust is therefore a duty; the host must be believed to be generous, genuine, and the guest must be grateful and show good manners. That both might be acting out a performative code reveals the danger of duplicity. The disarmed guest may be in mortal danger from a seeming host, and vice versa, though at the risk of ending in the penultimate circle of Hell with Fra Alberigo. But the dangers of hospitality are not simply when things go wrong; the etymology established by Emile Benveniste shows that Latin *hostis*, divagates into two opposite senses as both *hospes* host /guest—and as *hostis*, enemy.[1] The stranger in my house might harm me; there is "apotropaic hospitality" as Ladislaus Bolchazy calls it, a welcome offered to avert harm.[2] There is an element of contest and contestation in hospitality, as there is in the gift, and the reverse side of hospitable welcome is, in medieval romance, the challenge. Thus Derrida coined the term "hostipitality" to capture both faces of the host / guest relationship.[3] The challenging nature of hospitality is most evident in *Sir Gawain and the Green Knight* as Ad Putter has demonstrated.[4]

One example of such a hostile welcome is found in the thirteenth century *Suite de Merlin* when the knight Balin sits brooding at a feast:

1 Émile Benveniste, *Dictionary of Indo-European Concepts and Society.* Trans. Elizabeth Palmer. Hau Books, 2016.

2 Cited in James A. W. Heffernan, *Hospitality and Treachery in Western Literature*, Yale, 2014. 60.

3 Jacques Derrida, "Hostipitality" in *Acts of Religion*, trans. Anidjar Gil. Routledge, 2002.

4 Ad Putter, Sir Gawain and the Green Knight *and French Arthurian Romance.* Clarendon, 1995. See also Matilda Bruckner *Narrative Invention in Twelfth-Century French Romance: The Convention of Hospitality (1160-1200)*. French Forum, 1980.

> Garlon the Red, who went among the tables serving,
> took good note of this and
> saw that this man had neither drunk nor eaten, and
> he thought it very rude of him,
> for he thought he left his food out of disdain. Then he
> came up beside him and,
> lifting his hand, gave Balin a great slap across
> the face, so that it became all red,
> and then said to him, "Raise your head sir knight, and
> eat like the others what the
> seneschal sends you. Ill health to him who taught you
> to sit at a nobleman's table
> and do nothing but think."[5]

Garlon is acting as a host in his brother's household, where courtesy demands that the hosts serve at table. But obviously, good will is not a striking part of the bargain. Balin is brooding about killing Garlon, which he shortly does, in breach of all the "sequences of hospitality" that the story details.[6]

The perils of the gift are somewhat different, because the obligation to return a gift is more evident. The structure of the gift is described by Seneca as a circle: giving generously, receiving gratefully and reciprocating in time. These three are represented, in *De Beneficiis* as the three Graces, in the dance painted by Botticelli in "Primavera." The gift indebts the receiver even if it does not intend to; accepting a gift puts one in a duty to pay back, to return, to oblige, even if only with the subjective attitude of gratitude. The gift can be imperilling or even literally poisonous—like the poisoned apple Guinevere inadvertently gives to Sir Patryse at a

5 Lancelot-Grail: *The Old French Arthurian Vulgate and Post-Vulgate in Translation.* V.IV. Norris J. Lacy, ed. Trans. Martha Asher. Garland, NY 1995. 210-11. All subsequent citations of the Merlin are to this edition.

6 The term is Bruckner's, *op cit.*Chapter iv.

"pryvy dynere" she hosts, in Malory.[7]

The first of my minor instances in the annals of hospitality is drawn from the thirteenth-century prose *Merlin*. This work is the second part of the great Vulgate cycle of Arthurian romance, whose other parts are the *Estoire del Sanct Graal*, the prose *Lancelot*, *Le Queste de Sanct Graal*, and the *Mort Artu*. The *Lancelot* is the work Paolo and Francesca were reading, and it, and most of the rest of the cycle were wildly popular in the late middle ages. The *Merlin* has not had the literary attention it richly deserves, perhaps because it is embedded in a great prose cycle read only by those with a taste for thousand page Arthurian romances and all seven or eight volumes of Stephen King's *Dark Tower* series. It is best known in Malory's version, since it was one of his sources, though his version excises exactly the courtly flourishes to be considered here; I will quote from the middle English translation of *Merlin*, contemporary with Malory.

In the initial incidents leading to the conception of Arthur, in an instance of obligatory hospitality, Uther invites the Duke of Cornwall and his wife Ygraine among many, apparently as part of a great court, but really in order to seduce Ygraine. In fact, Uther has been expressly counselled *not* to go to Ygraine's court, but to use the ruse of hospitality to lure her to his. Giving gifts to all is also part of his duty as a king, but particularly aimed at Ygraine; Uther's pursuit of Ygraine is a campaign to get her to accept the many gifts he attempts to give her. She can accept the initial gift, because it is in the hospitable context where everyone is receiving gifts. Thereafter, Uther pursues a complicated strategy through his henchman Ulfin to manoeuvre Ygraine into receiving some special and particular gift. Ulfin's cynical counsel is:

7 Thomas Malory, *Le Morte Darthur*. Ed. Stephen Shepherd. Norton, 2004: 591.

> Who herde ever speke of eny woman, yef she were
> wele requereth but ye sholde
> have of her your volunté; with that to yeve he gret
> yeftis and juwels and to hem
> that ben abouten hir. I ne herde never speke of woman
> that cowde hir diffende
> ageyn this![8]

Ygraine 'defends' against this by managing to turn down all the jewels and so on, until she is tricked into taking a golden goblet; Uther and Ulfin manage to get the duke himself to act as intermediary, and send on the cup with the command that Ygraine "sholde it take and also to drynke for the kingis sake" (60). The general formula, to drink for the king's sake, or for the king's love, now has a much more particular double meaning. Both Uther and Ygraine realize the significance: "And glade was the kynge that she hadde resceyved his yefte" (60). The receipt of this gift causes her to finally confide in her husband; the implicit obligation in receiving a gift means she either gives in to Uther, or entirely breaks the bonds of gift and hospitality. The duplicity underlying the apparent 'gifts' cannot be acknowledged, and even Ygraine has an interest in prolonging the charade of peaceful entertainment as long as possible. In Malory's version, where less is usually more, the complex cat-and-mouse game of the King is summed up by "desyred to have lyen by her … and thenne she told the duke her husband, and said, 'I suppose that we were sente for that I shold be dishonoured; wherefor, husband, I counceille yow that we departe from hens sodenly…'" When their flight is known, Uther sends for them, in what is the strongest possible invitation, an invitation become a summons; it is their refusal to accept this invitation that changes covert hostility into open war (3).

8 *Prose Merlin*, ed. John Conlee. TEAMS, 1998: 59. All subsequent quotations are to this edition.

One version of Froissart's *Chronicle* (for the years 1339-42) details a strikingly similar situation of a coercive gift inside hospitality. Edward III, having just defeated the Scots and relieved the siege of Salisbury castle, is welcomed there as a guest of the Countess of Salisbury. It is repeatedly stressed that the countess is an exemplary host. She welcomes the king "et l'enmena ens ou castiel pour lui festyer et honourer comme celle qui très bien le savoit faire" [she led him into the castle in order to celebrate and honour him as one who knew very well how to do it[9]].[10] She knows how to run a dinner party: "ala les autres seigneurs et chevaliers festyer et saluer moult grandement, et â point, enssi que elle savoit bien faire, chacun selonq son estat ..." [she went to the other lords and knights celebrating and greeting them very grandly, and perfectly, as she well knew how, each one according to rank](455). But the king has fallen in love at first sight, aflame with a spark of courtly love ["une estincelle de finne amour" (454)] not soon to be extinguished. The king broods about his sudden passion, earning a kind of gentle rebuke from the countess, for he is holding up dinner: "vous devriés tousjours faire bonne chière pour vos gens mieux reconforter et laissier le pensser et le muser" [you ought to always put a good face on it for the better to reassure your people, and leave off thought and musings] (456). This is the same accusation of rudeness that Garlon levelled against Balin—thoughtfulness and brooding is not good manners, and is an impediment to the enjoyment of others. This is made very explicit; we are told that the king "avoit eult en-devant usaige de rire et de jeuer, et de vollentiers oïr aucunnes trufferies pour le temps oublier, mais là il n'en avoit cure, ne talent" [before this he had had the habit to laugh and play and to wish to listen to trufferies to pass the time, but now he had not

9 For this text, I provide the French because the translations are my own and therefore likely to be full of errors.

10 Froissart, *Oeuvres*. T. 3. Ed. Kervyn de Lettenhove. Bruxelles: Victor Devaux, 1867: 454. All subsequent citations are to this edition.

taste nor interest](457). The scene is exactly that of the joyful and light-hearted court of romance, damaged by melancholy.

The king confesses his love to the countess, a declaration met with shame and astonishment and pleas for self-control. But the terms of the hospitable situation mean the countess must continue to receive her guest, who is avowedly looking for a 'better answer'. He manages to engage her in an apparently neutral game of chess, and then proposes that if she wins, he will give her a large and valuable ruby ring. She protests the inordinate value of the ring; he manages to let her win, and then insists on her taking the ring, forcing it on her finger over her protests. Plainly, he has managed to engineer a state of affairs in which, even though she 'won', she owes him some return gift.

The next day, he rides off after the Scots, and the countess instructs one of her gentlewomen to return the ring, but only once the king has mounted his horse and begun his journey (apparently another point of etiquette, for the king will not mount until he has made his adieu to the countess). The king refuses to accept the ring; he leaves it with the damsel to take back to the countess; she refuses to accept it from the damsel. So the obliging gift ends up in limbo: not given, not received, not reciprocated. The king thinks better of his passion, especially considering the Earl of Salisbury's service and usefulness, and lets the love affair too slide into the indeterminacy of the unacheived.

What to make of the events described by Froissart? For one account, the *Merlin*, is fiction, while the Froissart purports to be history and eye-witness history at that. Other chronicles agree with Froissart about Edward's infatuation with the Countess of Salisbury; but instead of the romance narrative given here, Jean le Bel claims Edward raped her.[11] Again, only one redaction of

---

11 Jean le Bel, *Chronique*, T. 2, ed. Jules Viard et Eugène Déprez. Renouard, 1905: 30-34. According to these editors, Froissart disputed Jean's claim (30, fn. 1).

Froissart's chronicle contains the elaborate ruse of the game of chess and the forced gift of the ring. Is this a 'literary' embellishment, whereby the courtly classes are held to have behaved according to the paradigms established by literature like the *Merlin*? Or perhaps, steeped in such literature, did they behave in 'literary' ways? For Jean le Bel is in fact just as literary, inasmuch as in his account, the aggreived Earl of Salisbury left England for the conventional course of fighting the Saracen in Spain and dying a heroic death at Algesiras. Froissart is pro-English, roughly, and Jean pro-French. Do propaganda agendas enter in to it? I leave the separation of art and life, the authentic from the ersatz, to the originator of the "Fake or Facsimile" webpage.[12]

In both my cases, a sovereign is involved, and in Froissart the countess makes explicit the difficulty in dealing with someone "qui mes drois souverains naturels sires estes" [you who are my rightful sovereign and natural lord] (457). It is the sovereign who best epitomizes the obligatory or quasi-obligatory nature of the economies involved; when it is the question of the sovereign, an invitation cannot be refused, a gift is harder to return, absence is treason or revolt. The figure of the sovereign reveals the 'law' of hospitality and gift operating under its guise of freedom and generosity.

There are obvious sexual risks for women inside the hospitable welcome. Their risk is not disarmament but proximity; 'going to bed' is in fact one of the sequences of hospitality described by Bruckner, and that sequence often involves a visitor to the bedchamber.[13] The hospitable welcome is to the inside of the home, a place of intimacy and enjoyment, and thus sexuality. The host/guest position is interchangeable; the Froissart example shows the host/countess in much the same sort of risk as the guest/duchess

12 https://recherché.com/fake-or-facsimile

13 Bruckner, *op cit*, 193.

of the *Merlin*. In chivalric romance, the woman is not literally disarmed, but appears in the intimate interior as vulnerable, needing elaborate ruses to protect her chastity. The ingredients found in my two examples are also found in *Sir Gawain and the Green Knight*, but there it is the man in apparent sexual danger, pressured by an over-involved host into an exchange of winnings, while being received and entertained at the New Year's festivities at a remote court. Much has been written about both gift and hospitality in *Sir Gawain*[14] but the texts I have chosen testify to strength of the motifs in play.

But all three texts show a pattern, and that is: hospitality, game, gift. Inside the setting of hospitality, a gift is offered that is part of a larger game.[15] *Sir Gawain and the Green Knight* indeed repeats the pattern internally, for the poem begins with Arthur's New Year's feast, an unwelcome guest, a beheading game and the 'gift' of the axe. In the Froissart, it is the strategem of the game of chess that allows the enforced gift. In the *Merlin*, the game is more understated, but the strategies of Uther and Ulfin are constructed to entrap Ygraine in a carefully discussed series of moves. This third term, game, complicates the structures of generosity that are here very obviously merely a cover for predation. Inside any complex social structure is the possibility of strategy, moves and play. All three are examples of gaming the system. Yet no game would work without existence of the absolute imperatives: give, welcome, receive. A subject for another paper …

14 On hospitality, see Putter op cit. On the gift, see Britton Harwood, "Gawain and Gift" *PMLA*. May 1991, Vol. 106(3), p.483

15 There is also much written on games in Gawain, starting with John Leyerle's seminal "Game and Play of Hero" in Benson, Larry Dean, and Leyerle, John, eds. *Chivalric Literature : Essays on Relations between Literature & Life in the Later Middle Ages*. Kalamazoo, Mich.: Medieval Institute Publications, 1980. Studies in Medieval Culture; 14.

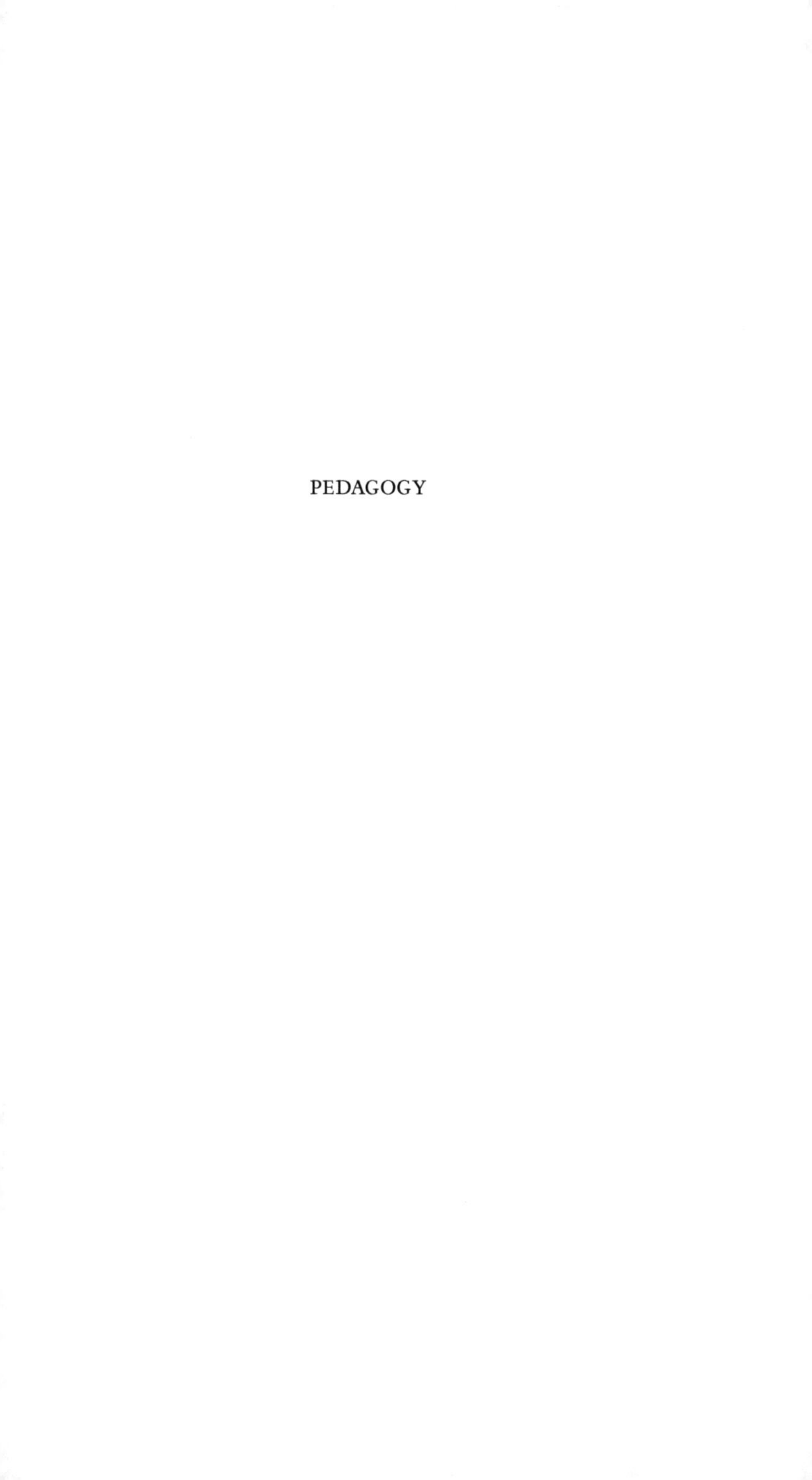

PEDAGOGY

LAWRIN ARMSTRONG

Reading, Thinking & Listening with Tom Curran

Dear Tom:

I recall from FYP 1976-7 the saying of Bernard of Chartres that we moderns "are like dwarves perched on the shoulders of giants, and thus we are able to see more and further than they. But this is not due to our stature or the acuteness of our sight, but because we are carried aloft by their great stature." You—more than anyone in the programme—helped me and many others clamber onto the shoulders of those giants through your lively tutorials, your (sometimes painfully) frank comments on writing and style, and your sage advice on reading, thinking, and listening (to music, especially). For all of which I've been in your debt ever since: when I think about how to present a topic or mark a paper or listen to an opera, I inevitably ask myself: "How would Tom have done this?"

You've reached 70: may you live to see many more such anniversaries and to share your insights with many more students and friends.

Ad annos multos!

—Lawrin

PETER MACLEOD

Learning

All of us know and love Tom, and treasure our conversations with him. They are always, by turn, illuminating and expansive but also fundamentally generous and kind. The best teachers show their students their own love of learning. For Tom, this is a reflex. Is it possible to have a conversation with him without his scribbling something down or looking something up or following along shortly after with a detailed note? But let's also talk about how Tom conducts a conversation, and what we all know is his infectious, if particular, manner of speech. You recognize it immediately. The pause. The scowl. The look of acute pain that crosses his face, as he apologizes once, then twice. The claims to ignorance and inadequacy and general bafflement. The performative humility and determined equality and irrepressible puzzling that are a levelling force in every conversation, and which make him so human. You are in awe of him, and still he treats you like a peer. This is Tom's ethic and just one among his many gifts.

—Peter MacLeod

KIM KIERANS

Split Infinitive

To boldly split an infinitive is wantonly to seek the wrath of Curran.

Tom Curran introduced me to the split infinitive in the fall term of 1979 with a big circle around three words on my FYP paper. The correction stood out like a zit on my nose on prom day. I have no memory of what adverb I had wedged between "to" and the verb, but I will never forget the pointed message from my beloved tutor. I had committed the mortal sin of splitting the infinitive. My shame.

I had sailed through primary and secondary school at a time when the public education system embraced phonetics and had abandoned grammar instruction "based on the argument that it was irrelevant to language and writing development" (Vanstone, 2017). Obviously, no one had thought to consult Tom Curran about this. Had they, he might have suggested that attention to grammar is important because complex sentence structure and complex thoughts are mutually dependent (Vanstone, citing Nunan). And Tom was determined that his tutorial would know the rules of grammar and never split another infinitive—or at least if they did, there would be a darn good reason.

As we worked our way through Plato and Augustine, I thought about that split or cleft infinitive, the cave and conversion. Tom Curran led me from the cave of grammatical ignorance towards grammatical enlightenment and clarity of expression. Through grammar Tom opened a door that gave his tutorial what Amy Benjamin describes as metalanguage, "language about language" (2016, p.18). How FYP is that? As a Curran convert, I took it as my mission over these past 40 years to school hundreds, maybe even thousands of working journalists and journalism students on the perils of the split infinitive.

Who knew that the topic was so controversial and for centuries has pitted "non-split die-hards" (Fowler, 1926) against free-range linguists. Jeremy Butterfield, the editor of Fowler's *A Dictionary of Modern English Usage* (2015) opens the section on the split infinitive by noting: "Few other grammatical issues have become such a cultural meme." In this age of social media and text messages "prescriptive grammar" is considered quaint. The history of the split-infinitive could be said to be one of British rule and Victorian (in)sensibilities, because as colleague D.I. Suttonius wrote to me: "There is no structural or grammatical historical reason why it should not be done; English had been happily splitting infinitives for about six centuries without any problems before someone told it to stop. It's purely a question of style."

Fowler (2015) cites F. Th. Visser's *An Historical Syntax of the English Language* (4 vols., 1963–73) about the emergence of the split infinitive in the 13th century. One example comes from the renowned and revered John Wycliffe, Biblical translator, reformer, and who wrote "*hat movede the pape of Rome to thus accepte mennes persones,*" (c.1380) (as cited in Fowler, 2015). "From about the beginning of the sixteenth century to about the last decades of the eighteenth century the use of the split infinitive seems to have been as it were tabooed in the written language," Fowler notes.

That did not stop George Gordon, Lord Byron (1788-1824) from using his poetic licence to split an infinitive for drama and emphasis in the poem, *Love and Death.*

> Thus much and more; and yet thou lovs't me not,
> And never wilt! Love dwells not in our will
> Nor can I blame thee, though it be my lot
> To *strongly, wrongly, vainly* love thee still.

A Smithsonian magazine article in 2013 blames the "infinitive taboo" on one "misguided Latinist" Henry Alford, a dean of Canterbury Cathedral. His publication of *A Plea for the Queen's English* in 1864 calls the split infinitive a crime. The 20th century brings a softer less rigid consideration of this contentious issue. Grammar guru H.W. Fowler in *The King's English* (1908) offers sage advice:

> The 'split' infinitive has taken such hold upon the consciences of journalists that, instead of warning the novice against splitting his infinitives, we must warn him against the curious superstition that the splitting or not splitting makes the difference between a good and a bad writer. The split infinitive is an ugly thing … ; but it is one among several hundred ugly things, and the novice should not allow it to occupy his mind exclusively. (Part II.25)

Furthermore, Fowler in his seminal work *A Dictionary of Modern English Usage* (1926) notes "a real split infinitive though not desirable in itself is preferable to either of two things, to real ambiguity and to patent artificiality" (560). Meanwhile, Strunk and White in *Elements of Style 4th ed.* (1999) urges avoidance "unless the writer wishes to place unusual stress on the adverb" (58). Is one "to diligently inquire" or "to inquire diligently"?

So where should we stand when it comes to the use of the split infinitive? I'm with Tom Curran. In 1979 and now in 2019,

I support learning and applying the rules of grammar. So, when I split an infinitive, my objective must be to further cement a point. Or as detective fiction writer Raymond Chandler wrote in a letter to a meddling copy editor at *Atlantic Monthly* in 1947: "When I split an infinitive, God damn it, I split it so it will remain split." I wonder how Tom would have responded to Chandler's letter.

—Kim Kierans
May 29, 2019

References:

Benjamin, A., *et al.* (May 2006). "Teacher to Teacher: What Is Your Most Compelling Reason for Teaching Grammar?" *The English Journal*, Vol. 95, No. 5, pp. 18-21 URL: http://www.jstor.org/stable/30046583.

Byron, Lord GG. "Love and Death." *Poetry Foundation*. Retrieved from https://www.poetryfoundation.org/poems/49266/love-and-death

Fowler H.W. *A Dictionary of Modern English Usage*. Oxford: Oxford University Press, 1926.

Fowler, H. W. *The King's English* (2 ed.). Oxford: Clarendon Press, 1908 and New York: Bartleby.com, 1999 https://www.bartleby.com/116/503.html

Fowler, W.H. *A Dictionary of Modern English Usage* (4th ed.). Oxford: Oxford University Press: 2015. https://www.oxfordreference.com/view/10.1093/acref/9780199661350.001.0001/acref-9780199661350-e-5585

O'Conner, P.T. & Kellerman, S. (February 2013). "Most of What You Think You Know About Grammar is Wrong."

Smithsonian Magazine. https://www.smithsonianmag.com/arts-culture/most-of-what-you-think-you-know-about-grammar-is-wrong-4047445/

Strunk, W. & White E.B. *The Elements of Style* (4 ed.). New York: Longman, 1999.

Personal communication Brian A. N. Bitar, May 28, 2019.

Personal communication D.I. Suttonius, May 29, 2019.

Vanstone, M. (2016). *Grammar Instruction in Toronto District School Board English Classrooms* (A research paper for Master of Teaching, Department of Curriculum, Teaching and Learning Ontario Institute for Studies in Education of the University of Toronto). Retrieved from https://tspace.library.utoronto.ca/bitstream/1807/77238/1/Vanstone_Matthew_201706_MT_MTRP.pdf. CC BY-NC-ND 4.0

DANIEL BRANDES

On Klopstock and Tom Curran the Teacher

In Praise of Dr. Tom Curran

I suspect that I will not be the only long-time friend and colleague who struggles to describe the scholarly commitments of the Rev. Dr. Tom Curran. Those of us who have had the immense privilege of keeping company with Tom—of teaching alongside him, of learning from his example, and of reading and writing and labouring with him—may nevertheless struggle to situate Tom's distinctive posture within a single school of thought or theoretical denomination. This is certainly not because Tom has been secretive or has concealed himself from us. No one could accuse him of playing his cards close to his (signature, ever-present, even in the summer months) vest. On the contrary, Tom has been the most candid and generous among us; he has held nothing back, has made himself wholly present in his teaching. When I say, then, that Tom's scholarly commitments cannot be easily listed, this is owing neither to concealment nor to esotericism, but because the thinkers who have meant the most to him—Dante, Goethe, Schiller, Eliot—have not been approached, or at least not primarily, as objects of scholarship. Tom's "scholarly" commitments are existential ones; they are deeply felt and urgently expressed. The thinkers that I name here, then, are not of antiquarian interest for him. They are sources of inspiration and instruction, ennobling and endlessly fascinating company, and reliable points of orientation in his own profound engagement with a broken, beautiful world.

It is Dante, I think, who has spoken to him most directly, and it is in his lecturing on Dante that Tom has come closest to offering what might be described (inadequately) as his worldview. He annually reminds students that what is at issue in *The Divine Comedy* is not the afterlife, a poetic vision or prophecy of what awaits us when we die; and therefore the poem must not be read as a pious exhortation to readers to attend to their sinful souls. Its force is not "religious" in this reduced sense. Rather—and on this matter Tom is fond of citing Dante's famous epistle to Cangrande de la Scala—the poem is to be read as a work of ethics ("composed for practice rather than theory"); and far from directing its readers' attention to the life beyond this one, its aim is "to remove those living *in this life* from the state of misery and to lead them to the state of bliss." It is impossible to capture in writing the singular urgency (or glorious theatricality) with which Tom communicates this point to our students. Since the entire poem, for him, hinges on coming to terms with it, there is no point in moving ahead before it is fully appreciated. It is a point that must be lingered over, reflected upon, turned over and over … and if that lingering and reflecting and turning should require a postponement of our engagement with the assigned reading, then so be it. Better to engage in a serious and thoughtful way with this single potentially transformative point than to rehearse without comprehension the countless details and personages and punishments that follow. For Tom, just how Dante himself might have understood the poetic conversion from misery to bliss, and why he insisted that such a conversion belonged neither to the domain of religious instruction nor to the vagaries of aesthetic contemplation but must be appreciated as an (unfinished) ethical undertaking, are questions that our students cannot afford to overlook. He does not pretend or presume to answer them. Instead, he seeks to pose them as questions that are not beyond our students' powers of understanding, that demand their attention, and the answers to which promise to change their lives; and no one—at least not in my time at King's—has done this more effectively.

Of course, the Rev. Dr. Tom Curran does not pose questions of this weight in any ordinary way. In the service of such exalted questions, he brings to bear his formidable arsenal of pedagogical devices: rhetorical riddles, pregnant pauses, perambulatory exercises, an ever-present box of mysterious supporting documents and materials, comical and touching expressions of exasperation and bafflement at his failure to yet realize the implications of the questions in his own life, asides and detours devoted to popular culture's still greater failure in this connection ("who is … Beyonce?"). Sometimes these enactments may court confusion; but in all cases, what is beautifully modeled for our students is a deeply sensitive and thoughtful scholar engaging in his own singular way with matters of the highest human concern.

What matters here, I am suggesting, is not the doctrinal takeaway but the encounter itself. To see Tom lecture on Dante—and I have never missed this chance, not once, even when I've not been teaching in FYP—is to be present for a highly charged, often quite emotional affair. There really are moments in these lectures, as also in the Werther lectures, at which one feels present for something deeply intimate. This is what accounts, in my opinion, for the theatrical strain in Tom's presentation, his outsize embarrassment at even the hint of anything untoward, profane, sexual. It is not that he is monkish by nature (see here his fascination with Las Vegas), but rather that the intimacy in question is of a different kind. I have never encountered in any other lecturer either the heights of exaltation or the depths of sadness that I have encountered in Tom. He is often forced to pause, to gather himself, when a poetic turn of phrase strikes him as perfectly expressive of its object. (If I were to speculate, I might find here traces of his German Romantic inheritance: a conviction that creatures, objects, and events seek to bring themselves to expression, seek articulation through the human word, and that such expression, achieved only rarely in works of high poetry, can produce a kind of pain in the most sensitive among us.) The example that comes immediately to mind is from *Paradiso*, Canto 17, where Dante meditates, through the figure of his great-great grandfather Caccaguido, on the pain of displacement and exile. Describing the "shot from the bow of exile," Caccaguido warns Dante (the soon to be exiled poet) of his exile from Florence:

> Thou shalt leave each thing
>   Beloved most dearly: this is the first shaft
>   Shot from the bow of exile. Thou shalt prove
> How salt the savour is of others' bread;
>   How hard the passage, to descend and climb
>   By others' stairs …
> (*Paradiso* 17.55-60)

These lines have always brought Tom up short in his lectures, sometimes bringing him to tears. I believe he finds in them a perfection in poetry that is hard to bear. Perhaps he experiences here something akin to what Werther experiences in that fateful moment when nature is roaring outside (he is staring out the window at a great thunderstorm) and Lotte utters the name "Klopstock." Overcome by the power of his own feeling, Werther describes himself as "lost in the sensations that flooded [him] on hearing the name," thereby registering a hidden correspondence or continuum—expressed in the figure of the "flood"—linking the natural world and human nature. The storm raging outside is mirrored in the storm raging inside of him, but it is only the poetic word that is capable of effecting and expressing this correspondence. Here, too, in his reflections on Werther, Tom has often been arrested in his presentation. And how else *should* one respond in the face of such a divine correspondence between the poetic word and what it poetizes, between mind and matter, word and thing? How otherwise would we wish our students to experience such things?

I'd like to linger on Werther for a moment longer, for he is a figure whom Tom deeply loves. He has sometimes remarked to our students that an inability to feel sympathy for Werther's plight, a failure to empathize with the heartache of such a man, must be judged not simply an intellectual failure—say, a failure to catch some detail or other in the text—but a moral failure, a failure of compassion, or a failure to exercise one's imagination in the service of another living creature. I have thought quite a bit about Tom's fellow feeling for this young man whose uncompromising war with convention seems so at odds with Tom's own good manners, his characteristic sobriety and rectitude. And more particularly, I have wondered whether one might find here the key to understanding his solidarity with our students, our own convention-testing romantics, whose afflictions always strike him with such force. That there is a real link to be found here is suggested by Tom's reading of the end of "The Sorrows of Young Werther." Without suspending his compassion, and without for a moment doubting the nobility of Werther's lofty intentions, he nevertheless cannot abide Werther's fateful decision. He considers it (correctly, in my view) a selfish and finally indefensible gesture, the concrete effects of which on Werther's closest friends and neighbors are disastrous. Tom has not been afraid to pass judgment on Werther—who has prized his own concern with authenticity and his own reckless nature over the health and happiness of those closest to him, and who has ultimately kept faith only with himself. This stern judgment has sometimes been experienced by our students themselves as jarring, as striking a discordant note—as if sympathy with Werther required an unconditional approval of his actions, even at their most excessive and harmful. Of course this sort of reckless suspension of judgment only mirrors the recklessness of Werther himself; it does not characterize the empathetic imagination that I mentioned earlier and it is not the kind of compassionate attention that characterizes good reading; in any case, it is certainly not the kind of friendship that Tom Curran has extended to those he has befriended (either in fictions or in the classroom) in the time that I've known him.

The kind of friendship that he prizes, and for which he has an extraordinary gift, is not without judgment or expectation. It is not accepting of all things and it does not encourage its beneficiaries to indulge their lowest, or loftiest, impulses at the expense of others. When he served as Associate Director, his handiest tool was the gentle admonition, precisely calibrated to elicit the best efforts in our students. And it is worth reflecting, finally, on the powerful effect that Tom's teaching—but also his manners, his tone, his bearing—has had on them. We are familiar, all too familiar, with the growing fragility that has afflicted our student body, and in these dark times, where the slightest hint of expectation or of disappointment risks destroying a student's confidence for weeks or months, one might suppose that a middle-aged, white, and well-mannered man, wearing a moustache and a three-piece suit, who insists on addressing students formally (as Mr. and Miss) would meet with an implacable opposition (or, worse, sullen indifference) from the student body. What, then, accounts for the universal admiration, even adoration, inspired by Tom in our students?

For a small few, I suspect, it is the unabashed eccentricity of the man (the natty clothing, the above-mentioned omnipresent box, the seemingly discordant but oddly comprehensive knowledge of popular culture). But—again I will allow myself to speculate—for the overwhelming majority it is something simpler: Tom takes his students seriously and he treats them as adults. He abhors, as he ought, the grim and reductive pieties of identity politics. His old-fashioned expectation is that all students, regardless of their colour, class, or gender, owe it to themselves to think, to exercise their imagination and understanding, to form and reform their opinions. He takes as his governing assumption that our students are capable of thinking beyond their inherited identities and that each of them may be led *to see* (and more, *to say*) what is just, what is beautiful, what is true. That Tom maintains these expectations for all students, and that they love him for it, is a very heartening sign. It suggests that our gloomiest speculations about the future of our precious program (inasmuch as it shares Tom's humanistic and aspirational ethos) are likely to be overblown. If our students are still capable of responding to Tom Curran—if they are still eager to discover in themselves that more humane, more receptive, more imaginative, and more capacious self to which he bears witness in his reading, and which he elicits in his teaching—we may continue on apace, assured that we are not toiling in vain.

WILLIAM BARKER

Tom Curran: Fake or Facsimile?

For Tom Curran, of course

Regarding Tom Curran, who is always carefully invested with splendid manners, who bows and nods as he observes you carefully, and who speaks in a curiously indirect manner, the question will sometimes arise: "Is he for real?"

I will pursue this question by examining his on-line essay *Fake or Facsimile?* I will then turn to a recent conversation I had with Tom: "What is happening in the humanities?" This question, his essay, and his identity are all closely related. One of the central issues in the study and practice of the literary humanities is authenticity—our careful mastery of languages in order to achieve a more direct and true relationship with the past and with other cultures, the identification of texts and determination of the genuine author, the making of commentary that assumes some kind of authentic engagement with the text, and debates that depend on the attention and good faith of others. How willing and able are we to connect with texts and with each other in an authentic manner? What happens, in our ironic age of simulacrum, parody, appropriation, and false news, when the desire for that authentic connection falls away?

First, a quick account of the fifteen-part essay. You can read the whole of *Fake or Facsimile* online at www.recherché.com (don't forget the accent). The first part is dated 26 May 2017 and the last, number 15, is 25 October 2017. I had been put on a mailing list announcing these essays and I read them as they first came out. I found them quirky, ironic, charming and challenging. I was amused and impressed. It is a strange project. To quote from Essay 9, "this series, entitled Fake or Facsimile, is about designer handbags and art galleries, and how both of these cultural institutions can be seriously damaged by high quality 'off-brand' substitutes—sometimes derisively referred to as 'knock-offs.'" How did a student of Schleiermacher's hermeneutics end up reflecting on the truth and fiction of the Hermès Birkin handbag? The pleasure I received from these essays was similar to what I felt when I first read the highly eccentric Hillel Schwartz, who had had also essayed the problem of authenticity in his *Culture of the Copy*. But this was not Schwartz, it was Tom Curran, and knowing the author seemed to intensify the experience, as I could determine a distinct voice in the writing. In fact, it seems difficult to call this voice anyone but "Tom" as I proceed. This sense of friendship, sometimes real, often imagined, is essential to communication in the humanities (a point to which I will return).

Let me, by outlining you the argument, tempt you into reading this series of essays. The first, "The Myth of the Yuandan," is a reflection on the problem of fake purses, watches, and the like, now for open sale on Chinese web sites, and the irony that a fake Louis Vuitton bag may for the non-professional be indistinguishable from the genuine, or that it may be easily distinguishable and that there are reasons to sometimes prefer the fake to the original (cost being the most obvious). Outright fakes thus have their complications, but the matter becomes even more difficult where we move to consciously planned and openly declared fakes, more politely known as facsimiles.

Tom's next four essays cover replication in the museum world. He begins with the complex site for the Caves of Chauvet, which were constructed at enormous cost by the French government to allow us to experience prehistoric cave art in a meticulous reconstruction after the authentic Chauvet site had been permanently sealed. From there we move to the beard of King Tut, a poorly executed repair of the ancient head, even though the life-size replications of his tomb (in Essay 4) has been so carefully prepared as to provide the sensitive viewer with a sense of actuality. But not all of such exhibitions have such a clear function. When we turn to the problem of the Terracotta Army (Essay 5) we can see how the complications pile up. The so-called Emperor's Army is comprised of thousands of terracotta life-sized statues of warriors found in 3rd century BCE burial sites in Shaanxi Province of China. The exhibitions that followed in New York, Frankfurt and elsewhere were a sensation. Yet many of the "authentic" items were in fact reproductions. And what can we say about the actual statues, all formed from moulds? Is the mould the "original"? A question for Walter Benjamin, who takes this essentially political question into the late modern era and our embrace of all forms of replication and yet who strangely never appears in this or any of the other essays.

Tom then turns to something that would, however, astound the world-weary Benjamin, the Otsuka Museum in Japan, in which every work on display is a reproduction. The Museum opened in 1998. The existence of these copies in a formal museum challenge our ideas of the fake: these specially prepared works are "not 'fakes': in the precise sense that "they are created on a unique medium (ceramic boards), which ensures that they will not be mistaken for the originals"; they are not 'fakes' or 'counterfeits' because they could never—because of their ceramic manufacture—be passed off as originals." The next essay looks at the motives behind this museum and in the spirit of contradiction, Tom declares that he has "come to praise Otsuka, not to bury him!" He gives a vigorous defence of the right to reproduce art and to display the reproductions. In the next essay (8), he continues with this argument, by arguing that reproductions are necessary given that many outstanding works of art after purchase disappear into private collections or warehouses, hidden away from the rest of us. If we cannot ever see the original, he pleads, give us the reproduction.

The next essay, with the brilliant Shakespearean title "The Handbags of Two Households: 'Both Alike in Dignity,'" compares the competitive philanthropy of two French billionaires, Bernard Arnault (LVMH—Louis Vuitton, Dior, Dom Pérignon) and François Pinault (Artémis—Gucci, Yves Saint-Laurent, Chateau Latour), both of whom are engaged in creating major cultural venues in Paris. Up to now the art world and the world of the handbag had been separated in his series. Now we can see the handbag and the art gallery begin to come together through the power of commerce. One person who unites these two worlds is the American artist Jeff Koons. Essay 10 ("Appropriation Artist") looks at the joint project of Louis Vuitton and Jeff Koons—the Mona Lisa handbag. Here we sense a certain acidity in the humour.

We are now in the world of the absurd, with the handbag, based on a reproduction, being sold as an original, even collectable, work of art, with the commercial processes of accessorizing, purchasing and reselling all built into an aesthetic of luxury consumption. Koons is seen as a genial satirist of our time, someone who celebrates his ability to appropriate forms in popular culture, and who at the same time, carefully guards his own artistic look (his "signature") through copyright. Essay 12 ends with an amusing warning: "do not appropriate the intellectual property of an American appropriation artist." This essay, principally on designer Marc Jacobs' failed show in 2007 ("The Magpie Collection") takes us further into the world of post-modern appropriation in the convergence of art and fashion.

In Essay 13 we are taken further down this hole—to "Paris Semi Couture" and the work of Martin Margiella, the avant garde fashion designer: "'Semi couture' is the place where art begins again to imitate life; where the fashion world appropriates the street, and where the most luxurious fashion may also be stylish, attractive, and comfortable—all at once." In other words, distressed, ripped, and tired clothing now becomes chic. The essay also takes a sideways look at the salesmanship of Aldo Bensadoun, the founder of Aldo shoes, who by copying European styles and importing them swiftly to North America became enormously wealthy. Style, and the art of style, is seen as fluid and fast.

Essay 14 continues this theme of appropriation with observations on sampling in music. The point is summed up by Marc Jacobs: "All these things belong together." We are in an era which does not separate but merges our tastes. At the end of this essay, there is a sudden aside on hermeneutics, the most theoretical moment of the entire series, but this is not an academic moment. Instead we are asked to contemplate Borges' famous parable "Pierre Menard, Author of the Quixote." Menard is said to have written the entire *Don Quixote*, on his own, three centuries after Cervantes, and, astonishingly, this new Quixote is a word for word match with the original. This astonishing feat challenges our notions of temporality and originality. (I feel I must here contribute an example that seems inspired by Borges, the *Getting Inside Jack Kerouac's Head* project of 2009; day by day Simon Morris typed short passages from *On the Road*, then after many months of work, presented the final typescript—in reverse order of his typing—as his own ontological masterpiece.)

The final essay in series is on the film *Blade Runner* and the originating novel, Philip K. Dick's *Do Androids Dream of Electric Sheep?* We are now moving past the commercial reproduction of the Mona Lisa or street grunge into the world of living replicants, the world of the post-human. And with the post-human the series concludes. It's as though Tom has hit a dead end, though he does not admit it. Do androids dream of the Hermès Birkin handbag? Could they ever desire the Jeff Koons Mona Lisa from Louis Vuitton? It seems unlikely. To end with the second *Blade Runner* seems entirely appropriate.

This longish summary is presented to give you a sense of the whole, which though presented in a fragmentary and apparently whimsical manner, has a structure. Tom Curran's study of "Fake or Facsimile," with its principal focus on the relationship of the handbag and the modern museum, is written with a mixture of serious thinking and ironic juxtaposition that seems to mirror the playful absurdity of the contemporary world of art and fashion. Furthermore, it is not clogged with the normally required references to various deities of theory whose names inevitably arose in my mind as I read this work, for instance: Barthes (mythologies, death of the author), Benjamin (reproduction), Debord (spectacle), Bürger (avant-garde), Krauss (avant-garde), Bataille (excretion and appropriation), Foster (re-photography, the "real"), Lyotard (post-modern sublime), Baudrillard (simulacrum) and not a single citation from the journal *Fashion Theory*. Instead we have Tom musing in an unmediated manner on phenomena that have attracted an enormous amount of commentary. This essay (I now call the whole project an "essay" in the old sense of "trial balloon") is thus not so much a contribution to scholarship as it is a expression of personal thought that engages the reader with the complications of authorship, copyright, plagiarism, our present-day relation to the past, the relation of commerce and art, and the wonderful topsy-turvy world of modern art. Because his essay is whimsical, opinionated, with unexpected turns, you get the sense of an authorial presence that engages the reader. His essay encourages thought, not mastery. So, I have to thank him for writing this work, a gift freely offered on the internet. We are in an improved position to enjoy the conundrums of our condition.

Now that we have had a preliminary look at *Fake or Facsimile* I want to turn to a related conversation I had recently with Tom at a local bakery and coffee shop where I do much of my writing (including this essay). During our chat I noticed Tom was taking notes. It was a few days later, when I realized I had promised to write this essay, that I turned back to our conversation, which I knew was important to me, but the details of which I had already forgotten. I asked him if I could have his notes. Here is what he wrote down in his little notebook.

> Bill Barker (May 10th, 2019): The Age of Post-Humanity
>
> There is now no spiritual Transcendent Dimension
>
> In Identity Politics we are Self-Created Beings
>
> Therefore we are now in an historical moment where it is nearly impossible to connect with the texts.
>
> CSP (et al.): not a critique of the tradition, but a carrying-on of tradition … the self-critique is what the tradition has been doing all along … the critique is actually part of the tradition … Nietzsche: part of the process … Clearing out of the cobwebs … We treat the tradition as if it were unable to critique itself.
>
> The Turmoil in the Humanities … a tradition of continuing contestation … so rather than a sweeping away …
>
> "The Human Zoo" ~ Humanities create Community …
>
> A Critique of the Critique
>
> Our age is one of unsubtle and reductive critique, where ideas are domesticated …

The conversation, which I admit was at moments more of a monologue, all comes flooding back.

Even though we had started the conversation with a few observations on King's Foundation Year Program and its perpetual attempt to define the Tradition, we were now looking at the end of the chronological narrative of FYP, where Tom's essay had also ended, with the prospect of the post-human, which presents a significant challenge to any notion of the human, not to say the humanities. With the increasing presence of AI and robotics in our lives, it is not impossible to see our human existence as a prelude to a future age of machines, with our humanity merely a step in an evolution towards a future that is only hinted at in science fiction. In this vision, love, death, the self, divinity, will all undergo redefinition or indeed may be swept away as early manifestations of something we do not yet understand.

Perhaps this fantasy of a human-less future is a symptom of our own sense of displacement or confusion that come from two major shifts, the gradual and inexorable disappearance of a cultural élite that had existed for centuries in the West and our current sense of being swamped in an accelerated media-driven environment. The canon of great works, our history, the idea of what it means to be "educated" are all in a state of change. And interestingly, some of the agents of this change are the very people who also know how to regret this change the most—academic critics, artists, and intellectuals. We have taken the methods of critique that go far back in philosophy and literature and historical writing, and we have continued to apply them, now to our own tradition. Nietzsche the philologist and philosopher is our leader in this ironic self-analytical, ourobourotic self-devouring. He sets out the contradictions and hidden dishonesty and also the greatness of the analytical tradition that he knows so intimately.

I have been spending a lot of my time in the early sixteenth century with Erasmus of Rotterdam. I now find an almost unbridgeable gap between the work of this writer (and others of his time) and our contemporary world, where a number of once basic truths are now being scattered or set aside as part of a larger historical process which I do not pretend to understand, however much I can feel it. The canonical text, the historical frame of that text, and its spiritual aspect all seem to be evaporating, and as a sample text we could use the New Testament, which for Erasmus carried the living authentic voice of Christ. It is a captivating way of approaching a text, to see it as holding such abundant Presence. Yet, for me, increasingly, "All that is solid melts into air, all that is holy is profaned." As I read Erasmus on the New Testament, I find there is an increasing gap between the experience he calls me to witness, and the experience that I actually recover from his writing.

The historical process of this inexorable falling away to which I have been subject is now over a century old yet continues in such a way that it is still possible to use those century-plus words from the *Communist Manifesto* of Marx and Engels ("all that is solid ...") to describe my present-day predicament. Yet, with new media and their flooding of our experience, the sense of distance and of loss has been accelerated. We really are in a strange moment, the moment which Tom's *Fake or Facsimile* also witnesses. One may well ask if what we read in our classrooms is now an appropriated fake or facsimile. Because we no longer in our wisdom are able to meet the text on its own terms, we remake it according to our specific needs: this remaking is now accepted as an indisputable and inevitable feature of interpretation. But is the text now an authentic witness, or a projection of our own longings? Has our own horizon basically overwhelmed the horizon of the text?

I recently came across an essay that perhaps I should have read some time ago. It has helped me to understand what has been happening to the humanities in our historical moment. This is "The Human Zoo" referred to in the notes above. Peter Sloterdijk's "Rules for the Human Zoo: A Response to *The Letter on*

Humanism" ("Regeln für den Menschenpark: Ein Antwortschreiben zum *Brief über den Humanismus*") is a reconsideration of Martin Heidegger's long essay of 1946, now read in the context of genetic engineering. Sloterdijk's piece was published in 1999 in *Die Zeit*, the Hamburg weekly. Because Sloterdijk looked at what he called "breeding the human" as part of the tradition of humanities (from Plato through Nietzsche and onwards) he was seen as somehow proposing rather than describing eugenics, an unnameable subject in post-Nazi Germany; the furore at the time was in part driven by a secretly mobilized attack on Sloterdijk organized by Jürgen Habermas, the leading sociologist in the Frankfurt School tradition (curiously, the very kind of subterfuge that was often found in the humanist world of Erasmus and Luther). The essay, translated by Mary Varney Rorty, a distinguished bioethicist, appeared in *Society and Space* (27 [2009]: 12-28) and is available on line.

Sloterdijk announces the end of the humanities as they have been studied and theorized in antiquity and since their revival in the Renaissance. His idea of the traditional humanities brings together a group of themes that are entirely familiar to those who study Renaissance humanism: friendship, community, letters, books, and education. He begins thus:

> Books, as the poet Jean Paul once remarked, are thick letters to friends. With this phrase, he aptly articulated the quintessential nature and function of humanism: It is telecommunication in the medium of print to underwrite friendship. That which has been known since the days of Cicero as humanism is in the narrowest and widest senses a consequence of literacy. Ever since philosophy began as a literary genre, it has recruited adherents by writing in an infectious way about love and friendship. (12)

This recognition that humanism, books, and friendship are all of a piece is astonishingly accurate. It could serve as an introduction to Erasmus' *Antibarbarians* (1520), a dialogue among five young friends about their revolutionary desire to recover the ancient texts in a program that will overcome the professors of late medieval scholastic philosophy, whom they deem "the barbarians." Instead of dialectic and the syllogism, Erasmus and his friends seek a new world that is essentially non-academic, that relies on enthymeme, metaphor and story telling, thought that is shared by letters and books amongst the good friends of *bonae litterae*. The Bible can and should be read as part of this authentic communication.

These friends belong to an élite social class that is determined not by birth, wealth, or position, but by an education by friends (even friendly teachers) into a specific canon of works from antiquity and by a shared manner of speaking (mostly in the refined Latin of Cicero). These friends were all members of a nascent republic of letters (the concept already named by Francesco Barbaro writing to his hyper-learned friend Poggio Bracciolini in 1417). Learned friends were the glue that held the community of the humanities together, that taught one another, recruited new members to the community, and taught them the right way to speak. (To bring this into our own time, one might turn to Pierre Bourdieu who claimed that the principal aim of schooling is to teach students the "magisterial language," the way to speak like a professor; Francoise Wacquet has written a history of how we have learned "to speak like a book.") These friends communicated by letter and by books. And it is no exaggeration to say that Erasmus wrote his books as "thick letters" (the festive style of his correspondence is found in even the longest and most technical of his over one hundred works, all of which are also prefaced by letters to his "friends"—scholars, students, popes, kings, and a Rhine toll collector.

Today, we may still identify remnants of this kind of communication in the florid introductions that academics like to give each other at conferences or in the prefaces or footnotes to academic books. The preface often names the friends who supported the book, and the reader can identify in which specific province of the republic the author dwells. Indeed, the book itself is still often given as a gift amongst friends and colleagues. It is unclear, however, at what point "friendship" begins to assume an administered quality and becomes a way of speaking. Our institutional language still insists on these tropes of friendship. This informal essay you are now reading and the book in which it appears could serve as evidence for the persistence of this theme.

But back to Sloterdijk. In his essay he argues that the traditional humanities are really a political response to an essentially human quality: our "bestiality." The humanities, the texts, the moral messages, the educational process, are there to tame "the wolf" in us, to make us "loyal dogs." Writing is the means to attain this, for by the technology of writing we can extend our friendship and our care to others at a distance, even create communities. In the nineteenth century, the heyday of this community, humanism was a national phenomenon ("to incline the young towards the classics and to reaffirm the universal validity of the national canon," 14). But now "the art of writing love-inspiring letters to a nation of friends, however professionally it is practised, is no longer sufficient to form a telecommunicative bond between members of a modern mass society" (14).

Of course the humanities have continued to exist, but now as a marginal sub-culture. Even though this collapse into marginality has a long history, beginning with the first world war, the dream is often revived, and was during one of these conditional periods of revival, immediately after the second world war, in 1946, that Heidegger wrote his "Letter on Humanism," a document that can be seen in terms of the old way of the humanities—a letter to a stranger, seeking the stranger's intellectual affection (the recipient,

Jean Beaufret, a member of the French resistance, became a leading exponent and defender of Heidegger in the post-war period). Yet Heidegger in his essay is ready to abandon the word "humanism" because the word is a barrier to thinking. After all, is not man the cause of man's own suffering? Isn't humanist thought part of a 2000-year denial that by treating man as a "rational animal" there is an admission that man is in some ways always an "animal"? Heidegger, on Sloterdijk's account, is emphatic: the human is ontologically separate from the animal. The human in its essence does seek to befriend humanity (and in saying this, Heidegger retains one of the essential qualities of the older humanist ideal). Yet in the language of Heidegger, man is the "shepherd of Being," and human language is the "house of Being," and these conditions place huge demands on man. "Heidegger's critique of humanism suggests an attitude which directs man toward an asceticism that goes far deeper than that achievable though any humanistic education" (19). Curiously, that is one of Heidegger's reasons for following the Nazi doctrine, as it "despised the constraining values of peace and education more than its opponents" (19). Basically, according to Sloterdijk, Heidegger is asking "What can tame men, when the role of humanism as the school for humanity has collapsed?" (20).

For Sloterdijk, Heidegger was correct that the humanities had ceased to play their effective role but he had become trapped by his notion of the human. Sloterdijk would rather see man as an animal who struggles with his animal nature in striving to become a "being in the world": for "man is a creature ... rooted in the characteristics of his species that reveal themselves in the basic ideas of premature-born-ness, neoteny, and the chronic animalian immaturity of man" (20). "We could even go so far as to suggest that man is the being in which being an animal is separate from remaining an animal." Man is an animal, but man also seeks to transcend this condition, to be a breeder and tamer of animals. As you can see in Plato, "Humans are self-fencing, self-shepherding creatures" (25) and the king (in the *Laws*) is above all a breeder of men, an anthropotechnologist. And so we have arrived to the era of genetic engineering, and the total displacement of the humanities as a way to overcome the animal in man. Sloterdijk concludes his essay with these words:

> Two thousand years after Plato wrote it seems as if not only the gods but the wise have abandoned us, and left us alone with our partial knowledge and our ignorance. What is left to us in the place of the wise is their writings, in their glinting brilliance and their increasing obscurity. They still lay in more or less accessible editions; they can still be read, if only one knew why one should bother. It is their fate – to stand in silent bookshelves, like posted letters no longer collected, sent to us by authors, of whom we no longer know whether or not they could be our friends.
>
> Letters that are not mailed cease to be missives for possible friends; they turn into archived things. Thus this—that the important books of the past have more and more ceased to be letters to friends, and that they do not lie any longer on the tables and nightstands of their readers—this has deprived the humanistic movement of its previous power. Less and less often do archivists climb up to the ancient texts in order to reference earlier statements of modern commonplaces. Perhaps it occasionally happens that in such researches in the dead cellars of culture the long-ignored texts begin to glimmer, as if a distant light flickers over them. Can the archives also come into the Clearing? Everything suggests that archivists have become the successors of the humanists. For the few who still peer around in those archives, the realization is dawning that our lives are the confused answer to questions which were asked in places we have forgotten. (27)

I think Sloterdijk's essay is similar in a way to Tom's *Fake or Facsimile,* in that it addresses a major challenge to the humanities with a singular eccentricity. I can't say if Sloterdijk has misread Heidegger, Nietzsche or Plato in his account, but for my purposes it doesn't really matter if he has. The main point of the essay for me is contained in the two passages that begin and end the work and the general problem that he outlines in his main argument. We have clearly moved into new conditions for the humanities. The central function of the humanities, "taming the human animal" is now displaced imaginatively by the possibility of "breeding." I think Sloterdijk is quite correct that the old humanist role of creating broad community through authentic communication has gone into retreat in the sense that it no longer manages the general world of our culture. The world of *Fake or Facsimile* shows that well. Yet whether we have displaced the traditional function of "training the human animal" by genetic engineering is still to be seen, though as an imagined direction, this too leads us into the world of replicant and facsimile. With this kind of vision ahead of us, the old notion that there can be authentic connection between thinking minds does become shaken.

What role will the old texts play in the future, a future that is already upon us? I feel that the essential thing to do is to continue to read as closely and as intently as possible, to attend carefully to one's own reaction to the texts and to connect with others in these acts of reading. We read in such a way as to bring the texts into our present, while at the same time acknowledging their otherness, their essential strangeness. They must be allowed to speak their strangeness to us. But there is a problem in the way we have been trained to listen to them, for our new immersive world makes it increasingly hard to enter into a meditative relationship with them. Our system of education is increasingly inadequate to the task of slow reading and careful thought that we need to read well. Our communities of readers are more fragile. Other media are attracting us. There is an unusual loneliness for many readers, especially those in search of some form of authentic connection with the past.

STEVEN BURNS

What Comes After?

In 2006, when I was retiring as Professor of Philosophy at Dalhousie, I was invited to deliver the FINAL LECTURE to the Foundation Year Programme. Since I had had a long association with FYP and had been cross-appointed to the Contemporary Studies Programme for more than two decades, I was especially honoured and happy to oblige. The whole lecture ("The Sound of Silence") can be accessed at the King's Library. Now, thirteen years later, I have been invited to contribute to this Festschrift marking the 70th birthday of our colleague, Dr. Thomas Curran. Again I am honoured and happy to oblige. I would like to do so by revisiting and expanding one of the several sections of that Final Lecture of mine, because it was inspired by Dr. Curran.

First, allow me a few reflections on the number 13. When I think of my own life in blocks of thirteen years I see a familiar pattern. In the *first* thirteen years I was raised to puberty by my parents. The *second* block of thirteen was dramatically different: puberty does that to you, but I also completed Philosophy degrees at Acadia University and the University of Alberta, and had a year of study at the University of Western Australia. My fellowship had the collateral benefit of almost unlimited travel. I flew west from Edmonton to Australia. On the way home I continued west, paying substantial visits to 15 countries. That was an eye-opening period. The *third* block of thirteen years was again radically different. I completed a Doctorate at the University of London; I found a job and learned to teach and to publish, and was granted tenure. I also found a wife and we started a family. It was the beginning of life as a grown-up. The *fourth* block was nose-to-the grindstone time. Children grew up, I helped with our Canadian Philosophical Association, and with our local Dalhousie Faculty Association, and I chaired my Department. The *fifth* block was a period of cruising. I completed a major research project at the University of Vienna, served a two-year term as Director of CSP at King's, and ended with a semester as Visiting Professor in Vienna. And I gave the FYP Final Lecture.

Why am I reflecting on all this stuff about ME, when my focus should be Tom? Apart from being intrigued by the seven ages of 'man', as we used to say, I am of course reflecting that Tom has had a similar life: a childhood, a period of study and travel, a job that required him to learn to teach and to publish (overlapping with establishing a family), a nose-to-the-grindstone period, and a flourishing fifth period. But what comes after that? Tom is reaching his three-score years and ten, in the middle of his sixth block of thirteen years.

My *sixth* block of 13 years has just finished, a long winding-down since the Final Lecture of 2006. I taught part-time at King's for half of it, and now just the odd conference or publication clouds the sky. But my knees creak as I mount stairs; my grandchildren outrun me. And although I am looking forward to a *seventh* block, I have no reason to expect to outlive this final period. Which brings me to my real topic: the afterlife. Here I pick up a theme from my Final Lecture.

As a metaphor for a significant transition in one's life, death and rebirth has great potential. Tom's passing his Biblical allotment is a sort of little death, and his eventual retirement will be a sort of rebirth into a different world. I read a long while ago in the King's Alumni Magazine (*Tidings*), a striking article by Dr. Curran. He was discussing the immortality myths of the Ancient Egyptians, and listed some of their similes: "death is really to be understood [as] like coming up for air, or like recovering after a long illness; death is ... like a 'clearing sky' after inclement weather, ... death can only be compared to a homecoming after many years of wandering, or the joy of release after long years incarcerated in a dungeon." I agree with Dr. Curran that these similes "remain unsurpassed in the whole history of our literature."[1] They are metaphors which seem to license us to talk of living after death, of being reunited with loved ones in the afterlife, of meeting beyond the grave. They introduce the eternal to the very finite, and give us a long-range view of the smallness of our intellects and of the time we have 'on earth', as we say. They have a striking presence not only in Egyptian literature, but they echo throughout world literature.

We also need to acknowledge that they share a place in the literatures of the world with other metaphors that we need to respect. What should we expect after death? Nothing. Silence. Just the ashes of the destruction of the world (as at the end of Wagner's *Ring*), but without Wagner's melody of renewal soaring above the final silence. (That was a sly reference to my frequent FYP lectures on Schopenhauer and the *Ring* cycle of Richard Wagner. My texts for the Final Lecture were centred on that silence metaphor.)

Now recall the Egyptian metaphors for life after death. Of course one also respects the views expressed in those metaphors. But those afterlife metaphors awaken a different part of one's mind. They have the form of an argument: you know what it is like to

1 Tom Curran, "Egypt's Sweet Hereafter," *Tidings* (Summer 2005), p. 8.

be under water and desperate for breath, and then to burst through the surface and gasp with relief. Well, being alive is like being underwater; dying is like coming up for air. One immediately wonders how to apply this metaphor; in what ways is living like being under water? And what could the relief really be like? We can apply a metaphor when we know both terms of the comparison. For instance, some FYP students must have felt that being in high school was like drowning—they felt constrained, desperate, airless; and coming to King's felt like a breath of fresh air—a new freedom, real sustenance for your mind, etc. In this case the metaphor works, and gives us insight into their experience. But in the case of death we have no experience to compare to living, and so we suspect that we do not really understand the metaphor.

Plato, as you know, was a master of the metaphor for what life is like after a great change. The Allegory of the Cave is the one we are all most familiar with. It is, however, not about the transition to an afterlife; it is about making a connection with the eternal while in the midst of temporal life. It leads us from a set of known things to a set of unknown but knowable things. Our afterlife metaphors, however, purport to lead us from known things to unknowable ones.[2]

There are texts enough in Plato which suggest that he did think that personal survival made sense, and others that suggest the opposite. Here's one that suggests both, from the last pages of *The Apology*:

> Let us consider in another way also what good reason there is to hope that [death] is a good thing. For the state of death

2 I am tempted here (but shall resist) to expatiate on Plato's use of one of Tom's Egyptian similes: we know what it is like to see underwater, and how much clearer things are when we come above the surface; imagine then what it is like to go up above the air and see things as they really are, clear and pure (*Phaedo* 109–10). He adds that from up there the earth looks like "those twelve-piece leather balls, variegated, a patchwork of colours, … colours far brighter still and purer than these" (110b,c). I refrain from concluding that Plato had been taken up in a space ship.

> is one of two things: either the dead person wholly ceases to be and has no consciousness of anything, or it is, as people say, a change and migration of the soul from this to another place. And if it is an absence of all consciousness, like a sleep in which the sleeper does not even dream, death would be a wonderful gain .... But on the other hand, if death is, as it were, a change of habitation from here to some other place ..., what would any of you [not] give to meet with Orpheus and Musaeus and Hesiod and Homer? I am willing to die many times over, if these things are true.[3]

Like Tom's Egyptian metaphors, Socrates' metaphors suggest that death is not to be feared, but to be welcomed as bringing peace, if not adventure. This is a profound lesson, however construed.

Plato offers many attempted proofs of the immortality of the soul in the course of his works. I discuss one of them in detail in my Final Lecture. But for the present occasion I shall confine myself to a more recent philosopher, and to the specific matter of the interpretation of religious metaphors.

Tom is an authority on Friedrich Schleiermacher. My Schleiermacher, so to say, is Ludwig Wittgenstein. In his *Tractatus Logico-Philosophicus* Wittgenstein writes: "Everything that can be thought at all, can be thought clearly. Everything that can be said can be said clearly" (*TLP* 4.116). And his book ends with the admonition "Whereof one cannot speak, thereof one must be silent" (*TLP* 7). This conclusion is the result of his theory of language, of the requirements for being able to speak of anything at all. The theory is also related to his attempt to draw the limits of what we can say about things like life after death. His aphorism on this subject is: "Death is not an event of life. Death is not lived through" (*TLP* 6.431).

---

3 Plato, *The Apology*, 40c–41a. I have used the translation by Harold North Fowler (Loeb Classical Library, Harvard University Press, 1971; first printed in 1914), but with minor modifications suggested by F. J. Church's translation (Liberal Arts Press, 1956).

I think he is right about that. And we would also probably agree with him that just living through death would solve nothing. "Is a riddle solved by the fact that I survive for ever? Is this eternal life not as enigmatic as our present one?" (*TLP* 6.4312). His argument is that to speak of such things is to go beyond the limits of sense-making language. But it may seem to be an objection to this stripping of the power of language, that it is precisely through metaphor that we can get beyond the merely factual use of language. I am happy to agree with that, and to embrace the power of metaphor to enrich our language, to make it possible for poetic language to lead us to new insights and perspectives. But the implication of all of the Egyptian metaphors is that temporal life is all miserable. It is like being in a dungeon, or underwater, or lost away from home, or without shelter in a storm. And the afterlife is much preferable. I am reminded of Nietzsche's aphorism, that for Christians, "world" is a term of abuse. This implies that it is an illusion that we can be at home in this world, that we have an inborn longing to be in a better place which would be our true home. But of course such a "longing for something completely different"[4] may itself lead to an illusion. And what about the possiblity of changing the metaphor? Why should we rule out: Life is like a sunny day, and death a silent night? The Egyptian similes might be a consolation, but can we think that they prove there's an afterlife?

Returning to our metaphors about life after death. Here's what Wittgenstein wrote in 1929, shortly after returning to Cambridge:

> In religious language we seem constantly to be using similes. But a simile must be the simile for *something*. And if I can describe a fact by means of a simile I must also be able to drop the simile and to describe the facts without it. Now in our

4 I refer obliquely to *The Longing for the Totally Other*, by Max Horkheimer of the Frankfurt School.

> case (of religious metaphors) as soon as we try to drop the simile and simply to state the facts which stand behind it, we find that there are no such facts. And so, what at first appeared to be a simile now seems to be mere nonsense.[5]

Our afterlife metaphors have the form of a comparison between a known thing and a completely unknown one; if Wittgenstein is right about the nature of metaphorical meaning, they cannot tell us anything.

There are limits to the power of metaphors, and there is sometimes emptiness in their promise of wisdom. Do I think that I have said the final word on the subject? Not a chance.[6] Wittgenstein's return to Philosophy in the 1930s was marked first by self-criticism. In his first book he had only written about one sort of language, fact-stating language. Now he began to work with the idea that that was only one sort of discourse (he, perhaps misleadingly, used the term "language game") among many. Religious language, in particular, has a much different logic, and much different uses. But that leaves us prone to other sorts of illusion, especially ones caused by thinking that religious language tells truths the same way factual language does.

There is life after 70. I wish Tom many more years of service. There is more to do. For all of us.

---

5 "Lecture on Ethics", in *Ludwig Wittgenstein: Philosophical Occasions 1912-1951*, eds. J. Klagge and A. Nordmann (Indianapolis: Hackett Publishing Company, 1993), pp. 42-3.

6 A challenge to what I have said would need to begin with a different account of metaphor. This shows the importance for me of (recent English) philosophy of language. For further reading one might try Richard Swinburne, *Revelation: from Metaphor to Analogy* (Oxford: Oxford University Press, 1991), or Stephen Mulhall, *The Great Riddle: Wittgenstein and Nonsense, Theology and Philosophy* (Oxford: Oxford University Press, 2015).

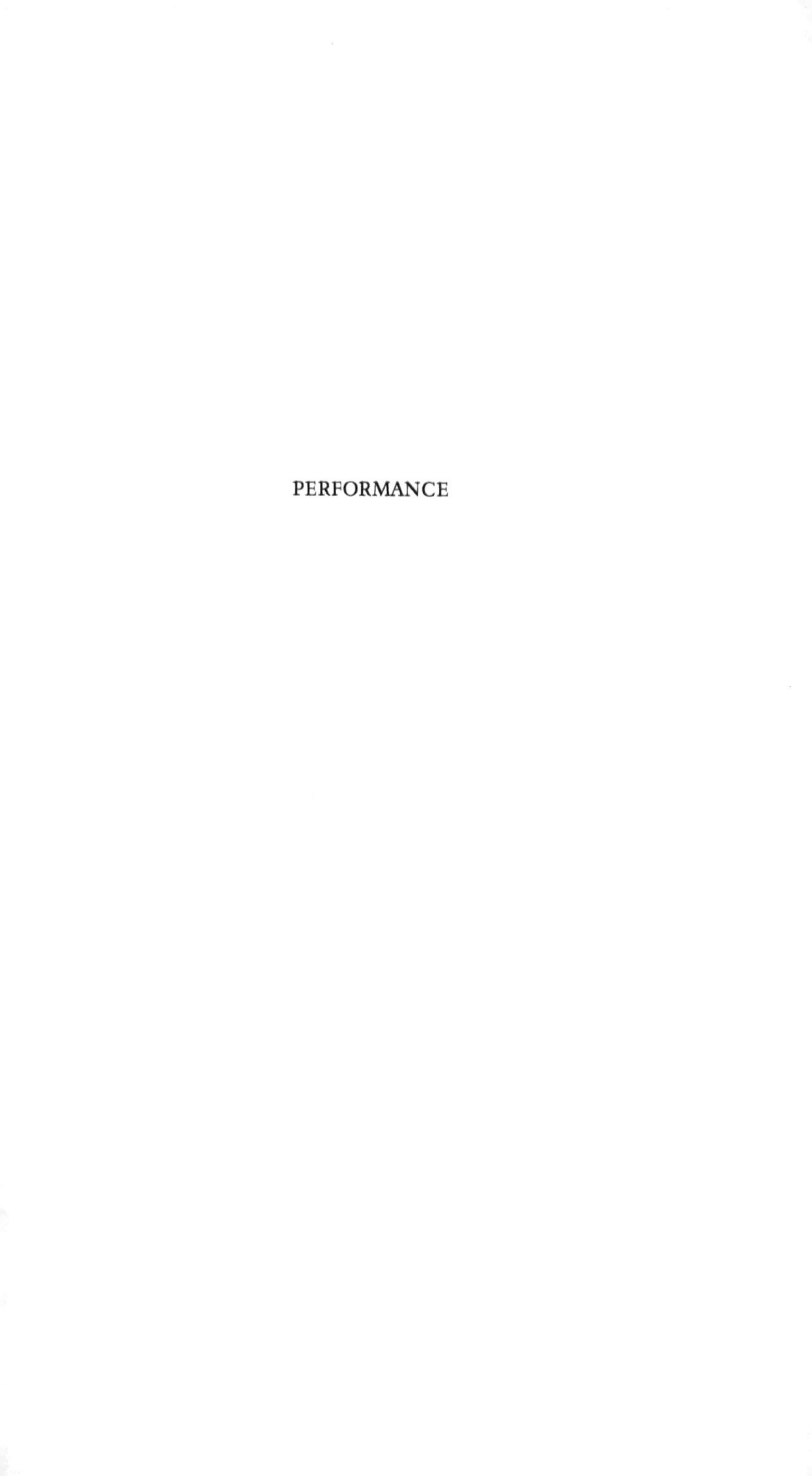

PERFORMANCE

ZACHARY FLORENCE

Presumption of Worth

More than fifteen years later, I remain moved by Tom Curran's many kindnesses. I first got to know Tom when, despite having no claim on his time and no expectation he would say yes, I approached him to write a programme note for my KTS production of Tom Stoppard's *Arcadia*. To my surprise and delight, he obliged. The note he delivered was wide-ranging, witty, and wise. It was tongue-in-cheek and it was thoughtful, and it invited an audience to enter into the world of the play. Thinking about what he wrote, what struck me most—both then and now—was the presumption of seriousness, of worth, that he credited all of us as meriting. He saw us, not just what we were doing, but the best and highest version of what we were trying to do, and he treated us on that basis. Feeling seen in that way is a hallmark of any encounter with Tom Curran. I am lucky to count myself among a group of people spread around the globe who are marked by his influence and his faith in us.

CHRISTOPHE FRICKER

Levinasian Facebook Status Updates

I

Reading Levinas's *On Escape* in the library ... The irremissible quality of being is nausea, and escape is both an imperious necessity and a strict impossibility within being's self-positioning. Coming back from the restroom I discover that some girl has claimed half my table. She is eating an apple and looks forlorn. Back in my office, my heater emits a gentle klicking sound but no heat. I am cold.

II

Went to get a haircut. Barber: "So how's your day been." Me: "Great. I've been reading Derrida's 'Word of Welcome,' on Levinas, where he says that the third comes to affect the experience of the face in the face to face, without waiting, and that, although this interposition of the third does not interrupt the welcome itself, this tertialité turns or makes turn toward it, like a terstis made to bear witness to it, the 'duel' of the face to face, the singular welcome of the unicity of the other." Barber: "Oh wow. Thank you for sharing this with me." Me: "You're welcome."

III

Walking back to my office, I contemplate the fact that "the chosen home is the very opposite of a root. It indicates a disengagement, a wandering which has made it possible." Standing in front of my door, I realize that I have locked myself out. A spare key is close at hand, and only a little later do I recognize that this "wandering is not a less with respect to installation, but the surplus of the relationship with the Other."—I am writing this in a café: we have had a power cut.

IV

"The face is growing old, even while being young," says Waldenfels in his reading of Levinas's *Otherwise than Being*, and "as a wrinkled face, it is a 'trace of itself.'" Fair enough.

V

"The face is not something I see, but something I speak to." And when Simon Critchley, in his introduction to Levinas, says "I," he means "you" of course. Thou. He means you—you speak to the face—because the "face-to-face relation with the other is always linguistic." The book of the face, which we are writing, is thus not a Thou-book.

VI

"The face always lends itself to a welcome" (Derrida, paraphrasing Levinas). Staring into the rain ("O wann winterlich?" Jetzt, bloody hell!), I read on. The welcome is real, although its political relevance remains uncertain. Yugoslavia, Rwanda, Syria remind us of the fragility of hospitality. The rains are relentless; years of ruthless drizzle. The street outside my window keeps a straight face. *Wann wird es endlich wieder richtig Sommer*? And I find myself thinking: at least there is no war here.

VII

When was the last time you were poked? Faced? Or even called? Tell me about it.

ELISABETH STONES

Gretchen am Spinnrade

Elisabeth Stones offers a recording of her singing Schubert's "Gretchen am Spinnrade", composed in 1814 based on a portion of Goethe's Faust. *To hear this song, please visit* www.tomcurranfyp.com.

Elisabeth writes:

Despite the somewhat heavy subject matter, it is my favourite Schubert *Lied*. The way the distinctive sound of the spinning wheel in the accompaniment is contrasted with the arching vocal lines beautifully illustrates the relentlessness of reality even as Gretchen's mind dwells on her dreams and her sorrows.

Partway through, we hear the spinning wheel stumble, and she struggles to focus and get back to the task at hand, while also coming to terms with her situation and forging ahead.

The accompanist/spinning-wheel impersonator is the marvelous Garth MacPhee.

JERRY WHITE

Surprised by the Joy of an Experiment in Criticism: Two Sequences in HORSEMAN ON THE ROOF

When I was an undergraduate in the late 1980s and early 1990s, "Star Studies" was something of a big deal among the cool kids in Film Studies.[1] Theories of authorship, never particularly stable in cinema because of the medium's (seemingly[2]) inherent collaborative nature, were falling apart left and right (mostly left), with slickly poststructuralist approaches moving in to fill the gap. Who even needs the text (that is to say the film), let alone the filmmaker or hey, even the star, when you can organize your analysis around Richard Dyer's famous contention (in his classic 1979 theoretical work *Stars*) that "a star, in films, publicity, and promotion, is a semiotic construction and the fact that the construction exhibits continuities does not prove that the star as person is responsible for them. S/he may be, but also may not be." The naively earnest semiotic self-seriousness of passages like that now seem so dated to me, so part of an approach that only an unworldly undergraduate coming to such stuff for the first time could possibly see as anything other than both self-evident and probably incorrect if subject to further scrutiny, that I can practically smell the stale doobage.[3]

All to say, works in "Star Studies" would likely have provoked eye rolls of vaguely parental scepticism and impatience from Tom Curran, had he been around when I was encountering them (and geez, wouldn't that have been good for me at that stage, although who knows if I could have kept up with the reading in FYP; see note 3). And yet he and I have had numerous conversations about the virtues of the French star Juliette Binoche: serious, thoughtful conversations about what makes her special, what it is that she contributes to French cinema. These conversations have been real challenges to my conventional approaches to film criticism, which tend to focus on both cultural history and authorship. That is because they always swing back to Jean-Paul Rappeneau's 1995 film *Le hussard sur le toit*, for which Tom has a tremendous enthusiasm.

Rappeneau is not a force in French cinema. He hasn't even directed that many films (nine in all), and the only one I had seen before talking Binoche with Tom was his 1990 version of *Cyrano de Bergerac*, which starred Gérard Depardieu.[4] Spoiler alert: it's OK, not great, your basic cinema-of-quality kind of stuff. It did not inspire me to see more of his films. Only Tom was capable of such a thing, and I was determined to follow his wise council. *Le hussard*, though, is not on Netflix; it is not on iTunes; there are no more DVD stores left in Halifax; the Dalhousie library does not have it on DVD. And so it was, late one rainy night, wife gone to Saskatoon, boyos in bed and me a little sleepless, that I decided that I would google the hell out of this thing and solve this problem once and for all in order to write something about this film. And so I did; I found, on Youtube, a complete version of the film, in a manner of speaking. The discussion that follows is actually based on my viewing of a very odd object known as *L'Ussaro sul tetto,* the Italian-dubbed version of the film that Tom speaks of so fondly as *Horseman on the Roof* and which I, with no more that touristic Italian, have duly watched all the way through.[5]

Two sequences are key, and for reasons that speak to the other half of these conversations that Tom and I have had about the film. That other half has to do with the French filmmaker Olivier Assayas.[6] If Rappeneau is the embodiment of the kind of French filmmaker that has always left me flat, then Assayas is just as profoundly the embodiment of the kind of French filmmaker that makes me thankful to have come upon Film Studies as a vocation. I am forever trying to get Tom to see some of these films, although the truth is that they're not a whole lot easier to see in these streaming-dominated days. The important film for my purposes here is *The Clouds of Sils Maria* (2014), a significant portion of which is set in the Swiss alps.

Almost exactly an hour into *Horseman*, there is a scene where Juliette Binoche (playing a countess called Pauline de Théus) and the aristocratic Italian revolutionary she's fallen in love with are fleeing through the mountains. This is a crucial moment in the film's story, but also crucial for an actually interesting understanding of the star-as-author thing, because it is where Binoche really starts to take over, to dominate the screen even when she's not in the image. She doesn't appear at all in *Horseman* until nearly 30 minutes in, and at first she seems to just be the exotic love interest for this macho idealist. But when the two are in the forest together he shows her how to sterilise her hands with alcohol and then burn the alcohol off. As the flames jump up from her hands she is transformed. In the open hills, drinking tea by the campfire, she takes charge. Her face is serious now; Rappeneau keeps her mostly in two-shots but we can see that she has now taken on the reality of her situation. When Rappeneau cuts to a dusky, shadowy image of them on horseback, there is a heaviness there, a heaviness that never leaves her character. It never left Binoche either. Her character in Assayas' *The Clouds of Sils Maria,* a middle-aged actress who goes to the open mountains to struggle with her debts to her art and her mentors, is still living with that moment, that sensation when the alcohol burns off of your hands and it's wild and exciting and really not that scary at all, it's just that the clarity it provides proves to be sublime. That is to say, it proves to be the gateway to that combination of the beautiful and the terrifying that *Horseman* provides glimpses of and *The Clouds of Sils Maria* meditates on.

And thus we come to the best sequence in the film, which is the last one. Safely back with her husband in their castle at Aix, she gets a letter from her lover. We never find out what it says (I don't think we do, anyway; with the Italian voice-over it's a little hard to tell), but Rappeneau closes with a series of extreme long shots of Binoche against the snowy alps: a tracking shot from behind that shows the mountains; a close-up of her face shot with a long lens which renders the castle something of a blur, which is just how it should be for her at that moment; and the film's last image, which is a really interesting combination of graphic elements, with Binoche herself tiny on the left corner of the screen, the mountains a bit blurry, the wall she leans on totally black in shadow, and a bare winter tree prominently taking up much (but not quite all) of the right third of the frame. It's awkward and lovely and cryptic and expressive all in equal measure, and that is not a bad way of explaining Binoche's approach to acting. That is also not a bad way of describing the whole narrative of *The Clouds of Sils Maria*, and having to actually write all of that out in a formal setting like this *festschrift* essay has really made it clear to me just how great a film that Assayas work really is, just how rare it is for a film to fully embody what its lead actress is all about, just how rare it is for a film to truly be *about* a performance.

So my tendency to minimise a filmmaker like Rappeneau was challenged in a big way by looking at *Horseman* via its lead actress; if this was a fuller, more expansive essay, I'd say something similar about looking at it via its screenwriter. *Le hussard sur le toit* credits three screenwriters: Rappeneau, the journeywoman-like

Nina Companeez, and, most significantly, Jean-Claude Carrière. Among European screenwriters, there is nobody quite so legendary as Carrière. He has written the screenplays for the French films of Luis Buñuel (*Diary of a Chambermaid*, *Belle de Jour*, *The Milky Way*, *The Discreet Charm of the Bourgeoisie*, *The Phantom of Liberty* and *That Obscure Object of Desire*), some of the nuttier mid-career films of Jean-Luc Godard (*Sauve qui peut (la vie)*, *Passion*), for Philip Kaufmann's adaptation of *The Unbearable Lightness of Being* (which also featured Binoche), just last year for Julian Schnabel's Van Gogh biopic *At Eternity's Gate*, along with, I kid you not, 81 other films (including shorts and television productions, as well as Jesus Franco's 1965 and thus Franco-era sex-horror film *The Diabolical Dr. Z*). In terms of versatility, he has no equal in film history.

How exactly this plays out in *The Horseman on the Roof* is hard to say. As with Binoche, though, Carrière's presence speaks to the deep diversity of "art cinema," a diversity which has a certain Frenchness to it, or at least requires a French-led perspective in order to see. As with Binoche, nobody would accuse Carrière of being a popular-entertainment type, and yet not only are there a few exceptions to that (the 2014 *Godzilla* for Binoche, the aforementioned Franco film for Carrière), but both have made a career out of doing some seriously different kinds of "serious" films. There is a major gap between *The Unbearable Likeness of Being* (which may be based on a Milan Kundera novel but which is basically a Hollywood movie) and the later films of Godard (which are much closer to experimental films than they are to the Hollywood-inflected material of his early new wave days). And yet all of this features both Jean-Claude Carrière and Juliette Binoche (who has a small part in Godard's completely nutty although sometimes intensely lyrical 1985 work *Je vous salue, Marie*, which I once dubbed his "Christmas movie"). Being compelled to look at *Horseman on the Roof* via Kundera and Godard: that is something fully unexpected, and genuinely enlightening (albeit in ways that I need more space to make any kind of real sense of).

I did not expect these kinds of discoveries at all; setting out to write about this filmmaker who I would generally not hesitate to dismiss has been quite a surprising exercise. My affection for Tom is what made me willing to see *Horseman on the Roof* (crikey, it made me willing to see *L'Ussaro sul tetto*!), and that is purely sentimental. But it is Tom's unique gifts as a teacher and scholar —his wide-eyedness, his seriousness, his generosity, his unspeakably intense sensitivity—that made me glad, nay joyful, made him urge me so forcefully to see *Horseman on the Roof*, and God damn if the old vicar wasn't right after all. That feeling of genuine and (because genuine) intellectually nourishing surprise, which doesn't come around all that often, is what criticism is supposed to be all about. Experiencing that feeling as I write this *festschrift* essay makes me thankful to have come upon criticism as a vocation. So all hail Tom Curran: the Olivier Assayas of criticism!

Notes:

1. I do some of my best writing in the footnotes; I certainly tend to spread out a bit more, even if I sometimes veer towards the self-indulgently rambling and extra-curricular. Suffice it to say that this essay has a lot more footnotes than, strictly speaking, it needs. I am assuming this will work for a reader who is not looking for a formal article but rather a more festive kind of *schriften*.

2. This is a misunderstanding, since there is a whole school of experimental filmmaking, particularly strong in the US and Canada, which is marked by great filmmakers working completely on their own, in the manner of a poet or a painter. Indeed, the greatest of these, Stan Brakhage (who made most of his films

in Colorado, although he died in Victoria in 2003), used to carry around a tiny wind-up 16mm camera everywhere he went. He told me that he thought of it like a painter going around with a little set of watercolours in order to capture material tentatively, to do better with later. I do regret that I never got to introduce Tom, or King's students generally, to Brakhage's work. I have, however, just published a book on him. I have a hard rule against citing myself, even in the footnotes, so I can only hope that Tom, or interested readers, will google Brakhage's name and discover it all on their own. His films are available in two very good Criterion Collection editions.

3. At the University of Oregon in the late 1980s and early 90s "Doobage" was the term of art for "cannabis," a word that in our era of legalisation sounds hopelessly pretentious to my ears. I myself did not indulge, because one aspect of my years as an undergraduate was that I was insufferably pious (partially in reaction to the truly ridiculous amount of doobage that was being smoked all around me in first-year residence; the preposterous level of alcohol consumption in those dorms also led me to immediately embrace teetotalling). It was all part of what I sometimes refer to as my "Quaker phase." Since coming to Dalhousie and connecting with King's it has occurred to me on many occasions how much I needed someone like Tom Curran when I was an undergraduate, someone who would take the often religiously-inflected trials of youth seriously but who was also seriously invested in questions of morality, of art, of joy. These are aspects of "Kingsiness" which are for me inseparable from Tom and the way he moves through the world, and these aspects account for most of the reasons why I tell people that King's is the most radical place in the world of Canadian universities.

4. I saw Rappeneau's *Cyrano de Bergerac* at the Telluride Film Festival in 1990. I was there as part of their student programme,

and Dépardieu was receiving a tribute. Although we did see the *Cyrano* film, the students didn't get to go the main Dépardieu event. Luckily, though, I came upon him at a party and screwed up the courage to speak with him in French. He was incredibly patient with what must have been my *very* inexact diction, in a way that I have basically never experienced with another Francophone ever again. *En tout cas,* I can remember telling him there about how much I loved him in Maurice Pialat's 1985 film *Police*, an edgy drama where he plays a cop who is attracted to a young drug dealer (Sophie Marceau). For a long time I held that contrast —the Dépardieu of *Police* and the Dépardieu of *Cyrano*—in my head as an embodiment of my own value commitments in terms French cinema especially but really for world cinema in general: I would be a strong defender of the former, an impatient adversary of the latter. One of the effects of writing this *festschrift* piece about *Horseman on the Roof* (in which Dépardieu has a bizarrely un-credited cameo—at least I think that's him!) has been the upsetting of such easy (and studently-ly pious) binaries, as I think you will see by the time you get to the end.

5. This is a particularly odd turn of events given the hero of the film, the horseman in question: a Piedmont Italian nobleman who plays an important role in the struggle for independence from the late Austro-Hungarian empire.

6. Assayas, it is worth mentioning, knows quite a lot about the kind of cinema that I was invoking in note 2, that is to say a cinema that is made by one person, working in the manner of a painter or a poet rather than a theatre director or a conductor. Assayas was at Telluride (also see note 4) in 1996 with *Irma Vep*, whose final sequence features Maggie Cheung's eyes being whited out by scratching directly onto the film. At that year's event I bumped into him on Main Street (a very common occurrence at Telluride[7]) and asked him (in somewhat better French this time) about this technique and about whether he knew about Brakhage and other

American filmmakers who directly manipulated the physical surface of the film in this manner. He responded enthusiastically that he did indeed know about Brakhage and Norman McLaren and other such North American experimentalists, but that he was actually influenced by a different experimental filmmaker, a French artist whose name I have long since forgotten. I did not take very good notes in those days, which is something that I profoundly regret and over the last decade or so have made a major effort to improve upon.

7. The Telluride Film Festival is a very intense event that unspools every Labor Day weekend in a tiny (and breathtaking beautiful) ski town in the south-western corner of Colorado. The town is maybe as big as a university campus, and so filmmakers and audience members mix very freely indeed; there is literally nowhere to hide. I worked for the operation for 22 years in total, and took students there every year from 1998-2010, when I taught at the University of Alberta. I came to Dalhousie in 2011 and so cut my ties with the event: too far away, too awkward to keep missing the first week of class. I did manage to get two King's students down there to participate in the student programme: one in 2012 and again in 2013. To return to the language of note 3, there is something very "Kingsy" about the intensity and high seriousness of Telluride, and I truly think Tom should consider attending.

ALAN HALL

Art to Enchant
Reflections on Teaching from a Mendicant Lecturer
(For Tom)

For just as bat's eyes are towards daylight, so in our soul is the mind towards those things that are clearest of all.

—Aristotle, *Metaphysics.* Alpha the lesser, 1

Estragon: We always find something, eh Didi, to give us the impression we exist?

Vladimir: [*impatiently*] Yes yes, we're magicians.

—Samuel Beckett, *Waiting for Godot,* 59

The Clown of God

When Max, my oldest, was born, Jeremy Schmidt, another FYP tutor at the time, gave us what became my favorite book to read to Max at bedtime. Jeremy claimed that the book was theologically coherent (he was strict about such things). I think he is right. Indeed, at the level of theology, I think there is very little that needs to be added to the book. Our version is by Tomie de

Paola who was a famous children's writer and illustrator through the 70's and 80's. But he says that he knows the story through Anatole France, another famous story teller.

The story is about a poor young boy named Giovanni. Giovanni makes his way in the world by juggling fruit and vegetables at the market. The juggling attracts customers and he is paid with meals prepared by the women tending the stall. It is a good arrangement. One day a small group of performers and acrobats come to the village where Giovanni lives and he is entranced. He begs that they take him with them as a performer. Eventually the leader relents and he joins the troupe. With them he travels the countryside, seeing the world and honing his craft. He becomes very good and quite famous. He is particularly famous for his trick called "the Sun in the Heavens," when he juggles an improbable number of balls and then, at the last second, he adds a spectacular golden ball which he is able to throw higher than all of the rest. It is his set piece, a real crowd pleaser. He will shout "the sun in the heavens!" to wild applause. He becomes famous enough to leave the troupe and branch out on his own.

One afternoon, as he is eating his lunch between towns, he is approached by a couple of Franciscan Brothers out asking for food. They ask him what he does and then they tell him that his juggling is a gift to God. He thinks this is nice but unlikely but the brothers seem harmless enough so he gives them some food and goes on his way. Time passes. Giovanni becomes older, less powerful, less coordinated. His tricks too become old. They have all been seen before, done better. Or they seem trivial and foolish next to what is new and surprising. His life unravels. He is mocked. He can no longer afford to live as he has been living. But then he remembers meeting the brothers and thinks that there might be a place for him in the monastery, if only for food and shelter. And so he goes to Assisi. He arrives during a great procession of gifts to the Christ child. Exhausted he falls asleep. When he wakes up the Cathedral is empty. He realises that the only gift he has is his now stale and ridiculed juggling trick. Drawing up his courage he approaches the statue of Mary and Christ. It is, it seems, the best performance of "the Sun in the Heavens" that he has ever done. But it is also his last. In the morning, when one of the Brothers finds his body, they also discover something miraculous. The Christ child in the statue is now holding a golden ball.

Max liked this story but I love it.

The Best Class I Ever Taught

> Vladimir: What do they say?
>
> Estragon: They talk about their lives.
>
> Vladimir: To have lived is not enough for them.
>
> Estragon: They have to talk about it.
>
> (*Waiting for Godot*, p. 53)

In the best class I ever taught the text was *Waiting for Godot*. The class was for an upper year course in the Great Books Programme here at St. Thomas called "Faith and Reason" in the fall term of 2017. I remember it as one class, but my students tell me it was three. No doubt they are right. This is what I remember: Jon, Ethan and Daniel are in a group. I have asked then to split into groups to perform small sections of the play. I have done this for a couple of reasons. It gets the quiet students talking, but with a script, which seems to cause less anxiety. It forces them to work through the text in a deliberate way, which can often be obscured in a wider ranging discussion. Mostly though, despite a rather committed amount of preparation and despite the fact that I have wanted to teach *Waiting for Godot* for years I have very little to say. I am beginning to worry that the play is almost impossible to teach.

This group work is a series of Hail Mary passes to different parts of the room … please God, someone spark something. Someone say something illuminating. (Except, of course, I have already told them what to say. Or at least Samuel Beckett had.) Jon is playing Estragon. Daniel has the look of ironic bemusement he has had since the first day of university. Ethan, as always, is all in. He was writing his Honours thesis that year on perseverance in the Grail stories. Jon, as Estragon, is fiddling with his shoe, half off his foot. It is his line but he has become focused on the shoe and he is holding it in both hands and slowly rolling back in his seat. He is well over six feet and pencil thin. Is this rotation intentional? He has moved well past his center of balance, but he is still moving, weirdly slowly and in control. He rolls backwards and out of the seat. He lands gracefully and finishes pulling the shoe on his foot. The class explodes in applause and cheers. Jon, slightly self-consciously, smiles.

I thought that we might want to talk about what the 'waiting' might mean and whether we could read the entrance of Pozzo and Lucky as the response to Vladimir and Estragon 'waiting for Godot'. Melly says that the problem isn't that Godot hasn't come. The problem is that we cannot really know one way or the other. Perhaps the silences in the play do not point out to the silence of the spheres but inward, at Vladimir and Estragon's confusion. Godot may have arrived and left, they may just be mistaken about who he is or was? No, says Melly, the problem isn't that it is one or the other but that we can't know which of the two it is. The play is simultaneously an opening tragedy about hope that is endlessly differed and disappointed and a closing comedy about our prayers being answered and us, in our own confusion, missing the reveal, even as we had our eyes peeled expectantly. I had nothing to add to this. This class looks at Melly delighted and grateful. We are in the right place with the right people they think. It is not the first time this has happened.

I thought we could talk about friendship. I know the students have read the *Nicomachean Ethics*. I taught it to many of them and I know that the others have read it in another class. Is this a friendship like any described in the *Ethics*? It's a compare and contrast, not the most graceful pedagogical gambit, but an old warhorse and, as I have mentioned, I was grasping a bit. The class picks at this for a while. Are Didi and Gogo living the best possible life? To be spending time philosophizing with your friends? Daniel, who is usually quiet and watchful, moves in an unexpected direction, it is a play about time and friendship, but not in the way we are describing. The only source of any coherence in time is when Gogo and Didi are together, talking. Outside of this, time appears to be incoherent, neither of them seem to be able to keep track. If there is a lesson about friendship it seems to be this: it gives coherence to things. It may even be the thing that gives us the sense of time's coherence. The conversation then moves into a comparison of Gogo and Didi with Pozzo and Lucky. Daniel's insight seems to hold. Compassion, reciprocity and coherence appear to be bound together. (As I write this I am beginning to worry about Vladimir singing alone at the beginning of Act II. Should I mention this to Daniel? He might find this weird, it was over a year ago now.)

It went on like this. If I had a virtue teaching that class it was this: I was silent, in the right way, at the right time, and about the right things. At least, I was closer to this virtue than I remember being in any other class. Mostly I was silent because I didn't have anything to say. Afterwards, I stood outside the class room dazed. "What was that?" I asked Michael, one of the students as he left the class. "I don't know," he said, with his usual ethereal kindness. "That was amazing," I said to Phil, my friend with whom I taught the course. "They are amazing" said Phil. He said that a lot that term.

Distracted and Delighted

Prospero has a number of pedagogical experiments on the go. Some are winners but many appear to be abject failures. Sebastian and Antonio remain mostly unrepentant, not only for Prospero's exile but even for their ongoing plan to unseat Alonso. Likewise, Stephano and Trinculo, though embarrassed to be caught scheming to take Prospero's life and island, are largely unchanged by the whole escapade. But of all his apparent failures the most obvious is with Caliban. "Thou most lying slave, / Whom stripes may move, not kindness" (120, 1.2,l.345-346). Caliban is angry, openly subversive, scheming, and unrepentant of his desire to rape Miranda. And although he has been marked by Prospero's lessons he rejects them, "You taught me language, and my profit on't/ Is I know how to curse. The red plague rid you/ For learning me your language!" (121, 1.2, ll.362-264). But this is not the end of the story. In the midst of his rebellion Caliban is still moved by enchantment, and easily confused. "Be not afeard, the isle is full of noises," he says to Stephano,

> Sounds and sweet airs, that give delight and hurt not.
> Sometimes a thousand twangling instruments
> Will hum about mine ears; and sometime voices,
> That if I then had waked after a long sleep,
> Will make me sleep again, and then in dreaming
> The clouds me thought would open and show riches
> Ready to drop upon me, that when I waked
> I cried to dream again.
>
> (*The Tempest*, 162, 3.2,ll.133 – 141)

Except, of course, in this case, it is not the island that is singing to Caliban but Ariel on a tabor and pipe, sent by Prospero. I can only be moved by Caliban here. He is delighted and confused, and cannot see the outlines of his own enchantment. He wants to stay in his beloved home, where sleeping and waking overlap. He can be led by the nose. It is contagious. "This will prove a brave kingdom to me, where I shall have my music for nothing," (l.142) says Stephano.

The other visitors are likewise enchanted. No visitor is totally immune. Being able to cast a spell is Prospero's great triumph. But in the end there is only one enchantment that really matters, Miranda and Ferdinand must fall in love, and fall in love at the right time, in the right way and for the right reasons. This is Prospero's great project and all of his hopes (leaving the island, regaining his Dukedom, securing Miranda's future) depend upon its success. Even the transformation of his former enemy Alonso, into something "rich and strange," is subordinate to this great end. It works, of course. But then, two young people falling in love is no real surprise, except to them. "So glad of this as they I cannot be, / Who are surprised withal, but my rejoicing/ At nothing can be more" (156, 3.1, ll. 93 – 95). And this is good and right, in the world as in the play. But we should notice this: Prospero's great triumph has very little to do with Prospero at all. For all of his fanatical planning and his careful staging there is very little Prospero can do in the case of Miranda and Ferdinand. The enchantment takes hold or it doesn't. Indeed, if the enchantment is going to work it cannot actually be Ariel hiding, playing the pipes. That is, if the enchantment is going to work, it cannot be Prospero's work but something else.

Even with the realization of this deeper magic Prospero's work isn't finished. But now he is running downhill. He feels the new couple need a lesson and a warning about the dangers facing them and so Prospero conjures a pageant, a strange, cryptic affair with stern demonstrations about fertility, desolation and the intricate balances of marriage. It is delightful, and unlike Caliban, Ferdinand is not easily confused: "May I be bold/ To think these spirits?" (178, 4.1, l.119). He is still enchanted, "Let me live here ever./ So rare a wondered father and a wife/ Makes this place paradise" (ll. 124-125). The pageant, or the young couple's response to the pageant, is so delightful that even Prospero is enchanted, even Prospero loses track. Prospero, master magician of time and space on the little island, is absorbed in his own creation, and the response to his creation, and has lost track of the rest of the plot, the "foul conspiracy ... against my life" (179, l. 140). His timing is off. He has fumbled. He suddenly needs to cancel the pageant. "This is strange" says Ferdinand, "Your father's in some passion/ That works him strongly." "Never till this day/ Saw I him touched with anger, so distempered" answers Miranda (180, 4.1, ll. 143 - 145). Prospero, now off his game, misunderstands their concern:

> You do look, my son, in a moved sort,
> As if you were dismayed. Be cheerful, sir;
> Our revels are now ended. These our actors,
> As I foretold you, were all spirits, and
> Are melted into air, into thin air,
> And, like the baseless fabric of this vision,
> The cloud-capped towers, the gorgeous palaces,
> The solemn temples, the great globe itself,
> Yea, all which it inherit, shall dissolve,
> And like this insubstantial pageant faded,
> Leave not a rack behind. We are such stuff
> As dreams are made on, and our little life
> Is rounded with a sleep. Sir, I am vexed.
> Bear with my weakness, my old brain is troubled.
>
> (*The Tempest*, 180-181, 4.1,ll.146 – 159)

Do not worry, says Prospero. It was just a play. You know how these things are. They come into being and pass away. The rest is silence.

It is a mopping up operation now. Caliban's plot needs to be stymied. Alonso, Sebastian and Antonio need to be forgiven and released from their spell. There needs to be a reunion with beloved Gonzalo. The king needs to be reunited with his son, his son with his father. Stephano, Trinculo and Caliban need to be punished, but this is a fairly lighthearted affair proportionate with their actual threat rather than their murderous intentions. More solemn tasks are also in the wings. Caliban needs to be acknowledged. Ariel needs to be released. (W.H. Auden said that properly staged, Ariel would now turn into pure light.) Prospero needs to drown his books and break his staff. The boat to take them to Naples needs to be relocated. (There it is! Miraculously untouched!) We need to appeal to Ariel for fair winds. We might even catch the rest of the convoy. "O rejoice/ Beyond a common joy, and set it down/ With gold on lasting pillars," says Gonzalo, delighted and amazed,

> … In one voyage
> Did Claribel her husband find at Tunis,
> And Ferdinand, her brother, found a wife
> Where he himself was lost, Prospero his dukedom
> In a poor isle, and all of us ourselves
> When no man was his own.
>
> (*The Tempest*, 199, 5.1, ll. 205 -213)

There is just one spell left to unravel. But it might be difficult to locate. *Our revels are now ended*, Prospero tells the audience. Did they work? Were you enchanted? Delighted? Were you worried that my spells might fail? That the King would be murdered before his brother could be stopped? That Miranda wouldn't capture the heart of Ferdinand? That Ferdinand would be a terrible match?

Was Caliban hilarious and sorrowful? I hope so, because I need your help.

> I must be here confined by you,
> Or sent to Naples. Let me not,
> Since I have my dukedom got,
> And pardoned the deceiver, dwell
> In this bare island by your spell,
> But release me from my bands
> With the help of your good hands.
> Gentle breath of yours my sails
> Must fill, or else my project fails.
> (*The Tempest*, 205, v.1, ll. 322-330)

I need to go my way back to Milan, back to my daughter's wedding, and then to my infirmity and old age, says Prospero. And you must go too, out into the streets outside the theatre, back to wherever you belong. But first the spell must be broken and this "baseless vision" will disappear. Possibly something happened and you were moved. That is my hope and was my aim. But this final spell has been conjured by you.

Our time with our students is short. We have a few tricks up our sleeves and, like Prospero, we have our beloved books. But all of our spells do not add up to very much unless the deeper enchantments take hold. It is our honour to serve these deeper spirits, the ones beyond our own tricks with smoke and mirrors. Whether these enchantments work and how they are taken up is, in the end, beyond our control.

This is how it should be. This is how it must be if we serve the deeper enchantments. And no matter the misfires and near misses, not to mention the triumphs and parades, our final trick must be a disappearing act. We can set this one up, but it is our students who break the spell.

This paper is written as a tribute to Fr. Dr. Tom Curran. A miraculous teacher.

References

Beckett, Samuel. *Waiting for Godot*. New York: Grove Press, 1954.

Shakespeare, William. *The Tempest*. Ed. Stephen Orgel. 1987. Oxford: Oxford University Press, 2008.

ROBERTA BARKER

GAME OF THRONES *as Schillerian Drama: A Meditation for Tom Curran*

Varys smiled. "Here, then. Power resides where men believe it resides. No more and no less."

"So power is a mummer's trick?"

"A shadow on the wall," Varys murmured. "Yet shadows can kill."

—George R.R. Martin, *A Clash of Kings*

WARNING: HERE BE SPOILERS FOR ALL 8 SEASONS OF GAME OF THRONES

When I first learned that the Reverend Dr. Thomas H. Curran was interested in the HBO TV series *Game of Thrones* (2011-2019), I was astonished. I was at a party when the topic came up. "Tom Curran and … *Game of Thrones*??" more than one person squawked. *Game of Thrones*, that big, messy, beautiful, awful, overblown, exquisite, offensive, tragical-comical-historical-fantastical pop culture phenomenon? The fact that people like myself, who have spent years wallowing in the bloody depths of Jacobean tragedy, should be fascinated by the show is not particularly surprising. But when one thinks of the wise, gentle, and courteous Dr. Curran, with his affinity for the crystalline intellectual architecture of Dante's *Divine Comedy* and of Hegel's *Lectures on the Philosophy of Religion*—well, *Game of Thrones*'s infamous mixture of sex, violence, political skullduggery, and dragons isn't necessarily the first thing that leaps to mind. Nevertheless, as I mulled further on the possible connections between them I began to realize that, even without asking Tom about *Game of Thrones*, I had already learned more about the show from him than I'd ever suspected. After all, Tom has taught me a tremendous amount about the work of the great German poet, philosopher, and historian Friedrich Schiller—and *Game of Thrones* is one in a long line of dramas that have grown from Schillerian seeds. As a small and unworthy tribute to Tom, this brief meditation will strive to draw out a few of the dramaturgical, thematic, and formal threads that tie HBO's blockbuster series to the theatre of Friedrich Schiller, in which philosophical and political ideas are embodied in flesh, blood, and the dialectical struggle between opposing characters.

Friedrich Schiller (1759-1805) was, among many other things, one of the greatest and most influential tragic playwrights in the history of the European stage. While still in his teens and trapped at a draconian school run by the Duke of Württemberg, he began writing a drama that would revolutionize the theatre of his time: *Die Räuber* (*The Robbers*, 1781). A famous account of its opening night in Hamburg describes how, with "[r]olling eyes, clenched fists, strangers falling sobbing into one another's arms … everything dissolved as in the chaos from whose night a new world breaks forth."[1] (This already sounds like *Game of Thrones*.)

1 Quoted in Robert David MacDonald (trans.), *Schiller: Five Plays* (London: Absolute Classics, 1998), 17.

With *Die Räuber* and his next play, *Kabale und Liebe* (*Intrigue and Love*, 1784), Schiller created some of the defining theatrical works of the revolutionary German artistic movement known as *Sturm und Drang*, which flew in the face of Enlightenment aesthetics by emphasizing the individual struggle for liberty and the extremes of human passion rather than rational order and neoclassical unities. In *Die Räuber*, a tragedy of Shakespearean proportions, Schiller embodied the rebellious spirit of the age in the persons of two warring brothers, Karl and Franz von Moor, whose titanic desires tear their community down around their ears. *Kabale und Liebe* depicts a more domestic world, centred around the star-crossed love of the aristocratic Ferdinand and the bourgeoise Luisa Miller. Here, too, passion and politics wreck lives and leave a pile of bodies onstage as the curtain falls.

The clash between desire and social order, individual freedom and harsh necessity, continued to dominate Schiller's drama as he grew older; but his work, while losing none of its emotional intensity, grew sparer and more austere. With *Don Carlos* (1787), set in Renaissance Spain, he created a new genre altogether: the historical tragedy of the mind. In the play's remarkable dialogue scenes—for example, the Act 3 debate between the autocratic, unhappy King Philip II and the idealistic Marquis of Posa over power, freedom, and the possibility of social change[2]—huge philosophical and political ideas play out through the bodies and psychologies of individual characters. This technique comes to further fruition in *Mary Stuart* (1800), where, in a stunningly theatrical scene that blithely ignores the historical record, Schiller imagines a meeting between Queen Elizabeth I and her prisoner, Mary Queen of Scots. At the peak of this scene, Mary seals her own death warrant by throwing in Elizabeth's face her illegitimization by her father, King Henry VIII:

2 Friedrich Schiller, *Don Carlos*, in MacDonald, 399-412.

A bastard has defiled the throne of England,
a noble-hearted nation is deceived
by a cunning cheat: if there were any justice
it would be you who should be lying here,
before me in the dust. I am your King![3]

This is quintessential Schillerian dramaturgy. A highly personal clash between two women whose anger and sorrow shape the fates of nations, it raises questions both political and philosophical. Who really has the right to the throne? Who is truly a wise and just ruler: she who rules from the "noble" heart, or from the "cunning" head? What do freedom of choice, of conscience, of action look like for a sovereign—and can a sovereign (or, indeed, any person) ever claim to be truly free?

As a scholar and a teacher, Tom Curran has always modeled the conviction that the great thinkers of the past are vital in helping us to understand the present. If we set Tom's work next to *Game of Thrones*, the dialectical pattern of Schillerian dramaturgy—in which the clash of individuals embodies the clash of ideas—begins to cast its powerful illumination upon the most popular television drama of the 2010s. In its early years in particular, *Game of Thrones* was famous for its stories of political intrigue and love (*Kabale und Liebe*), often encapsulated via intense exchanges between two characters. During the first season of the show, for instance, the audience was introduced to the brewing turmoil in Westeros (its fantasy version of late medieval England) via a long series of intimate scenes. We saw King Robert Baratheon (Mark Addy) beg his old friend Ned Stark (Sean Bean) to leave his home in the North to serve him in the capital; we saw Robert's queen, Cersei Lannister (Lena Headey), reach out to her husband in hope of salvaging one moment of affection from their long marriage, only to meet with

3 Friedrich Schiller, *Mary Stuart*, in MacDonald, 564.

a final rejection; and we saw Cersei seek solace in the arms of her twin brother Jaime (Nikolaj Coster-Waldau), who promised her that if their liaison should be threatened he would kill "the whole bloody lot of them until you and I are the only people left in this world."[4] In these scenes, and many others like them, were sown the seeds of the civil war that would dominate the ensuing seasons and end in cataclysm for the realm. In *Game of Thrones*, as in Schiller's drama, the political was always articulated through the personal.

In *Game of Thrones* as in Schiller, too, the political ideas in question often hinged on the responsibilities of power, the shaping force of established social structures, and the possibility of making free or moral choices while bound in the chains of authority, experience, and tradition. These are the issues that shape the debate between Posa and Philip in *Don Carlos*; when the younger man begs his king to free the people of Flanders from religious and political tyranny, Philip responds sadly: "You will think / differently, I know, when you have learned / as much of men as I have."[5] In *Game of Thrones*, similar questions of freedom, morality, and experience shape the argument—which turns out to be even more consequential than it appears at the time—between the ruthless, brilliant powerbroker Tywin Lannister (Charles Dance) and his cynical but good-hearted son Tyrion (Peter Dinklage) after Tywin orders the murder of the Stark family and its forces at the infamous Red Wedding. Their dialogue offers a perfect example of Schillerian dramaturgy, the simmering tension between father and son rendering tangible two opposing approaches to violence and moral choice:

> TYWIN: Do you disapprove?
>
> TYRION: I'm all for cheating—this is war. But to slaughter them at a wedding …

---

4 *Game of Thrones*, season 1, episode 3, "Lord Snow," written by David Benioff and D.B. Weiss, directed by Brian Kirk, aired May 1, 2011, on HBO.

5 Schiller, *Don Carlos*, in MacDonald, 410.

> TYWIN: Explain to me why it is more noble to kill ten thousand men in battle than a dozen at dinner.
>
> TYRION: So that's why you did it. To *save* lives?
>
> TYWIN: To end the war. To protect the family. You want to write a song for the dead Starks, go ahead; write one. I'm in this world a little while longer—to defend the Lannisters. To defend my blood.
>
> TYRION: The Northerners will never forget.
>
> TYWIN: Good. Let 'em remember what happens when they march on the South.[6]

Played with quiet, chilling intensity by two magnificent actors, this scene stages questions that are as crucial to the final seasons of *Game of Thrones* as to its beginnings. Should love and loyalty to family should be rated above moral absolutes? Is it justifiable to kill the few in order to save the many? And is there ever any real hope of ending a war, once it has started? Many spectators will likely feel sympathy for Tyrion's position, just as many will feel it for Posa's arguments against tyranny in Schiller's *Don Carlos*. As *Game of Thrones* and *Don Carlos* unfold, their evolution challenges these instinctive reactions; affirms them; and then challenges them again.

The evolution of *Game of Thrones* is, of course, a very different thing from the evolution of a tightly knit five-act tragedy like *Don Carlos*. Inspired by George R.R. Martin's as-yet unfinished series of novels *A Song of Ice and Fire*, *Game of Thrones* has often been read through the lens of adaptation studies in terms of its faithfulness to its source material. This perspective became more and more difficult to sustain, however, as the show first departed radically from Martin's fourth and fifth books (the last ones to be published) and then passed his series altogether. During this

6 *Game of Thrones*, season 3, episode 10, "Mhysa," written by David Benioff and D.B. Weiss, directed by David Nutter, aired June 9, 2013, on HBO.

process, lovers of the books were frequently heard to complain that *Thrones* was abandoning the philosophical and psychological depth of Martin's novels in favour of empty spectacle. Putting it another way, one might argue that the show swung progressively away from the Schillerian dramaturgy of idea-driven dialogue and toward the melodramatic dramaturgy of Schiller's nineteenth-century disciples, like the great French Romantics Victor Hugo and Alexandre Dumas *père*.

In historical dramas such as Dumas's *La Tour de Nesle* (1832) and Hugo's *Lucrèce Borgia* (1833), the French Romantic stage married the historical framework of Schiller's mature tragedies to the outsized passions of his youthful *Sturm und Drang*, adding in the sensationalism and spectacular settings of post-revolutionary melodrama for good measure. Brilliant vehicles for great actors, these scandalous plays aimed to provoke intense emotion in their spectators just as much as—if not more than—they aimed to stimulate dialectical thought. Just so, the late seasons of *Game of Thrones* provided extraordinary opportunities for actors like the indelible Headey, whose Cersei matches Dumas's Marguerite de Bourgogne and Hugo's Lucrèce in psychological complexity and capacity for love just as she matches them in murderous cruelty. In the grand melodramatic tradition, these seasons offered awe-inspiring spectacle at moments like Cersei's destruction of the Great Sept of Baelor by wildfire at the end of the show's sixth season.[7] Like *La Tour de Nesle* and *Lucrèce Borgia*, they also provoked controversy by using incest, sexual violence, misogyny, and torture as plot points. To be sure, *Game of Thrones* had crossed those lines from the beginning. But as it drew to a close, many missed what they regarded as the finer pleasures of its earlier seasons—precisely those pleasures,

7 *Game of Thrones*, season 6, episode 10, "The Winds of Winter," written by David Benioff and D.B. Weiss, directed by Miguel Sapochnik, aired June 26, 2016, on HBO.

one might argue, that had tied the show to Schiller's theatrical aesthetics.

Inspired by Dr. Curran, who is not only a sophisticated reader of Schiller but also a lover of critical thought, however, I'd like to challenge the too-simple notion that Schillerian dialectical dramaturgy can only occur when two people are talking together in a room. Television shows, like plays, are visual performance media in which ideas are made flesh not only by actors' words, but also by their bodies and by the objects and settings with which they interact. In this context, the Schillerian personification of ideas through character can take place even in the midst of the most over-the-top spectacle. Take, for example, the clash between the forces of Jon Snow (Kit Harington) and Ramsay Bolton (Iwan Rheon) in the Emmy award-winning Season 6 episode "The Battle of the Bastards."[8] In one of the most spectacular moments in the history of *Game of Thrones*, sadistic Ramsay tempts dear, stupid, noble-hearted Jon by threatening Jon's brother Rickon (Art Parkinson). Jon rushes into the field (as Jon is wont to do) and finds himself caught within range of Ramsay's bowmen with only Rickon's arrow-riddled corpse to show for it. For a moment, he and Ramsay stare at one another across the battlefield. Then Ramsay (of course) smirks malevolently and Jon (of course) spurs his horse straight into a barrage of arrows; gets thrown from his saddle; and winds up facing the oncoming tide of the Bolton cavalry on foot, with only his sword in hand. Jon being Jon, he throws the scabbard away for extra-fatalistic good measure. It doesn't get much more melodramatic than this.

Nevertheless, this grandiose sequence also embodies a philosophical skirmish in the same clash of ideas about morality,

---

8 *Game of Thrones*, season 6, episode 9, "The Battle of the Bastards," written by David Benioff and D.B. Weiss, directed by Miguel Sapochnik, aired June 19, 2016, on HBO.

responsibility, and leadership introduced by that intimate scene between Tyrion and Tywin Lannister all the way back in Season 2. With his body, his sword, and his horse, Jon performs the same belief that Tyrion put forward in words: that one should prize decency and the life of the individual—especially the loved individual—above all else. Ramsay, like Tywin, rejects these values with contempt. Clearly, we may think, Jon is behaving morally and Ramsay immorally—except for the fact that by his impulsive and doomed effort to save his brother Jon leads thousands of his men into slaughter. Who is the good leader, who the bad, in this case?

In the final, highly divisive season of *Game of Thrones*, these same questions play out on hectic fast forward. Both in rooms and on battlefields, the last characters left standing fight supernatural foes and—far more disturbing than any ice zombie or dragon—the inward enemies forged by their own repeated experiences of trauma, loss, and betrayal. At the last, for all of them, the struggle comes down—in ice, fire, and blood—to the same questions that Tywin and Tyrion debated with words and Ramsay and Jon debated with swords. Must one's truest allegiance always be to the loved individual rather than the unknown multitude, or is it right and just that the few should die for the many?

For two of the show's pivotal couples, the final answers are articulated in the most intimate possible way: an embrace. Jaime and Cersei Lannister die in one another's arms after Jaime abandons everything—including his friend and lover Brienne of Tarth (Gwendoline Christie) and his last hard-won scraps of honour—to return to his sister. "Nothing else matters," he assures her as their world falls down around them: "only us."[9] Jon Snow, too, embraces his beloved Daenerys Targaryen (Emilia Clarke), the "Mother of Dragons," after she brutally sacks and burns King's Landing. In the

9 *Game of Thrones*, season 8, episode 5, "The Bells," written by David Benioff and D.B. Weiss, directed by Miguel Sapochnik, aired May 12, 2019, on HBO.

last of the show's many cruel twists, Daenerys has proven herself a figure of terror as well as strength and beauty, a tragic heroine in the mold of Euripides's Medea rather than of Sophocles's Antigone. As Jon embraces her, he stabs her to the heart, convinced that he must kill her in order to save the world from her merciless brand of justice. Which of these embraces—Jaime's or Jon's—embodies virtue, which villainy, is up to the viewer to decide. "Was it right, what I did?" asks Jon once the deed is done. "It doesn't feel right." "Ask me again in ten years," responds Tyrion, who had counselled Daenerys's death.[10] By betraying the one to save the many, both of these 'heroes' have in a sense come round to Tywin Lannister's ruthless point of view.

Many viewers have argued, with some justice, that the show's rapid set-up of these final conflicts lacked narrative rigour and plausibility. Such lapses do not necessarily imply, however, that *Game of Thrones* abandoned the legacy of Schiller's theatre at the last. On the contrary, in its final movement the show was steeped in the influence of both Schiller's early *Sturm und Drang* works and his later historical dramas. Like the ending of *Die Räuber*, in which Karl von Moor kills his beloved Amalia because he cannot fulfil his vows to her while keeping his oaths to his fellow robbers, the last fatal conflict between Jon and Daenerys was a *Sturm und Drang* climax that prioritized the embodiment of extreme emotional and philosophical positions over the rational, proportional logic of cause and effect. As for the hairpin turns, narrative dead ends, and emotional explosions of the show's last acts, they offered shades of the infamously sudden and ambiguous ending of Schiller's *Don Carlos*.

In that strange and remarkable denouement, the Marquis of Posa sacrifices his own life to save his friend, the eponymous

10 *Game of Thrones*, season 8, episode 6, "The Iron Throne," written by David Benioff and D.B. Weiss, directed by David Benioff and D.B. Weiss, aired May 19, 2019, on HBO.

Infante of Spain, in hopes that Don Carlos will dedicate himself to the cause of the people of Flanders. Carlos responds by renouncing his love for his father's wife in order to embrace his destiny as a political savior—until, in a bitterly ironic last turn of the narrative screw, he is interrupted by the arrival of King Philip and the Grand Inquisitor:

> CARLOS [*To the QUEEN*] I go now to pursue an open action against Don Philip. From now on, I do not want there to be any secrets between us. You need hide no longer from the eye of the world. This is my last deception!
>
> *(He is about to put his mask back on. The KING steps in between them.)*
>
> KING It is indeed!
>
> (*The QUEEN faints.*)
>
> CARLOS *(rushes to her and takes her in his arms)*
>
> Is she dead? Oh, Heaven and Earth!
>
> KING (*Coldly and quietly to the GRAND INQUISITOR.*)
>
> Eminence! I have done my part. Do yours!
>
> *(He goes out.)*
>
> *The End.*[11]

With astonishing defiance of Aristotelian aesthetics of catharsis and closure, Schiller refuses to fulfil the promise of Posa's self-sacrifice and instead leaves his spectators in a state of uncertainty and shock. He introduces the terrifying figure of the Grand Inquisitor only in the play's last act, just in time for him to play executioner *ex machina* in this final scene. An audience who watches it all unfold onstage does not know whether the Queen is alive or dead, or

11 Schiller, *Don Carlos*, in MacDonald, 489.

what Carlos's fate will be. After seeing Gale Edwards's production of the play for the Royal Shakespeare Company in 2000, my peers and I were locked in debate over whether King Philip, by sacrificing his own son to the Inquisitor, is selling the last inch of his soul or making a tragically responsible—if tyrannical—choice in order to prevent the escalation of civil war. The dramaturgy of *Game of Thrones*'s final season, with its multiple about-faces culminating in the crowning of a very unexpected king, provoked similar debates about the natures of both narrative structure and political power. If the season was divisive, its divisiveness was highly Schillerian.

Perhaps, however, it was in its emphasis on the telling close-up that the final season of *Game of Thrones* drew most deeply upon Schiller's visionary dramaturgy. Great literary dramatist though he was, Schiller was also a master of the wordless tableau. At the end of *Mary Stuart,* for example, Elizabeth I finds herself utterly isolated after Mary's execution. Abandoned by her counselor Shrewsbury, who mourns that he "could not preserve / the better part of [her],"[12] and by her favourite Leicester, she is left alone onstage. Schiller's final stage direction reads, "*Sie bezwingt sich und steht mit ruhiger Fassung da. Der Vorhang fällt.*"[13] Robert David MacDonald translates it thus: "*ELIZABETH masters herself and stands, calm and composed. The curtain falls.*"[14] As his play ends, Schiller demands that his audience focus upon Elizabeth's apparently impassive face, guessing at the emotions—guilt? fear? anguish? pride?—that lie behind her rigid façade. The spectator's interpretation of the play's war of two queens comes down, at least in part, to their reading of Elizabeth's final expression.

The final season of *Game of Thrones* leans heavily upon this same, silent dramaturgy of the face. Cersei's wavering attempt

12 Schiller, *Mary Stuart*, in MacDonald, 615.

13 Friedrich Schiller, *Sämmtliche Werke*, Vol. 10 (Stuttgart, 1814), 223.

14 Schiller, *Mary Stuart*, in MacDonald, 615.

to maintain her accustomed mask of feline satisfaction while she watches Daenerys sack King's Landing; the spasms of fear, grief, and rage that cross Daenerys's countenance as she makes her fateful choice of all-out violence; Tyrion's bleak gaze at the devastating fruits of their conflict: in these faces, more than in its increasingly sparse dialogue or in the fiery spectacle of war, the show stages the terrible personal and social costs of the pursuit of power. In the last of all its close-ups, Jon Snow rides away from Castle Black into the wilds of the extreme North. As he glances back over his shoulder, his habitual expression of numb melancholy shifts a little. Some viewers have interpreted his final look as a smile that bespeaks his liberation from the realm of politics, others as a grimace of resignation to his permanent exile from it. Is he at peace with his choices? Should *we* be at peace with them? Here, as in *Mary Stuart*, the responses to such questions are left to the viewers. The answers they choose will inflect their understanding of all the tumultuous debates over power, freedom, and responsibility that have gone before.

On the surface of it, few seasons of television have ever resembled the elegant intellectual architecture of Schillerian tragedy less than the explosive, uneven last season of *Game of Thrones*. In the final analysis, however, the show's dramaturgy proved as Schillerian as ever as the game drew to its headlong close. Like Philip II at the end of *Don Carlos* and Elizabeth I at the end of *Mary Stuart*, the survivors and rulers of *Game of Thrones* found themselves compromised, with blood on their hands, as the show ended. The audience, meanwhile, was left to grapple with frustration, ambiguity, and uncertainty—as well as with a sense of their own responsibility for the task of imagining a wiser and less tragic way of living. Perhaps it was in placing such demands upon its viewers that *Game of Thrones* followed most truly in Schiller's footsteps. For help in understanding this—as in so much else—I am deeply grateful to the Reverend Dr. Tom Curran. Lover of Schiller that he is, I am not at all surprised that he is interested in *Game of Thrones*.

VERONICA CURRAN

Brecht, GALILEO, *and the scientific imperative in art*

In 1938, Bertolt Brecht (1898-1956) completed the first version of his play *The Life of Galileo* (*Das Leben des Galilei* [*Galilei*])[1]. He wrote the play while in exile from Nazi Germany, having sought refuge in Denmark. It dramatizes the life of physicist Galileo Galilei (1564-1642) as a thinly veiled metaphor for the truth-suppression and persecution that was already being perpetrated by the fascist forces in Germany. After eventually fleeing to the United States of America, Brecht began to work on an English version for his American audience with the help and collaboration of the actor Charles Laughton, entitled *The Life of Galileo* or simply *Galileo.*[2] This version of the play was completed in 1945, by which time Brecht had a fuller and more nuanced perspective on the events that had taken place in Europe and around the world over the previous two decades. Most significantly, Brecht and the world witnessed the first use of atomic weaponry and this changed Brecht's perspective on how to write these plays. In explanation, he wrote in his introduction to the English version of the play:

1 From this point on the 1938 version will be simply referred to as *Galileo I.*

2 The American version will be referred to as *Galileo II* from this point on.

> The 'atomic' age made its debut at Hiroshima in the middle of our work. Overnight the biography of the founder of the new system of physics read differently. The infernal effect of the great bomb placed the conflict between Galileo and the authorities of his day in a new, sharper light. ("The Author's Notes on 'The Life of Galileo'," 8)

The event at Hiroshima could not be ignored in the writing of the new version and thus the depiction of Galileo as a character changed significantly. No longer was he simply the persecuted scientist trying to ring in the age of reason, now he was the egocentric elitist whose scientific discoveries lead to the eventual weapons of mass destruction. Having returned to East Germany after the war, Brecht completed a third version of the play in 1956 in German; this version incorporated aspects of both of the previous ones, but it is this original rewriting, which took place between the first and second versions, that reveals the significance of current political events for Brecht's views on theatrical writing.

Brecht's theoretical texts and especially his *Short Organum for the Theater* [*Kleines Organon für das Theater*] outline the reasons that he argues the history of science must be engaged with at the level of art. For Brecht there is no separation between art and political imperative and thus the artist must reflect the greatest political needs of the time in the same manner that the scientist is responsible for the destruction caused by his science. Art allows society to engage with political issues in new and critical ways and therefore it is the duty of the playwright to bring these issues to the fore. *Galileo I* and *Galileo II* had to take the changing scientific landscape into account because, for Brecht, art, politics and science do not belong in separate spheres, but rather support and inform one another in an endless cycle.

Galileo I and *Galileo II* are not historically accurate, and, further, Brecht was not concerned with giving an accurate depiction of Galileo's life. Herbert Knust remarks in his study of the plays:

> Neither was Galilei so closely surveyed by the church, nor was his close relationship with his daughter as negative as Brecht depicts it. Some dates appear to hint less at events of the 17th than of 20th centuries. [3]
>
> [Weder wurde Galilei von der Kirche so scharf bewacht, noch war sein enges Verhältnis zu seiner Tochter Virginia derart negativ wie Brecht er darstellte. Manche Daten scheinen weniger auf Ereignissen des 17. als solche des 20. Jahrhunderts anzuspielen.] (49)

It is clear from this statement that the inaccuracies of Brecht's texts are generally acknowledged in the scholarship which deals with them. Furthermore, with regards to this claim about the historical inaccuracies of the text, Brecht scholar Eric Bentley explains that this is not actually a mistake on the part of Brecht, but is rather a well thought-out choice. He writes:

> [I]t is one of the open secrets of dramatic criticism that historical plays are unhistorical. They depend for their life on relevance for the playwright's own time—and, if he is lucky, all future times—not on their own historicity. (83)

This is the reason that Brecht's first two versions of the play end up being so radically different. Both Knust and Bentley recognize that Brecht's aim is not to honour Galileo's memory by depicting his life with historical accuracy but is rather to interpret the events of his life in broad strokes, in order to present his audience with something more applicable for their own experience.

This perceived reluctance to limit himself to writing the facts of Galileo's life, is supported by Brecht's theory of theater. In Brecht's longest theoretical text published in his life, *Short Organum for Theatre*, he presents these theories the most concisely. The text

3 All translations without citation are my own.

was written in 1948 and does reflect upon the Galileo plays, even referring to the scientist directly. Further, the arguments that Brecht outlines in the work are very easily applicable to the techniques and themes of the Galileo plays. He explains the importance the historical setting for plays like *Galileo I/ Galileo II*: the significance of the temporal setting has nothing to do with the time period, but rather the use of his theoretical technique, the *alienation effect [Verfremdungsaffekt]*. This refers to his idea that by distancing or alienating the audience from the characters in the play, the playwright can more affectively create a political understanding in the audence about the true message of the drama. Brecht believes that the first principle of the theatre is "fun" [*Spaß*] (§3), but that the alienation effect must also be invoked as a kind of call to action. How is this achieved? Brecht is known to "alienate" his audience through his unsettling use of music and the strange stage directions, but in *Galileo I/ Galileo II*, the main alienation stems from the decision to greatly remove the main subject of the play from his audience temporally. Brecht explains:

> If we ensure that our characters on the stage are moved by social impulses and that these differ according to the period, then we make it harder for our spectator to identify himself with them. He cannot simply feel: that's how I would act, but at most can say: if I had lived under those circumstances. And if we play works dealing with our own time as though they were historical, then perhaps the circumstances under which he himself acts will strike him as equally odd; and this is where the critical attitude begins. (§37)

From this statement, we can understand just how the alienation effect works. Brecht's characters have flaws, but they must have flaws that are applicable to the current state of things in Brecht's age. The audience recognises the dilemmas with which the characters are faced, as they also exist in the modern era, but can examine them with a sense of removal that is impossible with a contemporary subject. It is a type of sober analysis that Brecht hopes will lead to sober self-reflection. Rather than attempt to create a sense of empathy or a strong emotional connection in his audiences, he wanted them to think about the actions of the characters, understand their motivations and form opinions of them without being manipulated by emotional content in the plays. This is clearly the strategy that he takes with Galileo. We never feel in either version of the play a strong connection to the character of Galileo, but we understand and form opinions on both the ways in which he is unfairly treated and the ways in which he treats others unfairly. Once we understand the connection that Brecht is making to his own time, for example seeing the Catholic Church of the play as a representation of the fascists of Brecht's day, one can also think more logically about the present, about a time which no one can remove or alienate themselves from in order to view it from the outside. Ernst Schumacher further describes the significance of the alienation effect for the Galileo texts in particular because they are what he calls "Exiliteratur" (68). That is, these texts were written by Brecht while he himself was in exile and they represent an anti-hero who undergoes his own exile of sorts as a type of self reflection on the part of the author. The alienation from the inherited history of the development of physics is mirrored by Brecht's own alienation from his culture.

The *Short Organum* also explains Brecht's interest in the scientific subject. Brecht believes that the post-industrial age is the age of science and therefore that theatre must reflect the strong influence it has culture of the day. It also aids the alienation effect. Roderich Grimm hypothesizes that the very use of science in the narrative is meant to distance the audience who would in the majority not be familiar with the specifics of these discoveries. Since the *Short Organum* was written three years after the

English version of the play was completed, the developments of that version are clearly reflected in the manner in which he engages with the scientific plays. In the text, Brecht makes it clear that he views the inclusion of science in literature as taking Marxian, and therefore political, principles into consideration. He writes that the bourgeois class ["burgerliche Klasse"] controls the ability to create the new scientific advances and therefore creates things that are specifically beneficial to its own advancement and not to the aid of society as a whole (670). The depiction of Galileo, for example, as a spineless member of this bourgeois elite adds to his condemnation in the second version. Furthermore, Brecht points out the destructiveness of the newest inventions of science, further strengthening the connection between modern scientific advancements and post-war *Galileo II*.

The inclusion of questions of relativity in both versions of the play demonstrate how Brecht engaged with modern science as well as historical science during the writing process. Patricia Paulsell, in her text on Brecht's use of the scientific method, points out one example from the first scene in particular:

> Important to our considerations here are Galileo's words 'und bewegt sich fur dich nicht,' [and does not move for you] for the historical Galileo had indeed been the first to postulate a theory of relativity in which he explained that the determination of motion depended upon the frame of reference. (273)

The phrase Paulsell writes refers to the perspective of the observer that the sun that is moving and the earth is still. The earth "does not move for you" because that is the perspective of the person on earth, but in reality, the earth is moving, while the sun, which appears to be rising and falling, remains motionless. This is a preliminary explanation of the theory of relativity, in which everything relies on perspective. In the first scene, Galileo is not simply arguing for one single interpretation, but rather one amongst other possibilities, a hypothesis. Not only does this sentiment bring the science of Galileo more clearly into the tradition of Einstein, it also supports a more diverse reading of the text, especially when considering this link to Einstein in both versions, rather than simply in the more explicit later text.

With respect to the scientific and cultural significance of the plays, it is no secret that the character of Galileo is significantly altered between the first two versions. The significance here is not simply in that there is a difference, but in what the specifics of these differences mean for understanding each version of the text unto itself and understanding Brecht's approach to art altogether. Bentley writes that "*Galileo I* is a 'liberal' defense of freedom against tyranny, while *Galileo II* is a Marxist defense of a social conception of science against the 'liberal' view that truth is an end in itself" (190). Khalid Ahmad Yas puts it in different terms, writing that while the first version "possesses similarity with Faustus as an overreacher dealing with the concept of religion versus science, the 1947-version presents Galileo as Faustian villain performing cheap tricks" (59). In Bentley's statement it is the emphasis on the political alliances that Brecht wants to highlight, while Yas's statement focuses on the folly of Galileo himself and how the follies differ between the plays. Both of these statements do, however, set up a dichotomy that many Brecht scholars get trapped in when considering these plays. This is in a large part due to the statement about Hiroshima that Brecht made in his introduction. The tendency is to simply view the first play as anti-Nazi and the second as anti-atomic warfare. In reality the relationship between these plays is a lot more complex and by not limiting them to these polarities, the reader is opened up to a whole array of different interpretations. Knust argues that by the very nature of the alienation effect technique of setting the play in the past, Brecht opened up its interpretation into many more avenues (49). The overarching stories of these plays do represent very similar plots, so the question becomes, why do the descriptions of Galileo differ so greatly? For the answer to this we must turn to the text.

In the first scene, after having explained to Andrea Sarti (the son of his housekeeper and future pupil), in *Galileo I*, that his theories are what one calls a "hypothesis," Andrea asks what the theories of the church are called. Galileo responds, "Oh, that is also a hypothesis. But it is worse. There are many laws, with little explained, but the new hypothesis has few laws and much explanation" ["Oh, das ist auch eine Hypothese. Sie ist aber schlechter. Es sind viele Gesetze, die weniges erklären, aber die neue Hypothese hat wenige Gesetze, die viel erklären"] (*BBW* 14). This sentence sums up the metaphor that connects the Catholic church with the German Nazi party. The laws, on which their ideology is based, are founded in an unfounded hypothesis. The Nazi laws, like the Church, did not simply control the actions of those who followed them, but also dictated their ideology and controlled the rhetoric of "truth." The Catholic Church also had an extremely strong political hold on Italy at the time. Interestingly, this distinction draws out the way in which this metaphorical connection between the Nazi party and the Catholic Church is in fact an analogy of opposites. It can be argued that the spiritual role of the Church has no business in the work of the state, while a political organization such as the Nazi party has no place dictating the ideological beliefs of the citizens under its power. However, Brecht's Catholic Church and the Nazi party are linked. There is a promise for a better future that seduces the masses, which in Brecht's view is unfounded and will not ultimately be delivered. Galileo's work, in contrast, is not attempting to impose a strict system that is pregnant with philosophical and theological implications, rather he is reporting on what he observes. Later in the text, he refuses to argue that he has eliminated the existence of God, but merely the location in which society previously believed that God dwelled; he also insists several times that he has remained pious (25). He continually distances himself from the supposition that he is attempting to destroy an ideological framework and believes himself to be simply destroying a scientific one.

There are several significant scenes which are included only in *Galileo I* and which have substantial value in interpreting the metaphorical meaning of this original work. For example, the play includes a scene in which the plague forces Galileo and household decide to either stay in Venice in peril or to flee. This takes place soon after their arrival in Venice to further pursue Galileo's scientific work, having left his previous home in Florence. Galileo chooses to stay behind as the others flee and in the next scene he is found back in Florence, carrying on with his research. The inclusion of the plague is a poignant metaphor. It brings to the fore the sense of exile that Brecht felt having left Germany and his attitude towards the authorities which forced him to this extreme. The Nazis are depicted as a plague on German society, destroying anyone that they come into contact with. Further, Galileo's persistence at continuing his research despite the impending danger, becomes a justification for the entire play. Brecht, like Galileo, is continuing his work in exile, hoping that the truth will prevail despite outside destructive forces.

In the American adaptation, Galileo is far less the victim, becoming the maker of his own misfortune. One particularly notable example of how this change manifests itself lies in his relationship with his daughter, Virginia. In the German version, Galileo shows a real affection for his daughter and a concern for her future. In the American version, she becomes someone that Galileo barely thinks about and whose life he completely destroys without seemingly caring or even being aware of this fact. This destructiveness comes to a head in the scene in which he finally cuts ties with her fiancé, Ludovico. In the German version, this is done in front of his daughter and it becomes clear that although it is regrettable to both of the men involved, they cannot remain connected to one another due to ideological differences, or rather the fiancé's desire that Galileo give up his insistence on teaching heliocentrism (*BBW* 77). In the American version, however, this interaction takes place while Virginia is out of the room and is far less amicable. Virginia arrives on scene soon after Ludovico has departed, although Galileo seems to have completely forgotten how the results of his last interaction would affect his daughter. Under the scene title, "Galileo's young daughter is the first victim of his decision," Virginia enters the room with the line "Did you send him away?" Galileo's silence is followed by Virginia fainting and a scene blackout (*BBW* 160). The striking contrast paints the picture of a man for whom ambition in his work is of more consequence than his ties to his friends or family. This change in style is significant when viewed with respect to the atomic event that frames the entire narrative. If Galileo is no longer the victim of circumstance, but chooses to pursue his scientific ambitions with no regard to who may be hurt by his actions, then he is also partly to blame for the events made possible through his discoveries.

The most significant moments of contrast and adaptation take place in the final scenes of each play. The plays end entirely differently, the 1938 version including an entire additional scene at the end. Both versions come to their most gripping, however, with a scene in which Galileo's students wait with Virginia to find out whether or not Galileo will recant his claims in the face of the threat of execution. In both versions Galileo does recant, much to Andrea's disappointment and to Virginia's joy; Virginia has subsequently become a deeply pious person and is praying throughout the scene that her father may not be damned. Both versions end the scene with the lines, more or less:

> Andrea: Unhappy is the country that has no hero!
> Galileo: No. Unhappy is the country that is in need of heroes.
>
> [Andrea: Unglücklich das Land, das keine Helden hat!
> Galileo: Nein. Unglücklich das Land, das Helden nötig hat. (*BBW* 93)]

While there are strong structural similarities in these scenes, once again the meaning of this scene and these lines, in particular, alters depending on which version one is reading. On first glance, it seems as if Galileo has said something fairly profound about the problems facing society. These are the thoughts of a genius living in a broken system who had no real choice in the outcome of these events. However, for post-war Brecht this excuse is not acceptable. In the English version, there are many subheadings which give us more direct understanding of Brecht's own interpretation of his text. Right before this line a subtitle gives us the prompt, "Faced with the accusation of his favourite pupil, Galileo blames the general state of things in Italy" (*BBW* 173). With this subtitle, working within the context of the subtleties of the entire work, the meaning of Galileo's line changes suddenly. Now he is the coward who will not take responsibility for the ramifications of his actions, but rather blames the system. This sentiment would have been a familiar one in the aftermath of the Second World War, a time when no one wanted to be called responsible for the untold number of lives taken in those few short years.

There are many of these additional headings scattered throughout each scene in the second version. They are only included in the written text, and are not part of the spoken action, which means that an audience seeing the play performed would not have access to Brecht's method of framing each scene. The reference to Virginia as Galileo's "first victim" falls under this category as well.

However, Brecht adds another characteristic technique which also allows for his own view of the events of the play to be presented to the audience. This comes in the form of short, sung chorus lines which situate a scene both temporally and thematically. For example, the chorus sings the first lines of the second last scene: "June, twenty-second, sixteen thirty-three,/ A date momentous for you and me./ Of all the days that was the one/ The age of reason could have begun" (*BBW* 170). This line certainly supports the reading of this adaptation as a condemnation of Galileo, because his recanting is to blame for the "age of reason" not beginning. However, sentiment also problematizes a straightforward interpretation of the play. Bentley summarizes this difficulty as such:

> Had those who wished to stop Galileo and scientific advancement had their way, there would be no atom bomb. Conversely, if we accept the Brechtian premise that Galileo could have changed history by making an opposite decision, by joining hands with Matti-Vanni the industrialist, and the atom-bomb might have been invented a little earlier—say, by Wernher von Braun. (194)

The reference that Bentley makes here to "Matti-Vanni the industrialist" refers to a short sequence that is inserted in the English version, in which Matti suggests to Galileo that he can help him flee in order to continue his work in either Amsterdam or London, places in which the Church does not hold the same level of control (*BBW* 165). This suggestion that Galileo is the person who has halted the "age of reason" leads one to ask what the alternative options would have looked like. If Galileo had held steadfast, his final work, the *Discoursi*, would never have been completed as it is in the end of the play. However, the common people of Italy would have known what he really believed rather than hearing his false recantation. Despite this, it could be argued that the new text, the *Discoursi*, contributed more to the development of science than

Galileo's steadfastness ever could. In addition to this problem, the suggestion seems to be that in order for the "age of reason" to begin the "truth" needed to prevail. Yet, the same truth that Galileo is denying is the truth that Brecht's introduction attributes as leading to the destructive atom bomb.

Once again, it is important to note that Brecht is not arguing for the scientist of Galileo's time, but his own. However, in order to the reconcile the contradictory messages about the relationship of the age of reason and truth, we must look at the power dynamic that is at play in this scene. The problem with Galileo denying the truth is less about the specifics of what he denied, and more about his choice to do something he knew to be wrong in order to save himself. This issue becomes even more problematic when we are presented with the Galileo in the final scene, after his years of imprisonment. He is not in a jail cell; indeed, he has a servant making his meals for him. He confesses to Andrea, who has come to see him one last time before leaving Italy to practice science in Holland, that "on account of the depth of my repentance, I live in comparative comfort" (*BBW* 176). Galileo chooses the bourgeois lifestyle at the hands of his oppressors, instead of protecting those more vulnerable than himself by standing up to the authorities. He is even using the language of the authority, claiming that his recantation was an act of "repentance" rather than admitting that it was a betrayal of his own teachings and his true beliefs. A few scenes earlier, the commoners sing a hopeful song about the possibilities of science in changing their fates, but Galileo affirms the status quo a little bit longer. He becomes a member of the oppressing class by publicly representing their position. Seen in this light, the denial of truth does work in connection to the atom bomb critique. The critique is not simply focused on science leading to the atom bomb, but the way that the authorities use science and rhetoric to remain in power to the disadvantage of those in the lower ranks.

Furthermore, when Bentley cites the "Matti scene" he implies that Brecht's suggestion by including the scene is that Galileo made a mistake in not taking up Matti's offer and by trusting in the Church. In an earlier paragraph Bentley writes, "Galileo is offered a conceivable way of escape [...] But he is not an astute enough politician to get the point, and prefers to believe not only in the authorities but in his own abilities to go it alone" (193). This does get to the heart of the issue with Brecht's rejection of Matti; he rejects him because he believes in the existing authorities, authorities who are bent on suppressing the truth. Scientists must think about what is for the good of the whole, not simply themselves or the bourgeoisie. However, looking directly at the text, Brecht again does not present this interpretation as the only one possible.

Once again, we are presented with a window into Brecht's own thoughts on the matter through one of his subtitles: "Galileo refuses the support of the rising Bourgeoisie, he relies on the friendship of the prince and the pope" (*BBW* 165). The subtitle certainly criticizes Galileo's pride and folly and his choice to cater to the powerful, but it does not put Matti in the positive light of a savior. Matti is a representative of the "rising Bourgeoisie," which Brecht blames for the negative affects of science in the *Short Organum*. Perhaps the inclusion of this scene is in fact meant to point to the complexities of these issues both for scientists and the public. By accepting Matti's offer, Galileo would have been trading in one corrupt authority for another. Brecht's message here is complex: Discovering the truth of the universe and inventing new methods of understanding the world is not inherently wrong, but the attitudes of those who invent and those who control the means of invention can manipulate the results of these inventions and discoveries for selfish and immoral purposes.

A straightforward reading of these plays is also subverted through the very nature of the scientific "method' that is central to the text. Galileo, as a historical figure, is most known for his telescope. It is a known historical fact that he was not the first to invent such a device, but Brecht's plays take this revelation a step further, by representing him as having stolen the idea for profit. Already in the first scene, when this intellectual theft takes place, there is a criticism of Galileo's method, but this criticism goes deeper if one considers the actual function of the apparatus by which Galileo makes his discoveries. The telescope is an instrument which allows for gathering more knowledge based on empirical evidence: what is seen by one's own eyes. However, on another level, the telescope *mediates* what one can see. If that which is observed can only be so through mediation, is the evidence developed through this mediation still considered empirical? This consideration can also paired be with the historical fact that Galileo's telescopes were not very accurate but were rather primitive. Galileo claims that he is simply reporting what he sees, but truly there is quite a bit of interpretation going on about the significance of what he is observing. He is not only claiming that he can see these things, but that he understands the meaning of what he sees through this mediation.

These questions of how we are meant to interpret Galileo's actions and the role of truth are most significantly addressed in the imprisonment scene. This is the final scene of *Galileo II*, but only the penultimate scene of *Galileo I*. In the earlier version, Galileo is now an old man living in forced confinement with his daughter. He has gone blind, a strong symbol of the gulf that has grown between himself and his work and the blindness of society due to his forced recantation. Blindness is an element of both versions, but more heavily emphasized in the first, in which it is claimed he lost his sight from looking too often at the sun. The sun here acts as a metaphor for light and knowledge, a symbol which recurs frequently throughout the text. In this scene Andrea visits him and then learns that he has finished the *Discoursi* in secret. The 1938 final scene depicts a grown-up Andrea carrying Galileo's secretly written work out of Italy to Holland. The text was given to him by the imprisoned Galileo in the previous scene with the warning, "Take care, when you travel through Germany and are carrying the truth under your cloak" ["Nimm dich in acht, wenn du durch Deutschland fährst und die Wahrheit unter dem Rock trägst"] (*BBW* 106). Here we see again a strong difference in emphasis between the two plays and a direct reference to the underlying message of the work. Germany has suppressed the truth and Galileo is a victim of this suppression. There is a stronger hopefulness in this text as well. Andrea is able to get the *Discoursi* away and he crosses the borders undetected. Holland becomes the place of refuge, but as for Brecht, the new territory is not desirable, it is simply the only way that truth can be kept safe. Excluding this final scene from the second version allows Brecht to focus the text more on the moral question of what Galileo ought to have done and whether he is redeemed by writing this final magnum opus. There is, however, a deeper sadder meaning behind the exclusion. This ending has no sense of hope, the destruction is already done, and the hero has definitely fallen. This is the post-war Brecht who knows too much, not the pre-war Brecht who hoped for change.

In the 20th and 21st centuries, as scientific advancements soar beyond a laymen's understanding into the realm of the exclusively specialized scientist, scientific developments can no longer be considered general knowledge, nor is there an expectation that an educated person would have a general knowledge of advancements in the scientific world. Despite this, in the 20th century and beyond there has been a rise in specifically scientific themes in playwriting, some examples of this include, Friedrich Dürrenmatt's [*The Physicist*] *Der Physiker* (1961), and Michel Frayn's *Copenhagen* (1998). Bertolt Brecht's Galileo plays have together been called "the prototypical science drama" from which this trend stems

(Orthofer 175). Both texts relate to the history of science in different ways and both take up the political imperative that Brecht places on the theatre in his *Short Organum* among many others. The citation in the introduction to *Galileo II*, which notes the influence of the events at Hiroshima, gets at something beyond the changes that are made to the second version as a result of this; it gets to the reason that there is a blossoming of scientific theatre that follows this text. The two detonated atom bombs and the Cold War era which follows their destruction made the general public all the more aware that, as Brecht already knew, the results of the scientific realm could have great implications for the daily life of the rest of the population. M.A Orthofer elaborates on this phenomenon in his text, "The Scientist on the Stage: A Survey." He writes,

> Until [the bombings of Hiroshima and Nagasaki] the work of scientists was often seen as abstract, having little to do with everyday life. The discoveries of Copernicus, Newton, Darwin, and others had profound but not always immediate implications. The atomic and then hydrogen bombs were very different products of science, posing a discernible, proximal threat of large scale annihilation from which no one could shield themselves. (176)

The Galileo plays are at once an anticipation and a response to this phenomenon. The fact that we have multiple official versions demonstrates the practical side to Brecht's thoughts on this topic better than his theories alone ever could. Art must interact with science, but not as an immovable stance. Rather, it must react to and converse with the developments and difficulties of the field. Art is not static and it does have a role in shaping cultural opinion; in this the artist and the scientist are equally responsible.

Bibliography

Ball, Philip. "Beyond Words: Science and Visual Theatre." *Interdisciplinary Science Reviews*, vol. 27, no. 3, 2002, pp. 169-72. http://dx.doi.org.myaccess.library.utoronto.ca/10.1179/030801802225005617. Accessed 2 Apr 2019.

Bentley, Eric. *Bentley on Brecht*. Evanston, Illinois: Northwestern University Press, 2008.

Brecht, Bertolt. *A Short Organum for the Theater*. http://tenstakonsthall.se/uploads/139-Brecht_A_Short_Organum_for_the_Theatre.pdf

Brecht, Bertolt. "The Author's Notes on 'The Life of Galileo.'" *The Life of Galileo*. New York: Methuen & Co, 1963.

Brecht, Bertolt. *Bertolt Brecht Werke* [BBW], eds. Bärbel Schrader and Günther Klotz, vol. 24. Suhrkamp Verlag, 1988, pp. 233-256.

Ewen, Frederic. *Bertolt Brecht: his life, his art, and his times*. Citadel Press, 1967.

Grimm, Roderich. *Verfremdung in Bertolt Brechts ››Leben des Galilei‹‹*. Verlag Peter Lang, 1987.

Hecht, Werner. *Bertolt Brecht: Aufzeichnungen zu ›Leben des Galilei‹*. Suhrkamp Verlag, 1963.

Hill, Claude. *Bertolt Brecht*. Twayne Publishers, go.galegroup.com.myaccess.library.utoronto.ca/ps/i.o?p=GTwayne&sw=w&u=utoronto_main&v=2.1&it=aboutBook&id=GALE|9780805749014. Accessed 22 Feb 2019.

Knopf, Jan. "Bertolt Brecht und die Naturwissenschaften: Reflexionen uber den Zusammenhang von Natur- und Geisteswissenschaften." *Brecht Yearbook/Das Brecht-Jahrbuch*, 1978.

Knust, Herbert. *Bertolt Brecht: Leben des Galilei: Grundlagen und Gedanken zum Verständnis des Dramas*. Verlag Moritz Diesterweg, 1987.

Orthofer, M. A. "The Scientist on the Stage: A Survey." *Interdisciplinary Science Reviews*, vol. 27, no. 3, 2002, pp. 173-83. http://dx.doi.org.myaccess.library.utoronto.ca/10.1179/030801802225003286u. Accessed 2 Apr 2019.

Paulsell, Patricia R. "Brecht's Treatment of the Scientific Method in His 'Leben des Galilei'." *German Studies Review*, vol. 11, no. 2, 1988, pp. 267-284 http://www.jstor.org/stable/1429973 Accessed 2 Apr 2019.

Schumacher, Ernst. *Bertolt Brechts „Leben des Galilei" und andere Stücke*. Henschelverlag, 1965.

Weimar, Karl S. "The Scientist and Society: A Study of Three Modern Plays." *Modern Language Quarterly*, vol. 27, no. 4, 1966, pp. 431-448. doi: 10.1215/00267929-27-4-431.

Yas, Khalid Ahmad. "The Evolution and Popularity of Science Play with Specific Reference to Marlowe's *Dr. Faustus*, Brecht's *Galileo* and Frayn's *Copenhagen*." *International Journal of Applied Linguistics & English Literature*, vol. 5, no. 7, 2016, pp. 56-62.

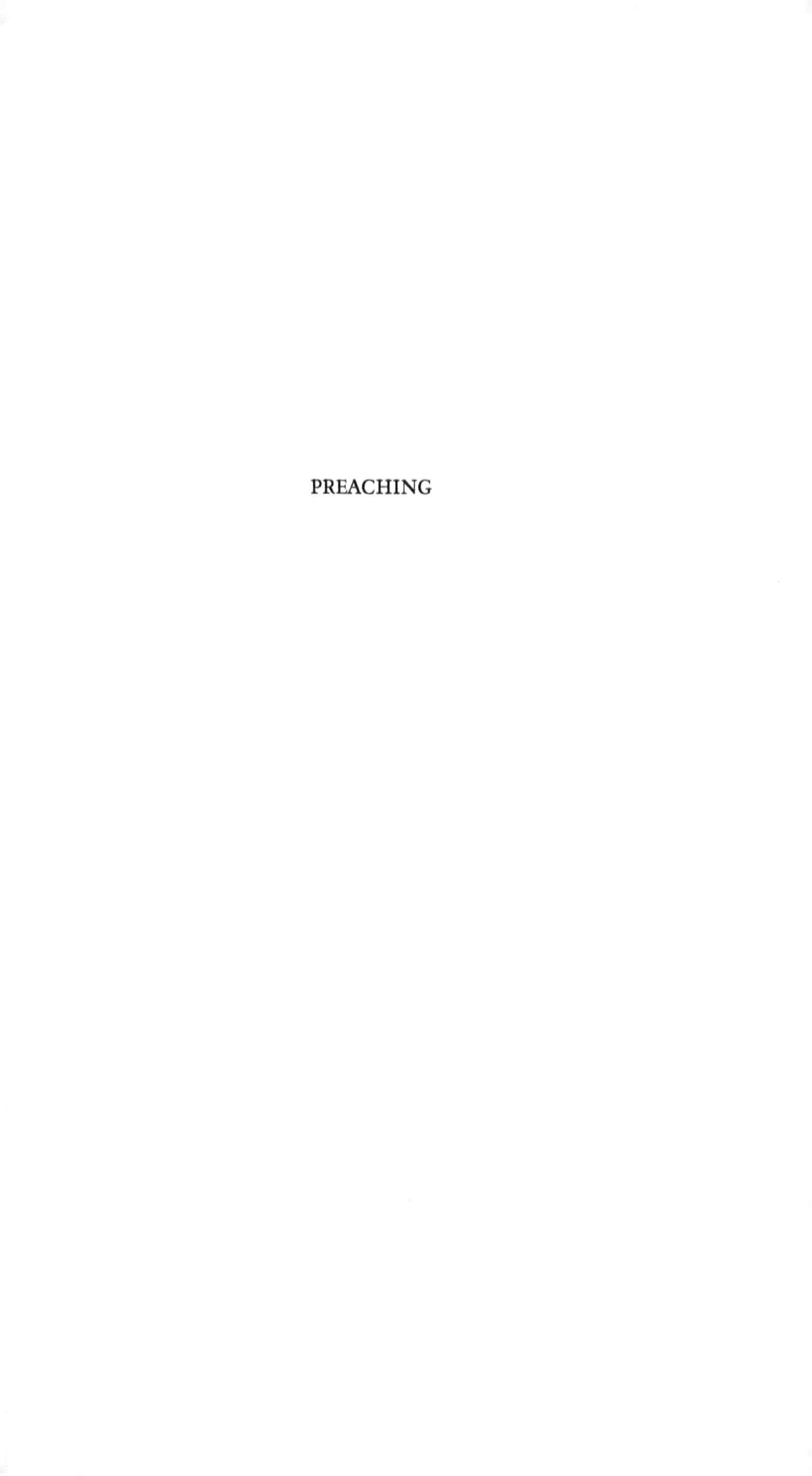

PREACHING

WILLIAM BARTON

Those who have heard Tom lecture in Alumni Hall or preach in the Chapel have almost certainly heard him quote from Dante Alighieri's letter to his patron, Cangrande: "My Commedia belongs to that branch of philosophy called ethics, and is intended to move the reader from a state of misery to a state of bliss, in this life."

The point Tom often makes about the *Comedy* in conjunction with this quotation is that Dante did not write it as a vision of the Christian afterlife, but rather as an allegory of the soul and its return to God now, *IN THIS LIFE*. If the images the reader encounters along with Dante the Pilgrim on his journey through Inferno, Purgatorio, and Paradiso have any urgency for us, they are urgent for us now—not after we die.

This point is worth driving home, as Tom has poured himself out to do for many generations of FYP students. But there are two other quotations that Tom often uses to help illustrate the urgency and flesh out the implications—both practical and spiritual—of this same movement of the soul.

The first is a quotation of a quotation. The character of

Vladimir in Samuel Beckett's *Waiting for Godot* says early on in the play, "One of the thieves was saved." In an interview, Beckett attributed this phrase to Saint Augustine, whose original phrasing Beckett gives as, "Do not despair, one of the thieves was saved; do not presume, one of the thieves was damned."The fine balance between salvation and damnation, hope and despair, receiving grace and taking it for granted, requires a vigilance and discipline which Tom admires and encourages, while making the humble claim not to possess in himself. Although Tom doesn›t usually make the following point explicitly, those who have listened to him often will see how Tom uses this quotation to help us hold in tension the "state of misery" and the "state of bliss" that Dante speaks of in his letter to Cangrande. Rather than simply achieving bliss and forgetting about misery, the bliss which Dante, Augustine, and Beckett speak of is a bliss which fully remembers the despair which preceded it. The soul does not simply move from one to the other, but is enlarged so that it may incorporate both positions. Tom often speaks of the magnanimous and pusillanimous—"large-souled" and "small-souled" Humbly, he always lumps himself in with the later category. But the enlarging of the soul such that it may hold opposites together is something he always encourages in others.

The second quotation is a somewhat longer passage from T.S. Eliot's *Murder in the Cathedral*—in fact it is the entire Christmas sermon that the character of Archbishop Thomas à Beckett gives between Acts I and II of Eliot's play! The essential point that Tom refers to is contained in the following passage (although he would strongly encourage the reading of the entire play!):

> It was in this same night that has just passed, that a multitude of the heavenly host appeared before the shepherds at Bethlehem, saying, 'Glory to God in the highest, and on earth peace, good will toward men'; at this same time of all the year that we celebrate at once the Birth of Our Lord

> and His Passion and Death upon the Cross. Beloved, as the World sees, this is to behave in a strange fashion. For who in the World will both mourn and rejoice at once and for the same reason? For either joy will be overborne by mourning, or mourning will be cast out by joy; so it is only in these our Christian mysteries that we can rejoice and mourn at once for the same reason.

So the conversion that Tom constantly encourages in us is a conversion to magnanimity—to great souled-ness. He is consistent in his encouragement of this growth of our souls, such that we may not only experience the inevitable misery and despair, but also the gifts of joy and bliss; and hopefully may come to a state where we may experience both, at one and the same time, for one and the same reason. Such has been the urgent nature of his message to students and the Sunday congregation for years.

RON HAFLIDSON

Biblical Comedy?

By the time I arrived at the University of King's College as a 'FYP' student, I had heard my fair share of sermons. Because I was an exceedingly pious and spiritually restless youth, I had listened to preachers from a variety of Christian traditions, from the folksy Roman Catholic priest to the pulpit-slamming Baptist pastor. Humor was one rhetorical tool I encountered no matter what the tradition, often in the form of some cute anecdote delivered early-on in order to draw listeners' in. I had come to the conclusion that homiletic humor was narrow and safe, incidental to whatever real theology was on offer once the introduction was over.

And then I heard Dr. Curran preach for the first time at the King's College Chapel. The main point of the sermon, if memory serves, is that Dr. Curran admired the Pharisees enormously and he thought his listeners should too: these were religious people who not only knew what they thought, but they actually lived accordingly; he aspired to that kind of holy integrity. Throughout the duration of the sermon, I was confused, at times horrified. Every preacher I had ever heard, not to mention my Sunday school teachers and Bible camp counselors, had demonized the Pharisees. They were the model of what not to do. Their religion, I was taught, consisted of little more than legalistic nit-picking and empty ritual.

Thankfully, I didn't simply forget the sermon. In the coming days it knocked around in my head as I tried to make sense of it. More sense emerged when I remembered that a small, but vocal, number of parishioners were chuckling all the way through it. At the time, I was not in on the joke. But it gradually occurred to me that, perhaps, Dr. Curran's sermon was a form of homiletic humor I had not encountered before. The jokes weren't confined to fleeting moments, especially at the beginning; instead, his whole sermon may have been an extended exercise in irony. I see now, I think, that Dr. Curran was setting himself up as a fool and inviting his listeners to laugh at him (a frequent posture of Dr. Curran's in my experience); but, in so doing, he was also making it easier for all of us to laugh at ourselves too, to acknowledge the foolishness we all share.

I argue in this paper that there is a genuine spiritual maturity in the humor that often marks Dr. Curran's sermons (and lectures too). A brief exploration of two instances of humor in the Hebrew Bible will serve as support for this claim.

The Book of Genesis tells of many beginnings; one such beginning—of God's relationship with Abraham and his descendants—comes with laughter.[1] God's promise to give Sarah and Abraham a baby, at the ages of 90 and 100, elicits skeptical laughter from both. We will focus on Sarah. When Sarah hears of God's plan, she laughs, but attempts to do so in secret; the text describes how she "laughed inwardly" (18:12).[2] We are familiar, I take it, with

1 My interpretation of this story is informed and influenced by an unpublished paper by Thomas Clement.

2 Unless otherwise noted, quotations from Genesis are from *The Five Books of Moses: A Translation with Commentary*, Robert Alter (New York: W.W. Norton and Company, 2004).

this kind of laughter, of one who is committed to being serious, to not taking the risk of playing the fool by believing in what seems unlikely. Though she tries to keep her laughter to herself, God doesn't let her. God asks Abraham why Sarah is laughing, and when she denies it, God responds, "Yes, you did laugh" (18:15). God, it seems, is nudging Sarah's laughter into the open.

After the birth of Isaac, Sarah's laughter erupts into the open, as she says, "'God has brought me laughter; everyone who hears will laugh with me'" (21:6). Sarah's solitary laughter has been transformed; because of the joy of this miraculous birth, she describes how her laughter is now shared, with the God who gave it to her, and with others who will laugh with her when they hear of her tale. She seems to delight in having been made a fool. She counts as a fool on two counts. I take it there is almost a slap-stick kind of foolishness when we imagine an elderly woman engaged in all the physical challenges of child-birth and caring for a baby. She also counts as a fool because what she previously denied as an impossibility has taken place. Yet whereas previously Sarah laughed at God, she now seems to laugh *with* God—at herself. Her recognition of her own foolishness comes because of God's faithfulness. God has invited her to laugh out in the open at the miracle of new life, of her new son, and of her new faith in a God who is capable of such things. As God said to Sarah after her private laugh, "Is anything too wonderful for the LORD?'" (18:14; New Revised Standard Version).

Our second example of biblical laughter is Jonah, who never laughs himself. But, in my reading, the tale consistently invites our laughter, and it ends on a cliff-hanger, as we are left not knowing whether Jonah, like Sarah, will laugh in recognition of his own foolishness, or whether he will remain stalwartly serious.

After he attempts to reject God's call to go to Nineveh, Jonah ends up in the belly of a large fish (1:17). Jonah's response to these dire circumstances may initially seem like boilerplate piety: he prays to God, asking for forgiveness and committing himself to do what God asked (2:1-9). His words echo those of other biblical prayers of repentance and commitment, such as in the Psalms. But with a closer look, at least a glint of humor emerges. Recall that Jonah is praying from inside *the belly* of a fish. If we imagine all that would involve, we will be immediately struck by the contrast between Jonah's exalted and eloquent words and his rank and raunchy surroundings. This contrast alone, it seems to me, is enough for us to at least crack a smile.

Things get still more amusing when we notice how Jonah seems to be doing his best to avoid admitting just how bad things are. While he makes numerous references to water ("seas," "waters," "flood," "waves," "billows"),[3] he never mentions that he is inside the belly of a fish. He does once mention "belly," but he does so to say he is inside the belly of "Sheol," a constant reference in the Psalms, which describes the land of the dead (2:3). Likewise he describes his distance from God, but again in language familiar from the Psalms, he places himself in a "pit" (2:7). Jonah is drawing on the great language of his tradition, in other words, to obfuscate where he really is.

We are no doubt familiar with other characters like Jonah from literature, films, sitcoms and cartoons: the relentlessly serious person whose life—despite his stalwart commitment to seriousness (especially when it comes to himself)—tends to keep making him into a fool. One sure way to make an amusing situation still funnier is to try to deny that there is anything worth laughing about. Such denial is a constant reaction of the serious person, like Jonah in the belly of the whale. Perhaps when God commandeered that large fish to swallow Jonah, then, God was inviting Jonah to take himself

3 Quotations from Jonah are from *Tanakh: The New Jewish Publication Society Translation According to the Traditional Hebrew Text* (Philadelphia, PA: The Jewish Publication Society, 1985).

less seriously, perhaps even to laugh at his foolishness in attempting to avoid God's request to go to Nineveh. This seems confirmed by the fact that God responds to Jonah's prayer by "spewing" him out of the fish's belly (2:11). Again, we might read this as God hearing Jonah's prayer and answering it. If we are on the look-out for comedy, though, we may also see that God responds to Jonah's attempt to maintain an air of spiritual seriousness with some scatological slap-stick.

The end of Jonah's story further points to how God may be inviting Jonah to laugh at his own foolishness. Jonah's mission turns out to be wildly successful: the people of Nineveh repented with gusto and as a result God refuses to punish them (3:10). Jonah, remarkably, is angered by this, and, in another posture of one who takes himself too seriously, he turns to a self-righteous pout, even telling God he wants to die (4:1-3). One way to read his reaction is as a sign that he disagrees with God's decision to care for those who do not belong to the original covenant people of Israel. This view, too, would fit a certain kind of relentlessly serious character, who wants to draw thick, hard lines about who is in and who is out, who is beloved by God and who isn't.

As has occurred throughout this tale, we see God answer Jonah's seriousness with some slap-stick humor. Jonah is pouting outside the city, and God grows a large plant that provides him some shade for about a day; then, just as Jonah has gotten used to the luxury of his make-shift gazebo, God sends a worm to kill it (I think the humor of this scene becomes all the more evident if we imagine it animated). Jonah's pout gets even worse (4:6-7). At which point, God gets the last words of the text: "'You cared about the plant, which you did not work for and which you did not grow, which appeared overnight and perished overnight. And should not I care about Nineveh?" (4:10-11a).

God's words are one last invitation for Jonah to recognize his foolishness. How could God not care for the Ninevites as his creatures, given how much Jonah cared for this random plant he had nothing to do with bringing about. Like God's gift of Isaac to Sarah, then, we might see God as repeatedly inviting Jonah throughout this tale to laugh at his own foolishness. But because these are the last words of the story, we don't know how Jonah responds.

One possibility, it seems to me, is that Jonah would reflect on his recent days, and be amused by the almost farcical moments of extravagance: the large storm, the large fish, the large acts of repentance by the whole large city (including its animals), and then the large plant that temporarily shaded him. Despite it all, Jonah resisted his role in the Ninevites' repentance, and yet throughout it all God kept giving him another chance. He might become like Sarah, and laugh at what a ridiculous story he played a part in, and notice that that laughter was a gift from God that others will share when they hear it. Perhaps he might even discern God laughing too, and inviting Jonah to laugh at his foolishness, which was no match, finally, for God's faithfulness.

Or perhaps, instead, Jonah would remain relentlessly serious.

DAVID CURRY

Such a Long Journey

"Tom's doing his degree in '80 Bob'," the genial publican of Thom's local in Durham told us while drawing a pint of the fine bitter. It was the spring of 1983 and Marilyn and I were visiting Thom in Durham, England. He was living near the medieval precincts of Durham Cathedral, "half church of God, half castle against the Scots" in John Leland's fine phrase (1534), and working on the respective political theologies of Schleiermacher and Hegel for his doctorate.

The conjunction of things medieval and modern, the harmony of things intellectual and sensual, not to mention beer and theology, speaks to Thom's intellectual life and work as a teacher and scholar, as priest and friend. The quest for such a "harmony of intellect and sensibility,"[1] as T.S. Eliot styles it, belongs to Thom's intellectual endeavours whether in seeking the reconciliation of soul and state in Plato's "Republic" or of thought and feeling in Hegel and in Schleiermacher or in Goethe's "The Sorrows of Young Werther" and Lessing's "Nathan Der Weise," or of antiquity

1 T.S. Eliot, *For Lancelot Andrewes: Essays on style and order* (London: Faber & Faber, 1971), p. 16. Though published in 1928, a version of the essay "*Lancelot Andrewes*" first appeared in the *Times Literary Supplement* on Sept. 23rd, 1926.

and Christianity in his wonderful treatment of Cato in Dante's "Purgatorio," to name but a few of his interests and pursuits. At the very least, there is the attempt at a "reconciliation among the stars" as Eliot puts it in the "Four Quartets" (*Burnt Norton*, II),[2] the constant struggle to overcome "the dissociation of sensibility," the separation of thought and feeling, of intellect and sensibility, that Eliot claims occurred after Andrewes and Donne and from which he argues "we have never recovered."[3] It is all part of the long journey of the understanding.

Eliot found in Lancelot Andrewes that harmony of intellect and sensibility which he sought for in his own poetry. His collection of "essays on style and order" entitled "For Lancelot Andrewes"[4] provides an account of Eliot's conversion to orthodox Christianity in the form of early twentieth century Anglo-Catholicism which at that time was still grounded in the intellectual sensibilities of the Common Prayer tradition. The whole collection of essays achieves a kind of unity through the figure of Lancelot Andrewes.

The first poem that Eliot wrote and published after his baptism and confirmation into the Church of England in June of 1927 was the "Journey of The Magi" (Aug. 1927).[5] He wrote it, as he explained to his life-long friend and fellow poet, Conrad Aiken, "in three quarters of an hour after church time and before lunch one Sunday morning, with the assistance of half a bottle of Booth's gin" (13 Sept. 1927).[6] It was published again at Christmas of 1927 in the first series of "Ariel Poems."

---

2 T.S Eliot, *The Complete Poems and Plays, 1909-1950* (New York: Harcourt, Brace & World, Inc., 1971), p. 119.

3 T. S. Eliot, review of *Metaphysical Lyrics and Poems of the Seventeenth Century: Donne to Butler.* Selected and edited, with an Essay, by Herbert J. C. Grierson (Oxford: Clarendon Press. London; Milford) in the *Times Literary Supplement*, October 1921.

4 See note 1 above.

5 *The Annotated Text: The Poems of T.S. Eliot, Volume 1, Collected and Uncollected Poems*, ed. Christopher Ricks & Jim McCue (London: Faber & Faber, 2015), p. 759.

6 *The Annotated Text*, p. 760.

"For Lancelot Andrewes" and the "Journey of the Magi" show the formative aspects of Andrewes' thought and expression on T. S. Eliot's thinking and writing. The poem famously begins with a quote from Andrewes' Nativity Sermon of 1622 which reveals an aspect of Andrewes' prose that belongs equally to Eliot's poetry. Andrewes' prose has a poetic force and rhythm which Eliot understood and appreciated as well as strong lines which are so much a feature of Eliot's poetry. The opening of the "Journey of the Magi" quotes Andrewes directly but with some slight abridgements and small adjustments that Eliot makes to the text in the spirit of Andrewes' poetic prose. They show Eliot's endeavour to capture for twentieth century moderns something of the quality of Andrewes' remarkable synthesis of intellect and sensibility as well as indicating his own poetic sense.

The passage from Andrewes reads: "A cold coming they had of it at this time of the year, just the worst time of the year to take a journey, and specially a long journey in. The ways deep, the weather sharp, the days short, the sun farthest off, in *solstitio brumali*, 'the very dead of winter'."[7] Eliot concentrates the images ever more slightly yet powerfully. "'A cold coming we had of it,/ Just the worst time of the year/ For a journey, and such a long journey:/ The ways deep and the weather sharp,/ The very dead of winter'."[8] Masterful and concise, nothing is changed in substance apart from the 'we' in place of the 'they', in keeping with the collective narrative voice of the poem itself—'we'. The passage from Andrewes' sermon in its larger context shapes Eliot's exploration of the nature of human longing and its seeking for unity and harmony, for completeness and integrity. It is undertaken in the midst of the ambiguities of modernity with all of its certainties and

7 Andrewes, Lancelot, *Works*, ed. J.P. Wilson, James Bliss, Vol. 1, Library of Anglo-Catholic Theology (Oxford: J. Parker and Co., 1841-54), Sermon XV, p. 257.

8 *Journey of the Magi*, p. 68.

uncertainties. For Eliot, Andrewes points to the possibilities of such harmonies and unities however hard and long the journey may be.

For Eliot, the Magi embody an intellectual sensibility that belongs to the deep truth of our humanity. His poem captures what Andrewes notes in another one of his Christmas sermons on this point. There is "a star" for every one in accord with the capacity of the beholder to behold and to be transformed by what they are given to see.

> Christ applieth Himself to all, disposes all things, what every one is given to, even by that Christ calleth them. St. Peter, Andrew, James, and John, fishermen, by a draught of fish. These that were studious in the stars, by a star for the purpose …
>
> There is no star or beam of it; there is no truth at all in human learning or philosophy that thwarteth any truth in Divinity, but sorteth well with it and serveth it, and all to honour Him who saith of Himself *Ego sum Veritas*, "I am the Truth." None that will hinder this Venerunt, keep back any wise man, or make him less fit for coming to Christ.[9]

Eliot's poem makes no mention of the biblical star but assumes the passion of the quest. Andrewes' sequence of "*viderunt, venerunt, adorarunt*,"[10] the idea of seeing, coming, and adoring, that belongs to his treatment of the Christmas mystery is only implicit in the poem and never fully declared. Such for Eliot are the ambiguities of modernity. He can only point us to the quest and its necessity. Whether that is "(you may say) satisfactory"[11] or not remains our question. That it is a question is the strength and power of Eliot's allusive and yet powerfully suggestive poetry.

---

9 Andrewes, *Works*, Vol. 1, Sermon XIV, p. 245.

10 Andrewes, *Works*, Vol. 1, Sermon XIV, p. 235.

11 *Journey of the Magi*, p. 69.

Eliot's poem is about the hardship and the difficulties of the Magi, unnamed and unnumbered in the poem. He avoids many of the later legends added to the biblical account that give the Magi names and ethnic identities, biographies and no end of fantasies and adventures; no doubt, Facebook accounts as well. Yet Eliot honours the sparseness of the biblical account from Matthew's Gospel where the Magi, too, are unnamed and unnumbered. The poem shows the evocative power of the seeking and the journeying towards a mystery that is seen more darkly than "*in a glass darkly*" (1 Cor. 13.12) and yet remains insistent and compelling.

The poem is a *tour-de-force* of imaginative thinking, what Eliot called, in a December 13th letter to Alan Porter, his "own fantasy of realism." He recognizes in the same letter that "the whole story of the Magi is not, I believe, an essential matter of Christian doctrine" though he is clear in his intent and belief that he "did not put forward any view which would either conflict with Christian doctrine or any imagination which would tend to weaken belief."[12] In line with Andrewes, Eliot imagines and enlarges upon the difficulty of the journey: the "times we regretted/ The summer palaces on slopes, the terraces, /And the silken girls bringing sherbet."[13] In a reading at Vassar College in May 1933, Eliot spoke about the journey of the Three Wise Men as those who are "alienated from and lost among their more materialistic people,"[14] contrasting that image of "the silken girls bringing sherbet" with the disquietude of returning to our places "but no longer at ease," finding themselves among "an alien people clutching their gods."[15]

The hardships of the journey are at once physical and psychological. The Canadian and Maritime writer, David Adams Richard, in a little essay, "Travel," recalls an Arabic saying that

12 *The Annotated Text*, p. 760.

13 *Journey of the Magi*, p. 68.

14 *The Annotated Text*, p. 760.

15 *Journey of the Magi*, p. 69.

"travel is a foretaste of hell" after reminding us about the one thing we can't avoid in all our travelling, namely, "ourselves."[16] And so too in our intellectual journeyings. Eliot imagines the difficulties of the journey, "the cities hostile and the towns unfriendly/And the villages dirty and charging high prices,"[17] the modern traveller's common complaint with just a tinge of the xenophobic distaste for the 'other'. Indeed "a hard time we had of it," but even more there are "the voices singing in our ears, saying/ That this was all folly,"[18] the voices of doubt and uncertainty that beset the journey inwardly yet only add to its intensity.

Eliot in a critical essay on the Metaphysical Poets noted that the seventeenth century poets "possessed a mechanism of sensibility which could devour any kind of experience," suggesting that they had the special quality of "feel[ing] their thought as immediately as the odour of a rose."[19] To feel the thought. That is the kind of harmony of intellect and sensibility that intrigued and entranced Eliot, the perfect balance of thought and feeling. In the "Journey of the Magi," Eliot is constantly seeking that balance and unity which is theologically understood to be found in Christ, the Word made flesh.

The second section of the poem alludes to the Christian mystery albeit at first obliquely. The Magi come "down to a temperate valley/Wet, below the snow line, smelling of vegetation/ With a running stream and a water-mill beating the darkness,"[20] images that conjure up any number of European landscape scenes. For me it is Pieter Bruegel the Elder who immediately comes to mind, though for Eliot it may have been Giorgione whose

16 David Adams Richard, 'Travel', in *A Lad From Brantford and Other Essays* (Fredericton, N.B.: Broken Jaw Press, 1994), p. 102.

17 *Journey of the Magi, p. 68.*

18 *Journey of the Magi*, p. 68.

19 *The Metaphysical Poets* (1921) in *Selected Essays* by T.S. Eliot (London: Faber & Faber, 1932), p. 287

20 *Journey of the Magi*, p. 68.

painting the *Adoration of the Magi* may have been the inspiration for the title.[21] "And then three trees on the low sky/ And an old white horse galloped away in the meadow."[22] The Vassar Miscellany News (1933) reported Eliot as explaining that "three trees were mentioned which foreshadowed the Crucifixion."[23] They are, he says in "Excerpts From Lectures 1932-1933," an "anticipation of Golgotha."[24] But about the "old white horse,"[25] it seems, there is no necessary mythic meaning, only the remembrance of a French landscape, at least as Kristian Smidt recalls Eliot saying.[26] Not every image, it seems, has to be freighted with symbolic significance.

Yet the "six hands at an open door dicing for pieces of silver"[27] is an explicit Scriptural reference "recall[ing] both Judas and the soldiers casting lots for the garments of the dead Christ," as "Mr. Eliot explained" at Vassar.[28] It is a nice economy of expression connecting two aspects of the Passion narratives. The second section of the poem ends with what I think is almost a trademark feature of Eliot's thinking, at once ambiguous and yet alluring. "But there was no information, and so we continued/And arrived at evening, not a moment too soon/Finding the place; it was (you may say) satisfactory."[29]

The sudden irruption of the second person, 'you', even if parenthetically, draws the reader into the journey more directly. "No information" becomes existential and personal.

Eliot in "Choruses from 'the Rock'" (1934) famously asks "where is the wisdom we have lost in knowledge?/ Where is the

---

21 *The Annotated Text*, p. 762.
22 *Journey of the Magi*, p. 68.
23 *The Annotated Text*, p. 760.
24 *The Annotated Text*, p. 764.
25 *Journey of the Magi*, p. 68.
26 *The Annotated Text*, p. 764.
27 *Journey of the Magi*, p. 69.
28 *The Annotated Text*, p. 760
29 *Journey of the Magi*, p. 69.

knowledge we have lost in information?"[30] That triad challenges the nature of every quest and especially the assumptions about learning in contemporary academia. In the "Journey of the Magi," it is neither *information* that is sought, nor *knowledge* that is looked for, but *wisdom*, a way of understanding. In a deliberate kind of understatement, the place—the lowly scene of Christ's birth at Bethlehem—is again "(you may say) satisfactory," alluding perhaps to the ecclesiastical and theological concept of satisfaction or atonement for sin that belongs to the Incarnation as well to the paradox of Bethlehem at once "least among the thousands of Judah" (Micah 5.2) and yet "not the least" (Matthew 2.6). The greatest and least is one of those paradoxes of the Scriptures that belong to the accidents of translation, on the one hand, and to the transcendent truths of the Gospel, on the other hand, differences which Richard Hooker in the *Lawes* sought to reconcile: "the one regarding the quantity of the place, the other the dignity."[31] In Eliot's view, it was "the achievement of Hooker and Andrewes to make the English Church more worthy of intellectual assent."[32]

"Finding the place," the Magi arrive "not a moment too soon."[33] The Epistle reading from Galatians for the Sunday after Christmas suggests that Christ's nativity signifies "the fullness of time"(Gal. 4.4) and anticipates wonderfully the passage about the intersection of time and eternity in Eliot's "Choruses From 'The Rock'." The latter bears mentioning in full:

> Then came, at a predetermined moment, a
> moment in time and
> of time.
> A moment not out of time, but in time, in what we
> call history:

30 *Choruses From "The Rock" I*, in Eliot, *Completed Poems and Plays*, p. 96.

31 Hooker, Richard, *Lawes of Ecclesiastical Polity*, Bk.V, xix.3.

32 *For Lancelot Andrewes*, p. 14.

33 *Journey of the Magi*, p. 69.

transecting, bisecting the world of time, a moment in time
but not like a moment of time.
A moment in time but time was made through that moment: for
without the meaning there is no time, and that moment of
time gave the meaning.
Then it seemed a if men must proceed from light to light, in the
light of the Word,
Through the Passion and Sacrifice saved in spite of their negative
being;
Bestial as always before, carnal, self-seeking as always before,
selfish and purblind as ever before,
Yet always struggling, always reaffirming, always resuming their
march on the way that was lit by the light;
Often halting, loitering, straying, delaying, returning, yet
following no other way.[34]

The "Journey of the Magi" is the quest for that meaning in "that moment" with all of the uncertainties that attend the quest —"bestial as always before, carnal, self-seeking as always before," yet "always struggling, always reaffirming, always resuming their march on the way that was lit by the light." Such is the journey of the Magi.

The last section of the poem brilliantly concentrates "that moment" in the uncertainties that belong to the certainty of faith,

34 *Choruses From "The Rock" VII*, p. 107.

that in Christ God was reconciling himself to the world, and that birth and death belong inescapably and necessarily to that moment in time and yet beyond time. The quest is always a questioning and that is what the last section of the poem presents. But the questioning assumes the possibilities of our knowing, however incomplete, however partial. We see "in a glass darkly," yet we see.

The last section reminds us that there are really two journeys: the journey of the Magi *to* Bethlehem and *from* Bethlehem, an *exitus* and a *reditus*, as it were, a movement towards the principle that unites and contains and a movement from that principle in its unfolding. Andrewes, in an Ash Wednesday sermon to which Eliot alludes in his poem "Ash Wednesday," describes repentance as a *redire ad principia*, a return to a principle, "a kind of circling."[35] There is the return of the Magi "to our places, these Kingdoms"[36] but in this recollection of the going forth and return there is a sense of unease, a sense of uncertainty, a sense of something new and different that changes everything.

The last section begins, too, with a narrative shift from the first person plural to the first person singular that highlights the sense of recollection in the effort to understand what the journey was really all about. There is the sense that the meaning of the journey is still something that is constantly being sought and pursued. "All this was a long time ago, I remember,/ And I would do it again," we are told, but with a renewed sense of insistence about the quest. "But set down,/ this set down/ This: were we led all that way for/ Birth or Death?"[37] It is as if the return of the Magi is really the harder journey, the longer journey, at least in the quest to understand.

Birth and Death point to the mystery of Christ's Incarnation which changes our outlook and leaves us unsettled. "This

35 Andrewes, *Works*, Vol. I, Sermon IV, p. 358

36 *Journey of the Magi*, p. 69

37 *Journey of the Magi*, p. 69.

Birth was/ hard and bitter agony for us, like Death, our death."[38] The capitalisation of Birth and Death points to the mystery of Christ whose Birth and Death signal our birth and death into a new understanding and a new sensibility. We return but changed by what we have encountered, changed in ways that leave us "no longer at ease,"[39] changed by what we have seen. We can no longer be "assured of certain certainties,"[40] it seems, but only more aware of the mystery around which we are constantly circling. Such is the influence on Eliot of the Neoplatonic structure of Andrewes' thought, itself a constant "kind of circling."

"We returned to our places, these Kingdoms,/ But no longer at ease."[41] There is no simple and comfortable return to our old ways and patterns of thinking for that would be to deny the journey. The phrase "no longer at ease" has become almost iconic. It is the title of Chinua Achebe's novel which explores the conflicts and contrasts between cultures in their interaction, such as between the tribal Igbo culture and the English colonial culture on the eve of Nigerian independence. Nothing remains the same and some things change forever. There can be no simple return to "the old dispensation,"[42] to the old ways of thinking and being. The Magi in the poem return to "an alien people clutching their gods."[43] But they themselves cannot return to those old ways without betraying what they have come to see and must continue to try to understand more fully. This is Eliot's great insight about the long journey of the understanding.

"I should be glad of another death," the poem ends.[44] It is not a note of regret or sorrow but rather an acknowledgment that the journey of the understanding is about a constant birth and

38 *Journey of the Magi*, p. 69.
39 *Journey of the Magi*, p. 69.
40 *Preludes IV* in Eliot, *Completed Poems and Plays*, p. 13
41 *Journey of the Magi*, p. 69.
42 *Journey of the Magi*, p. 69.
43 *Journey of the Magi*, p. 69.
44 *Journey of the Magi*, p. 69.

death, a constant return to the mystery which enfolds us and yet compels us and one in which we seek that unity of intellect and sense, one in which just maybe "the flowing back will correspond to the flowing out," as Meister Eckhart wonderfully suggests (*Sermon* LVI).[45]

Such is the long journey, the long journey of the understanding, to which Thom's intellectual labours and life bear eloquent testimony and which continue to have a marked influence on so many of his students and friends among whom I count myself and for which I am most grateful.

—David Curry
Palm Sunday, 2019

45 *Meister Eckhart, The Essential Sermons, Commentaries, Treatises, and Defense*, The Classics of Western Spirituality, Trans. & Intro by Edmund Colledge & Bernard McGinn (New York: Paulist Press, 1981), Intro, p. 30, n. 37.

RANALL INGALLS

A Sermon for Evensong, Wednesday in Easter Week, 2018

From the Song of Songs (2:10),

> My beloved spake, and said unto me, Rise up, my love, my fair one, and come away. For, lo, the winter is past ...

In the Name of the Father, and of the Son, and of the Holy Ghost. Amen.

A quick look at the table of lessons at the front of the Prayer Book suggests that the only time we hear from the Song of Songs in the course of the year is on Wednesday afternoon in Easter week. Why don't we read it more often? And why do we read it now?

Perhaps a certain reticence is not hard to understand. The Song of Songs is an ancient Hebrew love song. It is charged with erotic longing of lovers for one another and with their delight in one another. I use the word 'charged' advisedly. The imagery is rich and sensuous. And whatever we might happily listen to on Spotify or watch on Netflix at any other time, passages like those in which the Lover delights in the Beloved's eyes, teeth, lips, breasts, and legs may make us uneasy in Church. But even apart from all such scruples, what are we to make of this book? Who are these people?

Often they have been read allegorically, as representing God and his people, or Christ under the image of Bridegroom and his Bride the human soul or the Church. But how could that be?

Some among us may have looked at the Thirty-Nine Articles of Religion printed beginning on page 699—perhaps in a moment of boredom during a sermon by a guest preacher, for example. If you've ever looked at them, you may recall that the first article begins, 'There is but one living and true God, everlasting, without body, parts or passions; of infinite power, wisdom, and goodness …' and so on. 'Without passions,' notice. How can we imagine God might be conceived as a Bridegroom or a Lover if we take to heart such sober warnings against making God after our own image? Surely we should know better than that. If the prophets and the Articles are not enough, Sigmund Freud might put us on our guard against such anthropomorphism.

But let it first be said that historically nay-sayers with respect to the Song of Songs as allegory have been very much in the minority. Through most of the last twenty centuries the only books of the Bible more popular amongst Christians, for example, have been the Gospels and the Psalms. Origen wrote a commentary in the third century, Eusebius of Caesarea, St Ambrose of Milan and Gregory of Nyssa all wrote commentaries of their own in the fourth. St Gregory the Great wrote a commentary in the sixth century when he was not busy laying foundations for the medieval world. Roughly a hundred years later the Venerable Bede gathered together the fruit of what had already become many centuries of commentary in his own work. And the Middle Ages especially in the West saw many, many more sermons and commentaries, among them most notably a long series of sermons by St Bernard of Clairvaux. And not every great commentary has been written with words. There are musical commentaries, too. One thinks of the magnificent settings of these texts by Palestrina, and our own

Healey Willan's 'Rise up, my love', which we heard minutes ago.

Have all these simply been mistaken? Certainly some have thought it a mistake to ascribe eros to God, even in ancient times. But a mysterious sixth century monk known to us as Dionysius the Areopagite argued for eros, and his argument has borne much fruit. His argument informed writings on prayer and commentaries on the liturgy in both the West and the East for many, many centuries, and continues to do so. A recent scholar argues that it was his work more than any other which also provided a theological argument for the allegorical use of the Song of Songs so loved especially by monks, when an argument was needed. Dionysius writes,

> [I]n truth, it must be said too that the very cause of the universe in the beautiful, good superabundance of his benign yearning for all is also carried outside of himself in the loving care he has for everything. He is, as it were, beguiled by goodness, by love, and yearning and is enticed away from his transcendent dwelling place and comes to abide in all things, and he does so by virtue of his supernatural and ecstatic capacity to remain, nevertheless, within himself. [That is why those possessed of spiritual insight describe him as 'zealous' because his goody earning for all things is so great and because he stirs in [human beings] a deep yearning desire for zeal. In this way he proves himself to be zealous because zeal is always felt for what is desired and because he is zealous for the creatures for whom he provides. In short, both the yearning and the object of that yearning belong to the Beautiful and the Good. They pre-exist in it, and because of it they exist and come to be.] (*Works*, ed. Luibheid, page 82)

It is not that the Articles are wrong, then. God is indeed without 'body, parts, or passions'. The 'no' must be said. God is not pulled hither and thither by contrary passions, one time angry, one time generous; one time rejoicing, one time morose. God is eternal. That is, he is outside time, not limited by time. In Dionysius' words, he 'remains within himself'. But when we ascribe 'love' or 'yearning' to God, we are not talking about something less than human love, but something more—something which exceeds it in every way. In fact, on this argument, all human love is rooted and grounded in divine 'yearning'. But while we thus affirm human love as an image of divine love and a means to participate in it, at the same time we deny that our words capture or exhaust the reality to which they point. Love in one who is eternal and beyond time is something that we cannot adequately imagine or express.

There is reason, then, to ascribe to God burning passionate love for his creation and for us. And so also reason in the practice of a hundred generations or more who have read the Song of Songs and heard in them the voice of the divine Lover or Bridegroom, most of whom never read a word of Dionysius.

In sum, it might be a good thing to read more of the Song of Songs, and to take it to heart. But the question remains *why we read it now, in Easter Week?* And here we can only be grateful. It would be hard to imagine a more fitting or a more beautiful text to draw us into the mystery of Jesus' death and resurrection. For it draws us into desire and delight as the most appropriate response to what we have celebrated this past week.

> My beloved spake, and said unto me, Rise up, my love, my fair one, and come away. For, lo, the winter is past, the rain is over and gone; The flowers appear on the earth; the time of the singing of birds is come, and the voice of the turtle is heard in our land; The fig tree putteth forth her green figs, and the vines with the tender grape give a good smell. Arise, my love, my fair one, and come away.

Christ triumphs over every enemy of our humanity—indifference, contempt, cynicism, bitterness, treachery, rage, torture, violence, murder. His love and wisdom are not driven out or destroyed. All the way through his Passion he behaves as a King. He refuses to answer the charges, for he is not answerable to these courts. He wins freedom for a murderer by taking his place, exercising the prerogative of a king to grant pardon and reprieve, showing himself to be a true Shepherd even to those who in no way recognize his reign. To the penitent thief on the cross beside him he promises a share in his kingly bounty. For the soldiers who nail him to the Cross he prays, 'Father, forgive them, for they know not what they do.' And to those amongst his closest friends who abandoned him and denied him he says, 'Peace be with you.'

Christ triumphs over every enemy of our humanity—and the last enemy that is destroyed is death. Then he turns to his apostles and so to us, and says, in effect, 'Rise up, my love, my fair one, and come away.' He has joined himself to his beloved bride in her poverty 'for richer for poorer, for better for worse, in sickness and in health' and for him it has been for poorer, for worse, and in sickness. He has taken upon himself the sickness of the human race—our sickness. And he has done so that he may draw us into his own deathless life, his own eternal passion for the world he has made and everything and everyone in it. 'Rise up, my love, my fair one, and come away.' The winter is past. The winter of our humanity. The withering of desire and knowledge. The winter of our countless betrayals. As St Bernard says, the rains that cover the fields of our lives and hearts and understanding so that we cannot be tilled and made fruitful are 'over and gone'. Mercy brings forth the flowers of spring and the songs of birds: a springtime of the spirit, in a world that remains as mysterious, violent and broken as it ever was.

To read this text in this way is not meant to draw us into a flight of fancy. It is intended to open our eyes more fully to what is before us. It is intended to open to us the world around us as theophany, as the manifestation of the wisdom, goodness and beauty of God. The Resurrection is not about how God breaks into the realm of nature conceived as some great mechanism. The Resurrection is about how the order of the seasons and particularly the way in which all things extend themselves toward new and greater life in spring speaks to us of the highest and best manifestation of God's yearning—his eros. And what is that manifestation? His coming among us in our human nature. His living our life. His dying our death. His conquest of all that distorts and ruins our humanity. The union with him in humility and that repentance which continually works the renewal of love in us.

Let Peter be our example. Peter, bewildered, went fishing. He went back to what he knew. But nothing was the same. There was Christ, commanding him to put down his nets on the other side, as he had when they first met. There was Christ, feeding the disciples with bread and fish, as he had fed the great crowds in the desert. Peter would go fishing, but it would be fishing of altogether another kind as a result of the resurrection. Nothing would be easy. There would be loneliness, struggle, rejection, torture, a cruel death. But there would be Christ in all things, the reality of the conquest of death, the power of God to bring good out of evil.

Inevitably after Holy Week we will go back to what we know, to familiar routines and people and places. That is fine. But we may find we do not know it as we thought we knew it. We may encounter Christ there, and all that we thought we knew may be swallowed up in something greater, as it was for Peter—something more difficult perhaps, or even more painful—but something larger and better, something to draw us away from the distortions of desire that make us prisoners, and into an ever larger share in the divine yearning, the divine eros, to live as God's own beloved children, in a world God has loved to the uttermost.

GARY THORNE

Recent students of the Foundation Year Programme, but especially King's College Chapel attendees will know how Tom's visits to Egypt excited his imagination and opened up fresh ways of his thinking about both the ancient and contemporary worlds. Following his second visit to Egypt in 2013 Tom sent a letter to his family and friends in which he described Aswan (the natural southern border of Egypt where the Nile becomes impassible) as "the most extraordinary place on earth." That 2013 trip was a personal pilgrimage to visit in Aswan the Mausoleum of the Late Sultan Mohammed Shah, better known as the 3rd Aga Khan. Tom had obtained personal permission from His Highness the 4th Aga Khan (spiritual leader of Ismaili Shia Muslims) to visit the Mausoleum, normally closed to visitors.

That Tom Curran would perhaps be the only non-Ismaili Shia Muslim ever go to such lengths to seek permission to visit and pray in a specific Mausoleum on the Upper Nile will not surprise any of Tom's Sunday congregation. Each Sunday morning we sit on the edge of our seats, waiting for the unexpected, in both liturgy and preaching. One of his students recently described

Sunday morning as follows, "… The service starts late; the preacher always runs over time; he never talks about the appointed reading, but usually recycles material from lectures he heard or gave that week (with fresh commentary), the radio or assorted news outlets of varying reputations, literary reviews of the latest plays and performances from around the world, or reflections on his travels; the ceremonial is disordered at best … it is a high churchman's nightmare."

So it did not surprise me that when Tom and I visited the Museum of Egyptian Antiquities in Cairo in May 2015 I discovered that Tom thought highly of this museum. This Cairo museum on Tahrir Square must be one of the most disorganized, awkwardly lighted, poorly labelled, ill-kept museum in the world, yet it houses the most extensive collection of exquisite artifacts from the Old Kingdom to the period of Roman rule, including the contents of Tutankhamen's tomb and most of the mummies that have been discovered since the 19th century. Visitors are notorious for expressing exasperation in trying to find their way around and to make sense of the museum's layout.

But Tom relished in making the connections that defeated others. In fact, visiting this museum with Tom was like walking through one of his sermons. As he would point me to wonder after wonder among the 120,000 dusty and dirty Pharaonic artifacts of the Cairo Museum that had gone unnoticed by others, so Tom has helped countless students to make connections and see meaning in the most unlikely places and circumstances of life. I want to highlight a major theme from Tom's Sunday morning spiritual counsel, but I shall begin by describing an experience of mine in the Egyptian desert during the summer of 2015.

In 2015 I visited Egypt as the Anglican Foundation of Canada Saint Basil the Great Scholar, to learn about the contemporary Coptic Orthodox Church. My interest in the contemporary

Coptic Church began in the mid-eighties when I read a small collection of essays by Abouna (Father) Matta El-Meskeen (Matthew the Poor) called *The Communion of Love*, with an introduction by Henri Nouwen, and decades later I would read Abouna Matta's profound volume *Orthodox Prayer Life,* published in English in 2003. But as a parish priest in Nova Scotia I was particularly interested in the remarkable renewal of the Coptic Church that began under Abouna Matta's spiritual influence. How could a contemporary church enjoy such a renewal through a retrieval of ancient tradition, the devotional wisdom and practice of the Desert fathers, and a rigorous monastic discipline that offered itself as an escape from the clutches of the culture of global capitalism, greed and entitlement?

Matta el Meskeen was a prosperous pharmacist at the age of 29 when, like the great anchorite St Anthony (251-356 AD) he heeded the Scriptural call to "sell what you have" and follow Jesus. He disposed of his two houses, two cars, two pharmacies, etc. and for nearly a decade in the 1950s lived a solitary ascetic life in the caves of the Wadi El Rayan, a valley of the Western Desert 124 miles south-west of Cairo. Other Coptic Christians learned of Abouna Matta's withdrawal to the desert and sought him out. By the mid-sixties, there was a community of 12. They were determined to follow the example of Anthony's younger contemporary Pachomius who established a form of cenobitic monasticism in which solitary monks devoted themselves to ceaseless prayer during the week, but gather for the Liturgy on Sundays.

The valley was entirely cut off from the outside world and for more than a decade this group of monastics lived in ground-caves, read no newspapers and heard no radio. Some caves extended into the hillside and were covered in Coptic writings on plastered walls from early monastic settlements in the fourth century. They took turns to bake bread once a week: water was carried on a donkey in petrol cans from an oasis.

In response to an appeal from the Coptic Patriarch Kyrillos VI in 1969 Matta el Meskeen moved his community of 12 monks from the Wadi El Rayan north to the Wadi El Natroun into the monastery of St Macarius the Great, at that time inhabited by six elderly monks. Pope Kyrillos VI was aware of the increasing awareness and popularity of Abouna Matta's life in the desert, and he imagined that under Abouna Matta's leadership a renewal of the monastic life was possible. As the Pope received and welcomed Abouna Matta's community, he prayed "that the desert might bloom again and become the home of thousands of hermits."

Ten years later Abouna Matta had over 80 monks in community, in 1991 over 100, and today there are more than 150 monks at St Macarius Monastery. Most are university graduates in such diverse fields as agriculture, medicine, veterinary medicine, education, pharmacology, dentistry, engineering, etc., all having given up their professions to enter this monastery. Renouncing family ties and contact with the outside world, many monks never leave the monastery unless for medical emergency. During their consecration each monk had lain face-down on the ground covered by a sheet as the Prayer for the Dead was read over him, until he emerged from beneath the sheet reborn with a new name.

When I arrived at the monastery in April 2015 I was shown to my cell and began to wonder how I would learn about the recent renewal of the Coptic Church by being alone in a monastic cell. I had looked forward to interviews and conversations with monks that would help me understand the Coptic revival, but during my time at St Macarius monastery I would have few (though significant) conversations. I learned the wisdom of the Desert saying that one's cell is sufficient.

Everything was orchestrated to allow me to remain in my cell for many days in prayer and contemplation. Meals were dropped off for me outside my door: dirty dishes taken away. Other than joining the monks twice daily for communal prayer, there was no reason to leave the cell.

I arrived at St Macarius aware of my need for spiritual healing and conversion. I had a longing to rest in the Love of Christ. I sought the experience described by St John Vianney who noticed a person spending a lot of time in prayer in front of the Sacrament and asked him, "What do you say to our Lord?" He replied, "I say nothing to him. I look at Him and He looks at me" (Alfred Monnin, *Life of the Curé of Ars*, trans. H. E. Manning [London: Burns and Lambert, 1862], pp. 55–56). But I also knew that such an experience is not the beginning of our prayer life, but the end. This unitive experience of resting in God's embrace comes after the previous purgative and illuminative stages of the soul's conversion. The three-fold conversion of the soul through the stages of purgation, illumination, and union, first articulated by Dionysius the Aeropagite in the sixth century was my life's work: but in that cell, naked before the Lord, I was reminded of its reality.

For four days that isolated cell was busier and more chaotic than the traffic on the streets of Cairo. Alone in my cell, listening to the wind blow across the desert sands, I became aware of more distractions than I thought possible for one puny soul. I would leave my cell twice each day: at 3.45 each morning for the 4 AM prayers that would continue until sunrise, returning to my cell via a walk in the desert; then at 5 PM I would return to the chapel for Vespers. During these times of worship the monks sang their ancient pharaonic melodies in Coptic and Arabic for hours. With these melodies helping to settle the wildness of my untamed soul, I spent my time alone in my cell, seeking a rest in the Blessed Trinity. Around the fifth day there was a shift—the chaotic traffic was mostly gone—and finally I was able to hold individuals in my heart and to pray for them without a sense of hurriedness. I began simply to be present to God and to embrace those for whom I sought healing and blessedness. What a privilege to have the time to pray for others in an unhurried way for their healing and happiness: to pray that they would know the joy of being loved and of loving.

But on the 8th or 9th day of my solitude I became troubled with the question of just how much was I praying for others. I began to wonder if I was praying for others at all, or only for myself. I realized that my prayers for others were mostly for those whose health, happiness and joy were related to my own happiness and joy. I reflected upon my lifetime of prayer as a priest and wondered if even my frequent praying with and for those preparing to die were prayers that really issued from my own fear of death, subconsciously intended to build up my own resilience to that fear of death. I wondered if I was capable of truly praying for another.

Then my sense of being, self, and personhood began to shift. My praying entered a new landscape and I slowly was freed from seeing the other in relation to myself. I experienced a great release and found myself praying for others and their happiness regardless of their relationship to me. My prayers for those I saw as my enemies (those who wish me ill) were no longer that somehow we might be reconciled (that is, that the good might rebound to me) but I prayed simply that they might be granted the deepest experiences of Beauty, Truth and blessedness. I resolved to arrive at the monastery chapel an hour before the 3 AM morning office in order to pray for others. Through my imagined annihilation of self in order to affirm the goodness of being of others, paradoxically I became more specifically myself.

This conversion of my soul at St Macarius is, of course, a common enough experience. It is described as a state of 'de-creation' by Simon Weil (1909-43), achieved when we desire our "nonbeing" precisely in order to confirm our neighbor's being. I believe that my experience at St Macarius monastery is also what St Silouan the Anthonite (1866-1938) means when he exhorts us to "Keep your mind in hell and despair not." This principle of faithful living was only revealed to St Silouan after fifteen years of intense prayer as the remedy to his pride: "Thenceforth I began to do this, and my soul found rest in God." With your mind in hell there is nothing personal to strive for: we can pray wholly and entirely for others because we are already forsaken or, as Simone Weil might say, we have become 'non-being'. We are free truly to will the Good for another when we think of ourselves as already lost and unable to benefit from their healing.

I have come to see that this insight that came to me in my cell at the monastery in the Egyptian Desert was part of what Tom also learned from his own travels in Egypt and which he has been communicating to his students for years in Alumni Hall, but also in a more personal way in the Chapel on Sunday mornings.

Tom deeply appreciates the monumental and literary heritage of Ancient Egypt. The monumental architecture of pyramids, tombs, temples, palaces, and obelisks represent for Tom the majesty and awe with which the Egyptians confronted and contemplated the mystery of death in the midst of the fragility and contingency of their daily life. The literary heritage of ancient Egypt complements this message. Tom's interest in "The Dialogue of a man and his Ba," the most well-known and discussed literary work from the Middle Kingdom, is shaped by his deep study of Dante's *Divine Comedy*. Just as Tom insists that the *Comedy* belongs to the branch of *practical philosophy* called *ethics*, so a recent interpretation of "The Dialogue of a man and his Ba" understands it as an ethical text, resisting a common interpretation that the text is concerned with the after-life.[1]

As an ethical treatise the *Comedy* is not about a simple progression from the *Inferno* to the *Paradiso* through the *Purgatorio*,

---

1 Yordan Chobanov, "A New Interpretation of 'The Dialogue of a man with his Ba'," *The Journal of Egyptological* Studies, IV (2015), 84-97.

but rather each realm is present in the soul at every moment. The soul is always in the *Inferno* (death) even as the soul makes progress in the acquisition of the cardinal and theological virtues through *Purgatorio* and *Paradiso*. (Cf. the St Silouan principle above: "Keep your mind in hell and despair not.")

Our Middle Kingdom (2040-1759 BCE) text, "The Dialogue of a man and his Ba," embraces death to such a degree that suicide is often thought to be its theme. The text has been re-titled "A Dispute over Suicide."[2] A more careful recent interpretation is that the presence of death is not accompanied by despair but rather positively leads to the discovery of the possibility of an inner repentance. The text comes from the tumultuous times of the First Intermediate Period. Order has been replaced by disorder. Stability with chaos. Since the king is absent, Ma'at is threatened. Chaos and anarchy (Isfet) inhabit the soul of the Egyptians. Written in response to this crisis, "The Dialogue of a man and his Ba" concludes that confession is required to return to the path of Ma'at. Since there is no righteous person to receive his confession, the man must turn inward to Ba. That is, the man keeps his mind in hell but despairs not.

Conclusion

Many students who make their way to the King's College Chapel on Sunday mornings have had little previous contact with Christianity: they come to hear a favourite FYP lecturer speak directly and personally about how the most recent FYP lectures, or the monumental and literary heritage of Egypt, can help their particular soul's journey "from a state of misery to a state of bliss."[3]

2 "A Dispute Over Suicide," from *Ancient Near Eastern Texts Relating to the Old Testament*, ed. James B Pritchard, tr. John A Wilson. Princeton, NJ: Princeton University Press, 1950.

3 Tom very often quotes from Dante Alighieri's letter to his patron, Cangrande: "My Commedia belongs to that branch of philosophy called ethics, and is intended to move the reader from a state of misery to a state of bliss, in this life."

They meet a preacher who speaks to them of magnanimity and pusillanimity, encouraging them to become so "large-souled" that they hold together misery and bliss, death and hope. One of Tom's favorite pulpit texts is the Christmas sermon of the character of Archbishop Thomas à Beckett in T.S. Eliot's *Murder in the Cathedral.*

> It was in this same night that has just passed, that a multitude of the heavenly host appeared before the shepherds at Bethlehem, saying, 'Glory to God in the highest, and on earth peace, good will toward men'; at this same time of all the year that we celebrate at once the Birth of Our Lord and His Passion and Death upon the Cross. Beloved, as the World sees, this is to behave in a strange fashion. For who in the World will both mourn and rejoice at once and for the same reason? For either joy will be overborne by mourning, or mourning will be cast out by joy; so it is only in these our Christian mysteries that we can rejoice and mourn at once for the same reason.

To mourn and rejoice at the same time requires a magnanimity of soul that will allow one to keep one's mind in hell and despair not, mourning and rejoicing at once and for the same reason. From the countless students who have their discovered their blessedness and "great souled-ness" on Sunday mornings: "Thank you Dr. Curran."

—Gary Thorne, May 2019.

HENRY ROPER

The Halifax Explosion, Samuel Henry Prince, and the Tradition of Christian Social Action at the University of King's College

This short essay originated as an address delivered in the King's Chapel in December, 2017. It seems appropriate that it be included in a Festschrift honouring the Reverend Dr. Thomas Curran, for, like Samuel Henry Prince, Dr. Curran has for many years faithfully served King's as professor and priest.

The 6 December, 2017 was the 100th anniversary of the most traumatic event in Halifax's history. I use the word "traumatic" because the Explosion has received far more attention during the past thirty years than when I was growing up in this city during the 1940s and 1950s. The adults I knew, still in the prime of life, had lived through the event. Barbara Orr Thompson was very much part of my childhood, perhaps my mother's closest friend. She lost her parents, her five siblings, her grandfather and her uncle in the disaster. She herself lay in hospital for ten days before being discovered by a relative, who did not recognize her because her red hair had been dyed blue by TNT from the blast. I never once heard Aunt Barbara, as I called her, refer to the Explosion. Whatever terrible emotional scars may have remained she always seemed to me invariably upbeat, cheerful, and fun-loving.

Fortunately her story was recorded and you can read the horrific details on several websites and in various books.

In the same way that persons returning from combat rarely talk about their experiences, I think Haligonians wanted to forget the Explosion as much as possible. As a boy I routinely encountered people with explosion injuries. My first piano teacher had lost an eye; the skin on one side of her face was drawn taut and scarred with small blue grains like gunpowder. She was a beautiful woman and subsequently married. A teacher at my junior high school had also lost an eye. The Explosion was there in the background for those who lived through it, but there was little desire for commemoration. Indeed, the disaster had no civic memorial until the construction of the library on Gottingen Street in 1964. The first yearly commemoration was held as recently as 1994, nine years after the completion of the Memorial Bell Tower in Fort Needham park, erected through the initiative of private citizens. The Tower houses a carillon originally donated by Barbara Orr in 1920 to the United Memorial Church in memory of her family. Revealingly, construction of the Needham Park Memorial Tower received no financial support from the city of Halifax, although Dartmouth gave $10,000. The "tradition" of sending a tree to Boston is actually of quite recent origin. A tree was donated in 1918 as an expression of thanks for the massive relief sent from Massachusetts, but this gesture was not repeated. It was revived in 1971, initially as a marketing gambit by the Christmas tree growers of Lunenburg County.

The only significant work to address the Explosion before the publication in 1941 of Hugh MacLennan's novel *Barometer Rising* was a Columbia University Ph.D. thesis by Samuel Henry Prince, published in 1920 as *Catastrophe and Social Change.* Four years later Dr. Prince was appointed professor of sociology and Divinity at King's where he remained until his retirement in 1955.

From this position he was to have a lasting impact upon the College, the Diocese of Nova Scotia, and the development of social services in the province. At the time of the Explosion Prince was Curate at St. Paul's Church, the wealthiest parish in Nova Scotia, an Evangelical stronghold in a High Church diocese. Born in 1886, he was raised in New Brunswick as an Evangelical and so did not attend King's. He graduated from Wycliffe College, going on to complete an M.A. in psychology at the University of Toronto. High principled, austere, and a life-long bachelor, Prince devoted himself entirely to the Church, teaching and public service. It is revealing that although he played a significant role in the Explosion's aftermath by organizing the relief efforts of St. Paul's, he never refers to his own experiences in *Catastrophe and Social Change* or in "The Halifax Explosion—Fourteen Years After," a paper he read to the Nova Scotia Historical Society in 1931, which remained unpublished until 2018.

Prince joined St. Paul's in 1911, quickly becoming well known for a newspaper article in May, 1912 about the search for the *Titanic* dead which he had joined to perform burials and memorial services. His organizational talents made him the protégé of the formidable Rector of St. Paul's, Archdeacon W.J. Armitage, who was deeply disappointed when Prince resigned his curacy in 1919 to study at Columbia. Prince's motives for going to New York to pursue a Ph.D. in sociology are not altogether clear. His biography by Bishop Leonard Hatfield provides little insight into his intellectual development. However, much can be gathered from his later books and speeches, and by inference from the book *Catastrophe and Social Change* itself. As has been pointed out by a number of commentators, his thesis on the Explosion was shaped as much by his teachers at Columbia as by his own research, which was minimal. Prince argues that the Explosion galvanized a stagnant city. "Search where one will, it would be difficult to find another city which has more completely exhibited the causes of social immobility as set forth by sociology." The disaster impelled progress, which was achieved through the introduction of modern techniques of social science and public health; these in turn led to increased economic activity and civic improvement.

There are difficulties with this argument, which in some respects was factually inaccurate, and over-optimistic about the changes taking place in Halifax in 1920. However, *Catastrophe and Social Change* does reveal much about the framework of ideas that would guide Prince for the rest of his life. To Prince, human history is the history of progress, which frequently comes through disaster; for example, "the sinking of the *Titanic* has greatly reduced the hazards of the sea." The key to modern progress is empirical investigation, although "[p]rogress is not necessarily a natural or assured result of change. It comes only as a result of effort that is wisely expended, and sacrifice which is sacrifice in truth." These Delphic words, I think, mean that for progress to be meaningful it must result in a society animated by Christian principles.

This point is developed by Dr. Susan Dodd in *The Halifax Explosion: The Apocalypse of Samuel H. Prince*, her commentary on *Catastrophe and Social Change*. Dr. Dodd argues convincingly that the thinking behind the book is as much a product of Prince the priest–social activist as Prince the sociologist. The Christian foundations of his thought are at the core of an address he delivered in 1949 upon the occasion of his retirement from 20 years as Chairman of the Nova Scotia Diocesan Council for Social Service. After detailing the causes espoused by the DCSS, such as pressing for minimum wages for women, old age pensions and the creation of the Nova Scotia Housing Commission Act, Prince concludes: "… the opinion may be expressed that the most effective service of the Church in the future will lie … in the generation of a Christian atmosphere in which conditions which are anti-social must vanish as the mists before the rising sun. An informed Christian public opinion will do more than anything else to transform our society into one in closer accord with the ideals of the Kingdom of God ..."

Prince's appointment in 1924 as a professor of Divinity and as the first professor of Sociology in the Dalhousie-King's Faculty of Arts and Science had a profound effect upon the College and its future. His presence made King's more acceptable to Evangelicals like Archdeacon Armitage of St. Paul's who disliked the Divinity Faculty's High Church orientation; Evangelical support was crucial to financing the new King's buildings on the Dalhousie campus including its Chapel, which was consecrated in 1930. But more important was Prince's impact on students, particularly six future priests who arrived at King's during the depths of the Depression These included C. Russell Elliott, Mel French and Karl Tufts.

In Canon Elliott's words, "the Church in general seemed old and tired and weary ..." He illustrates this point with an anecdote. One day he and Mel French spied an elderly professor moving slowly and heavily across the quad. "There goes the Church militant," French remarked. To Canon Elliott and his friends, later known as "the Briefcase Boys," "Sammy" became "... an unconstituted [*sic*] and uncanonised patron saint." Because of their outspokenness about social justice issues Archbishop John Hackenley refused in 1940 to ordain five of them as priests; he also revoked their licences as deacons. Fortunately Archbishop Hackenley had a change of heart. Once ordained, the "Briefcase Boys" laboured tirelessly in their parishes for social and economic improvement.

Prince himself stayed away from politics, working within the existing power structure, for example in mobilizing support from the Liberal provincial government to found the Maritime School of Social Work in 1941. Some of those he influenced, however, were attracted by the predecessor of the NDP, the Cooperative Commonwealth Federation, or CCF. The CCF, led first by

J.S. Woodsworth, a Methodist minister, and then by M.J. Coldwell, an Anglican lay reader, espoused a socialist agenda in its founding document, the Regina Manifesto of 1933, which was deeply influenced by the social gospel movement of the early 20th century. Christian socialism and the CCF were closely linked.

In the late 1940s Father Elliott, Father French, Father Tufts and other "Briefcase Boys" joined the leftist Anglican Federation for Social Action, or AFSA, which proclaimed that "our present economic system frustrates brotherhood, as its appeal is primarily to self-interest and its basis is competition; therefore this system is un-Christian and immoral." Their involvement in AFSA created uneasiness in the hierarchy, as well as raising the ire of the conservative Diocesan Chancellor, Reginald V. Harris, KC. Chancellor Harris, describing AFSA as "atheistic and communistic," engaged in heated exchanges with Father Tufts and other AFSA members in the pages of the *Diocesan Times.*

Even more radical than AFSA, and a source of alarm to Bishop Harold Waterman, was the turn taken by a small group of King's theological students led by Robert Darwin Crouse. He and three friends rejected AFSA on theological and political grounds, establishing in 1951 a connection with Father Frederic Hastings Smyth's Society of the Catholic Commonwealth (SCC). The SCC fused belief in a Marxist revolution with an idiosyncratic Anglo-Catholicism. Father Smyth worked out this synthesis in his book *Manhood Into God* and other writings; he also founded an oratory in Cambridge, Massachusetts. In 1952 Robert Crouse became a member of Smyth's oratory while studying at Harvard. However, he soon broke with both Smyth and Marxism. Dr. Crouse eventually returned to King's, where he had as great an influence upon the College as had Dr. Prince in an earlier era. These two remarkable individuals brought different but complementary gifts to their vocations as priests and professors.

The activities of the "Briefcase Boys" in AFSA, let alone Robert Crouse's attraction to the revolutionary theology of Frederic Hastings Smyth, went far beyond Prince's conception of social improvement within the framework of the existing political order. But the seeds of these radical ideas nevertheless can be traced to Prince's evangelical vision. In ways that he could not have anticipated, his teaching and example brought into being an important King's tradition, that of Christian social action. The College accordingly owes a great debt to Samuel Henry Prince, priest, sociologist, reformer, and professor, who reminds us by his teaching and example that social action is inseparable from the Christian message of love of neighbour.

Sources:

Brown, Terry. "Metacosmesis: The Christian Marxism of Frederic Hastings Smyth and the Society of the Catholic Commonwealth." Unpublished Th.D. dissertation, University of Toronto, 1987. Anglicanhistory.org/academic/brown1987/

Cuthbertson, Brian. *A Journey Just Begun: A History of the Diocese of Nova Scotia and Prince Edward Island*. Halifax: Diocese of N.S. and P.E.I., 2010.

Dodd, Susan. *The Halifax Explosion: The Apocalypse of Samuel H. Prince*. Grandview, P.E.I.: Underhill Books, 2017.

Dynes, Russell R. and E.L. Quarantelli, "The Place of the Explosion in the History of Disaster Research: The Work of Samuel H. Prince," in Allan Ruffman and Colin D. Howell, eds., *Ground Zero: A Reassessment of the 1917 Explosion in Halifax Harbour* (Halifax: Nimbus Publishing and the Gorsebrook Research Institute, 1994), pp. 55-67.

Elliott, C. Russell. *The Briefcase Boys*. Hantsport, N.S.: Lancelot Press, 1996.

Hatfield, Leonard, F. *Sammy the Prince*. Hantsport, N.S.: Lancelot Press, 1990.

Prince, Samuel Henry. *Catastrophe and Social Change*. New York: Columbia University Press, 1920.

Prince, Samuel Henry. Ed. Heather Long and Barry Cahill, "The Halifax Explosion—Fourteen Years After: a paper read before the Nova Scotia Historical Society, 4 December, 1931," *Journal of the Royal Nova Scotia Historical Society* 21 (2018), 1-18.

Roper, Henry. "Evangelical-High Church Conflict at the University of King's College." *Journal of the Canadian Church Historical Society,* 36 (1994), 37-57.

Sutherland, David A., ed. *"We Harbor No Evil Design": Rehabilitation Efforts After The Halifax Explosion of 1917.* Toronto: The Champlain Society, 2017.

Thorne, G.W.A. Annual Report of the Chaplain and Priest-in Charge, King's Chapel, March, 2016.

TORRANCE KIRBY

Configuring God as Law: Richard Hooker's Neoplatonic poetics of law

> In sundry the workes both of art and also of nature, where that which hath greatest force in the very things we see, is notwithstanding it selfe oftentimes not seene. The statelinesse of houses, the goodliness of trees, when we behold them delighteth the eye; but that foundation which beareth up the one, that root which ministreth unto the other nourishment and life, is in the bosome of the earth concealed: and if there be at any time occasion to search into it, such labour is then more necessary then pleasant both to them which undertake it, and for the lookers on. In like maner the use and benefite of good lawes, all that live under them may enjoy with delight and comfort, albeit the groundes and first originall causes from whence they have sprong be unknowne, as to the greatest part of men they are.[1]

Richard Hooker commences his discussion of the origin of law—'that lawe which giveth life unto all the rest'[2]—with an appeal to two vivid metaphors, one artificial and another natural,

1 *Lawes* I.1.2; *The Folger Library Edition of the Works of Richard Hooker*, gen. ed. W. Speed Hill (Cambridge: Belknap Press of Harvard University Press, 1977), vol. 1, ed. W. Speed Hill, p. 57, ll. 4–16. All references to the *Lawes* below cite book, chapter, and section followed by volume, page, and line numbers found in the Folger edition.

2 *Lawes* I.1.3; 1:58.13–14

a constructed foundation and a nourishing root. As his argument unfolds, it becomes clear that his aim in his treatise *Of the Lawes of Ecclesiastical Politie* (1593) is to show that the Elizabethan religious and constitutional settlement of 1559—the 'stately house', as it were, of the established Church and the 'goodly tree' of the flourishing Commonwealth—is based upon 'good lawes' whose ultimate source is altogether hidden from view—'in the bosome of the earth concealed', according to the metaphor.

Is this subterranean root or foundation in any way knowable? The metaphor serves to introduce an extended analysis of the origin of law. Hooker goes on to identify this veiled 'first original cause' of good laws as that "lawe whereby the Eternall himselfe doth worke."[3] He defines law in general as "that which doth assigne unto each thing the kinde, that which does moderate the force and power, that which does appoint the forme and measure of working."[4] He goes on to affirm that the highest 'measure of working' in the divine activity on the ground that "only the works and operations of God have him both for their worker, and for the lawe whereby they are wrought. The being of God," he maintains, "is a kinde of lawe to his working: for that perfection which God is, geveth perfection to that he doth … God therefore is a law both to himselfe, and to all other things besides."[5] This identity of worker, the work done, and the activity of working anchor the assertion of his metaphorical speech in a non-metaphorical affirmative proposition, namely that God in himself is essentially law. As Aquinas puts this: "the end of the Divine government is God Himself, and His law is not distinct from Himself."[6]

---

3 *Lawes* I.1.3; 1:58.15

4 *Lawes* I.2.1; 1:58.26–29

5 *Lawes* I.2.2; 1:59.3–6; 60.17–18. On the character of sapiential theology and its applicability to Hooker, see Rowan Williams, 'Hooker: Philosopher, Anglican, Contemporary', *Richard Hooker and the Construction of Christian Community,* ed. A.S. McGrade, (Tempe, AZ: Medieval and Renaissance Texts and Studies, vol. 165, 1997), 369–375.

6 Thomas Aquinas, *Summa Theologica*, Ia IIæ q.91. a1

In the peroration to his exposition of the nature of law and its generic division into various derivative kinds found at the end of the first book of his treatise *Of the Lawes*, Hooker summarizes this argument in a striking passage evocative of the hymns to Holy Wisdom in the Scriptures:

> Of lawe there can be no lesse acknowledged, than that *her* seate is the bosome of God, *her* voyce the harmony of the world, all things in heaven and earth doe *her* homage, the very least as feeling *her* care, and the greatest as not exempted from *her* power; both Angels and men and creatures of what condition so ever, though each in different sort and manner, yet all with uniforme consent, admiring *her* as the *mother* of their peace and joy.[7]

As Rowan Williams has observed, Hooker's use of the feminine pronoun in explicit reference to law "would alert any scripturally literate reader to the parallel with the divine *Sophia*"—and indeed, what Hooker claims on behalf of Law the sapiential books of Proverbs, Job, and the Wisdom of Solomon affirm of the very Wisdom of God:[8] "The LORD possessed me in the beginning of his way, before his works of old. I was set up from everlasting, from the beginning, or ever the earth was."[9] "Wisdom reacheth from one end to another mightily, and *sweetly* doth she order all things."[10]

7 *Lawes* I.16.8; 1:142.9

8 *Lawes* I.2.5; 1:62.2-6. Rowan Williams, 'Hooker,' in *RHCCC*, 370. Proverbs 8:22-31; Job 28; Wisdom 6:12-9:18; and see also Rom. 11:33.

9 Prov. 8:22, 23.

10 *Wisdom* 8:1. In the Vulgate: *adtingit enim a fine usque ad finem fortiter et disponit omnia suaviter* / διοικεῖ τὰ πάντα χρηστῶς in LXX. See also the Advent antiphon 'O Sapientia', retained in the Almanack of the *Book of Common Prayer* (1559)—quoted by Hooker in *Lawes* I.2.3; 1:60.27–61.6. David Neelands has shown that this passage, favoured by Richard Hooker, is frequently quoted in Thomas Aquinas's writings, especially in the *Summa Theologica*, e.g. in discussions of divine government (Ia, q.103. art.8), grace (Ia IIæ q.110. art.2), charity (IIa IIæ q.23. art.2), the temptation of Adam and Eve (IIa IIæ q.165. art.1), Christ's miracles (IIIa q.44. art.4), the passion of Christ (IIIa q.46. art.9), and the manifestation of the Resurrection (IIIa q.55. art.6). See Neelands's essay on 'Predestination,' in Torrance Kirby, ed., *A Companion to Richard Hooker* (Leiden and Boston: E.J. Brill, 2009), 209.

For Hooker the sapiential theologian, then, it is because God *is* his own Wisdom that he may also affirm that God in himself *is* law,

> a law both to himself, and to all other things besides … All those things which are done by him have some end for which they are done; and the end for which they are done is a reason of his will to do them … They err, therefore, who think that of the will of God to do this or that there is no reason besides his will.[11]

This claim bears comparison with Aquinas for whom "the end of the Divine government is God Himself, and His law is not distinct from Himself."

Are such claims that God *is* his Wisdom, and consequently that 'God *is* law' mere metaphors? Are these figures of speech, comparable to the stately house or flourishing tree? Or, alternatively, can definitive, literal propositions about the divine nature be justifiably formed? There is perhaps something just a tiny bit transgressive about comparing God to a basement or a root, although it is clear enough that such images imply an "intuitive perception of similarity in dissimilars"—and as Aristotle says, "it is a great thing to be a master of metaphor."[12] The similarity of God to a basement is concealment from view. To propose that God is in some sense 'law' or 'wisdom' is not on the same footing, so to speak. In Q. 13 of the *Prima Pars* of the *Summa Theologica*, on 'The Names of God', Aquinas asks in Article 3 whether all names applied to God must needs be metaphorical, or whether some can be applied in a literal

11 *Lawes* I.2.5; 1:60.17–18. Compare Aquinas, *ST*, Ia IIæ q.91. art.1: "The law implies order to the end actively, in so far as it directs certain things to the end; but not passively—that is to say, the law itself is not ordained to the end—except accidentally, in a governor whose end is extrinsic to him, and to which end his law must needs be ordained. But the end of the Divine government is God Himself, and His law is not distinct from Himself. Wherefore the eternal law is not ordained to another end."

12 Aristotle, *Poetics* 22 (1459a5)

sense. He argues that "true affirmative propositions can be formed about God." This assertion depends upon drawing a distinction between signification 'in reality', what it is in itself, and what is for us (pro nobis) 'in idea'. God as considered 'in Himself', is altogether one and simple, yet "our intellect knows Him by different conceptions because it cannot see Him as He is in Himself (*in se*)." Hence diverse names are ascribed to God: God is One, Good, Infinite, Just, and so on. While it is possible to affirm diverse essential qualities or predicates, our intellect knows that in reality one and the same simple object corresponds to its conceptions. Therefore the plurality of predicate and subject, in Hooker's case 'Law' and 'God', represents the plurality of idea; nonetheless, for the intellect (*pro nobis*) this plurality represents 'unity by composition', that is by predication.[13]

For Hooker the primordial Wisdom is the law "which God hath eternallie purposed himself in all his works to observe";[14] this law is the 'highest welspring and fountaine'—a Plotinian image—of all species of law.[15] Hooker agrees with Aquinas when he speaks of the radical simplicity of God in himself when he states that God is 'one, or rather *verie Onenesse*, and meere unitie, having nothing but it selfe in it selfe, and not consisting (as all things do beside God) of many things.'[16] Of the divine simplicity, says Hooker,

> our soundest knowledge is to know that we know him not as in deed he is, neither can know him: and our safest eloquence concerning him is our silence, when *we confesse without confession* that his glory is inexplicable, his greatnes

13 *Summa Theologica*, Ia pars, q. 13, art. 12.

14 *Lawes* I.3.1; 1:63.7

15 In his essay concerning the Beautiful, Plotinus remarks: "But if you accurately distinguish the intelligible objects you will call the beautiful the receptacle of ideas; but the good itself, which is superior, the fountain and principle of the beautiful; or, you may place the first beautiful and the good in the same principle, independent of the beauty which there subsists." *Ennead* 1.6; see also 5.8.

16 Lawes I.2.2; 1:59.20-22.

> above our capacitie to reach. He is above, and we upon earth, and therefore it behoveth our wordes to be warie and fewe.[17]

As 'first originall cause', the First Eternal law has "her seate in the bosome of God." Simultaneously, this original 'Eternal Law' in its unity contains within itself a plurality of multiple derivative species of law—"as ofspringe of god, [all things which God hath made] are in him as effects in their highest cause, he likewise actuallie is in them, the assistance and influence of his deitie is theire life."[18] And so it is with original law and its diverse derivative laws. Hooker proceeds to distinguish between a 'First' and a 'Second' Eternal Law.[19] The latter is the ordering 'voyce' of the divine Wisdom, law as God's utterance proceeding from the ineffable unity the First Eternal Law and comprising within it all derivative species of law which 'participate' the eternal law as discrete emanations ordered dispositively in hierarchical 'procession', while the First Eternal Law is the original, self-constituting divine source as it remains ineffably simple, at unity within itself—as God's 'verie Onenesse'.[20]

> By law eternall the learned for the most part do understand the order, not which God has eternallie purposed himselfe in all his works to observe, but rather that which with himselfe he has set down as expedient to be kept by all his creatures, according to the severall conditions wherewith he has indued them ... All things therefore, which are as they ought to be, are conformed to *this second law eternall*, and even those things which to this eternal law are not conformable, are notwithstanding in some sort ordered by *the first eternall* lawe.[21]

It is the *Second Eternall Lawe* whose 'voyce is the harmony of the world' as distinct from that prior law whose place is in the 'divine

17 *Lawes* I.2.2; 1:59.14–19.
18 *Lawes* V.56.5; 2:237.23-25.
19 *Lawes* I.3.1; 1:63.6—64.3
20 *Lawes* I.2.2; 1:59.14-15
21 *Lawes* I.3.1; 1:63.6-10; 26-29

bosome'. The *Second Eternal Lawe* "does not work infinitely but correspondently to that end for which it works, even all things χρηστῶς, in most decent and comely sort."[22] Hooker's account of the Eternal Law as simultaneously unity in radical simplicity and participation of that unity by a multiplicity of derivative forms of law recapitulates the ontology of causality set out by Proclus in his *Elements of Theology* whereby "every effect remains in its cause, proceeds from it, and reverts upon it."[23] For Proclus the totality of reality beneath the One or the Good itself is structured by μονή [remaining or abiding], πρόοδος [going out procession], and ἐπιστροφή [return or conversion]. All reality is in the One, proceeds from it, and returns, is converted back towards its source when it achieves its proper good. In Hooker's formulation, this double motion of procession or emanation and return (*exitus/redditus*) is remarkably similar: "every effect doth after a sort conteine, at least wise resemble the cause from which it proceedeth: all things in the worlde are saide in some sort to seeke the highest, and to covet more or lesse the participation of God himselfe."[24] Hooker anchors his elaborate exposition and defense of the Elizabethan religious settlement in a metaphysical theory of law which itself assumes a Neoplatonic ontology of 'participation' in the Proclean tradition:

> All thinges are therefore pertakers of God, they are his ofspringe, his influence is in them, and the personall wisdome of God is for that verie cause said to excell in nimbleness or agilitie, to pearce into all intellectual pure and subtile spirites,

22 *Lawes* I.2.3; 1:60.27—61.6. "If therefore it be demanded, why God having power and ability infinite, the effects notwithstanding of that power are all so limited as we see they are: the reason hereof is the end which he has proposed, and the law whereby his wisdom has stinted the effects of his power in such sort, that it does not work infinitely but correspondently to that end for which it works, even all things χρηστῶς, in most decent and comely sort, all things in measure, number, and weight."

23 Proclus, *The Elements of Theology*, ed. E.R Dodds, 2nd edn. (Oxford: Clarendon Press, 1963), 38–39; proposition 35. Abbrev. below as *ET*.

24 *Lawes* I.5.2; 1:73.7–10

> to goe through all, and to reach unto everie thinge which is … All thinges which God in theire times and seasons hath brought forth were eternallie and before all times in God as a worke unbegunne is in the artificer which afterward bringeth it unto effect. Therefore whatsoever wee doe behold now in this present world, it was inwrapped within the bowells of divine mercie, written in the *booke of eternall wisdom*, and held in the handes of omnipotent power, the first foundations of the world being as yeat unlaide.[25]

Hooker's apophatic emphasis on law as it is written in 'the booke of eternall wisdom', having 'her seat in the bosome of God', raises doubt about whether God can be named literally as either Wisdom or Law. The extraordinary metaphor of 'the bowels of divine mercie' suggests that creation may be viewed as tantamount to a divine excretion. Is it possible to speak significantly about the first eternal law? Or is Hooker confined to solely figurative language. After all, of God's "verie Onenesse," says Hooker, "we *confesse without confession* that his glory is inexplicable, his greatnes above our capacitie to reach." And as Dionysius asserts in *On the Divine Names*, "Of Him there is neither name, nor can one be found of Him."[26] Ambrose of Milan, on the other hand, maintains ambivalently that "some names there are which express evidently the property of the divinity, and some which express the clear truth of the divine majesty, but others there are which are applied to God metaphorically by way of similitude."[27] Aquinas asks whether all names are applied to God solely in a metaphorical sense or whether any can be applied literally: "the names of creatures are applied to God metaphorically, as when we say, God is a stone, or a lion, or the like." After some discussion Aquinas eventually concludes that some names of God can be applied in an affirmative, literal sense:

25 Hooker, *Lawes*, V.56.5; 2: 236.26–31, 237.15–22.

26 Pseudo-Dionysius the Areopagite, *De Divinis Nominibus*, I.5 (PG 3, 593). Quoted by Aquinas, *ST* Ia, q.13, art.1.

27 Ambrose, *De Fide*, II, Prol. (PL 16.583). Quoted by Aquinas, *ST* Ia, q.13, art.3.

> There are some names which signify these perfections flowing from God to creatures in such a way that the imperfect way in which creatures receive the divine perfection is part of the very signification of the name itself as 'stone' signifies a material being, and names of this kind can be applied to God only in a metaphorical sense. Other names, however, express these perfections absolutely, without any such mode of participation being part of their signification as the words 'being,' 'good,' 'living,' and the like, and such names can be literally applied to God.[28]

Law and Wisdom are such names as express an essential property of the divinity. "The perfect unity of God requires that what are manifold and divided in others should exist in Him simply and unitedly. Thus it comes about that He is one in reality, and yet multiple in idea, because our intellect apprehends Him in a manifold manner, as things represent Him."[29] And so it is with the Wisdom of God read out, as it were, in the manifold species of law.

According to Hooker, the second eternal law, whose 'voyce is the harmony of the world', comprises the manifold divine order as "kept by all [God's] creatures, according to the severall conditions wherewith he hath indued them."[30] This law has a variety of 'names' depending on the different orders of creatures subject to the one divine government. The two principal derivative genera of the second eternal law are 1) the natural law and 2) the revealed law of the Scriptures, the latter sometimes termed by Hooker the 'divine law'—not to be confused with the eternal law itself. The entire system of the laws comprised within this second eternal law thus expresses the Proclean twofold motion of creative procession from (*proodos*) and return to (*epistrophē*) the original unity of the eternal law as expressed by this primary distinction between the

28 *ST* Ia, q.13, art.3, reply 1.
29 *ST* Ia, q.13, art.4, reply 3.
30 *Lawes* I.3.1; 1:63.9-10

natural and the revealed orders of law. Each of these two primary genera—Natural Law and divinely Revealed Law—is further participated by multiple derivative and dependent forms. The natural law, by way of a further procession, comprises in turn subordinate species of law which govern irrational natural agents as well as rational; the law governing the rational creatures is distinguished further into the 'law cœlestial,' which orders the angels, and the 'law of reason,' sometimes identified simply as the 'natural law' *per se*, which orders rational humankind. All of these sub-species represent the outward unfolding or processio ad extra of the second eternal law: 'reaching from one end to the other mightily.'

> Now that law which as it is laid up *in the bosome of God*, they call *æternall*, receyveth according unto the different kinds of things which are subject unto it different and sundry kinds of names. That part of it which ordereth natural agents, we call usually *natures* law; that which Angels doe clearely behold, and without any swarving observe is a law *cœlestiall* and heavenly: the law of *reason* that which bindeth creatures reasonable in this world, and with which by reason they may most plainly perceive themselves bound; that which bindeth them, and is not knowen but by speciall revelation form God, *Divine* law; *humane* lawe that which out of the law either of reason or of God, men propobablie gathering to be expedient, they make it a law.[31]

On the converse side of the second eternal law, the law of God's special revelation, the revealed law of the Scriptures, presupposes the disorder introduced into the cosmos by the Fall, and is provided in order to secure final restoration or 'return' of the creation to its original condition of unity under and within the primordial first eternal law. Hooker's distinction between these two *summa genera* of natural law and divinely revealed law corresponds to the cosmic logic of procession and return but also reflects the epistemological

31 *Lawes* I.3.1; 1:63.14-29

distinction of a twofold knowledge of God (*duplex cognitio Dei*), namely by the light of supernatural revelation and by the natural light of reason: in addition to the 'Book of the Eternal Wisdom' there are the 'Book of Nature' and the 'Book of Scripture', three books corresponding to three genres of Law. There are, moreover, composite species of law—such as human positive law and the law of nations, for example—which derive from a conscious, pragmatic reflection upon the general principles contained in the natural law. These additional derivative species of law are viewed by Hooker (here following Augustine) as a consequence of human sin, presupposing the Fall, and, like the divine law, they also constitute a corrective to the disorder introduced by Adam's disobedience. Augustine speaks of such law as a remedy of sin (*remedium peccati*).[32] Throughout this complex legal discourse Hooker presents the human creature as the *imago dei* at the focal point of the cosmic drama of procession from and return to the original fount of order established in divine simplicity of the first eternal law.[33]

As intellectual natures mortals share the desire of the angels for an infinite good in which alone such a nature can be finally satisfied: "Then are we happie therfore when fully we injoy God, as an object wherein the powers of our soules are satisfied with everlasting delight: so that although we be men, yet by being unto God united we live as it were the life of God."[34] Yet, "of such perfection capable we are not in this life. For while we are in the world, subject we are unto sundry imperfections, griefs of body, defectes of minde, yea the best thinges we do arre painefull ..."[35] The predicament of the human condition is to be of a mixed nature, partaking

32 For the use of coercive positive law as a remedium peccati, see Augustine, *de civitate Dei*, Bk XIX.

33 On the theme of the 'cosmic drama' see C A. Patrides, *The Grand Design of God: The Literary Form of the Christian View of History* (London: Routledge and Kegan Paul, 1972).

34 *Lawes* I.11.2; 1:112.17–20

35 *Lawes* I.11.2; 1:112.24–113

of both an intellectual nature shared by the angels and the physical shared by the irrational 'necessary agents'. For Hooker there can be no natural overcoming of this hiatus between a 'natural' desire for divine perfection and a complete natural incapacity to achieve that end desired. While the desire for *theosis* is a natural desire—"so that nature even in this life doth plainly claime and call for a more divine perfection"[36]—nonetheless

> the light of nature is never able to finde out any way of obtayning the reward of blisse, but by performing exactly the duties and workes of righteousnes. From salvation therefore and life all flesh being excluded this way, behold how the wisedome of God hath revealed a way mysticall and supernaturall, a way directing unto the same ende of life by a course which groundeth it selfe upon the guiltines of sinne, and through sinne desert of condemnation and death.[37]

The '*exitus-redditus*' structure of this generic division of law in Book I of the *Ecclesiasticall Politie* shows that Hooker has read Aquinas on law very closely, as indeed numerous scholars have noted.[38] Hooker's distinction between the first and second eternal laws constitutes, nonetheless, a highly significant departure from the Thomist scholastic model. The effect of the distinction between these two aspects of the eternal law is simultaneously to widen and to decrease the distance between the creator-lawgiver and the created cosmos.

In addition, the distance between the two principal aspects of the Second Eternal Law—that is to say between the Natural

---

36 *Lawes* I.11.4; 1:115.18–19

37 *Lawes* I.11.5, 6; 1:118.11–18

38 *Summa Theologica*, Ia IIae, qq.90–108. See Peter Munz, *The Place of Hooker in the History of Thought* (London: Routledge & Kegan Paul Ltd., 1952; repr. New York, NY: Greenwood Press, 1970), 49–57; Alessandro Passerin d'Entrèves, *The Medieval Contribution to Political Thought: Thomas Aquinas, Marsilius of Padua, Richard Hooker* (New York: The Humanities Press, 1959), esp. chaps. 5 and 6; John S. Marshall, *Hooker and the Anglican Tradition: an Historical and Theological Study of Hooker's Ecclesiastical Polity* (Sewanee, TN: University of the South Press, 1963).

Law and the divinely Revealed Law—is most pronounced in Hooker's account of soteriology. The final 'return' to God of all creation can only be by 'a way mysticall and supernaturall'. In *Notes toward a fragment on Predestination*, a MS in the library of Trinity College, Dublin, Hooker distinguishes between two species of the divine governance—a *duplex gubernatio Dei*:

> Government is that work of God whereby he *sustains created things* and disposes all things *to the end which he naturally* chooses, that is *the greatest good* which, *given* the law *of creation*, can be elicited. For, given the law of creation <is the rule of all> it was not fitting that creation be violated through those things which follow from creation. So God does nothing by his government which offends against that which he has framed and ratified by the very act of creation. The government of God is: general over all; special over rational creatures. There are two forms of government: that which would have been, had free creation not lost its way; that which is now when it has lost its way.[39]

This passage reveals the soteriological principle underlying the generic division of laws. On one side are laws governing the order of an unfallen Creation. Among these laws Hooker includes the law of nature in so far as it governs irrational and non-voluntary natural agents. This again is a significant departure from the usual, more restricted sense of Natural Law as an 'intellectual habit' of the soul, that is to say, the *summa ratio* as it is present and known to rational creatures.[40]

---

39 John Booty's translation of Hooker's original Latin notes in *FLE* 4: 86.28-87.12. Cp. Aquinas, ST. 1a, q.20, art.2; q.49, art.2, and q.103, art.7

40 See, for example, Aquinas's discussion of the definition of natural law in 1a2ae q.94., art.1; also, Cicero, *De Legibus*, 1.4. Gratian, *Decretum*, Part I, Distinct. 1: 'Natural law is that which is contained in the Law and the Gospel whereby everyone is commanded to do to another that which he would have done to himself.' Hooker cites Gratian's definition at Lawes I.12.1; 1:119.30-120.1. For further discussion of the significance of this distinction see Torrance Kirby, "Richard Hooker's Theory of Natural Law in the Context of Reformation Theology," *Sixteenth Century Journal* 30.3 (1999), 681-703.

To conclude, for Hooker, the form of law "to be kept by all creatures according to their several conditions" is comprised within three *summa genera*—the eternal law, the natural law and the divine law—where the latter two species are understood as comprehended within the first, and yet nonetheless distinct both in their operation and in our knowledge of them. Together these *summa genera* constitute a comprehensive division of the many diverse 'kinds' of law. To understand their derivation from the original unity of the First Eternal Law is to gain critical insight into the underlying ontological assumptions of Hooker's argument, and moreover provides a vital instrument for interpreting the manner of Hooker's reconciliation of Neoplatonic ontology of participation with a Reformed soteriology.

Viewed from the standpoint of their divine principle of origin—i.e. in the first eternal law where 'the being of God is a law to his working'—these three *summa genera* of law may be considered as simply one. The predication of law to God is not metaphorical for Hooker. Law is a perfection of the divine being and can consequently be affirmed literally so long as we understand that what God is 'in reality' is not to be confused with what he is 'in idea'. Our intellect apprehends God in the manifold manner of the expression of the voice of his Wisdom. Viewed from below, as it were, that is from the standpoint of mortal finitude, the original unity takes on the aspect of articulated multiplicity of kinds which nonetheless all 'participate' and 'proceed from' the undivided unity that is their common source.[41] This account of the simultaneous unity and diversity of law in its multiple species lies at the very heart of Hooker's vision of law as an expression of the divine governance:

41 On the concept of the *procession* of the forms of law see, for example, I.3.4; 1:68.6-8: "... the naturall generation and *processe* of all things receyveth order of *proceeding* from the setled stabilitie of divine understanding."

> Who the guide of nature but only the God of nature? *In him we live, move, and are.* Those things which nature is said to do, are by divine arte performed, using nature as an instrument: nor is there any such art or knowledge divine in nature herself working, but in the guide of nature's work.[42]

Hooker begins with metaphors of 'the nature of law in general'—law as the root of a flourishing tree, law as the foundation of a stately house, law as a wellspring or fountain, all hidden 'in the bosome of the earth'—and proceeds to identify these underlying, hidden sources with the primordial Wisdom of God. This Wisdom is in turn presented metaphorically as hidden 'in the bosome of God' and the 'bowels of the divine mercie', and manifest in the 'voyce' of cosmic harmony. In effect, when we mix these metaphors, what is 'hidden in the bosome of the earth' is in actuality 'hidden in the bosome of God'. The conclusion for Hooker is that God, in some literal sense, is Law. His law is not distinct from himself, and therefore it becomes possible to move beyond metaphor to a more literal affirmation.

This predication must be interpreted cautiously—it is composite in form, but refers the theological understanding to an essential simplicity, the ineffable unity and simplicity of all law in the divine self-regulating activity: 'the being of God is a kinde of law to his workinge' and on this working a manifold diversity of laws depend.

42 *Lawes* I.3.4; 1:67.16–20

POETRY

PETER BULLERWELL AND ERIN WAGNER

The End of Term

On the last day of class you get credit for just coming.
The teacher enters and acknowledges you with a bow.
You glance around to see who's left,
And the emptiness of the room makes you feel giddy—
though no one dispenses with formalities:
Like the teacher himself, they're the last to go.
The fat is cut and the frame is left bare.

The lesson has always been the same.
The trouble is that you could never remember how it had
begun once it was ending,
Or how it would end when it was beginning.
But now time has run out.
Looking up from his notes, the teacher seems to change his
mind.
Before you know what's happening, the lesson is present like
another in the room.
You swallow it whole.
The lesson is learned.

You empty the classroom, squinting in the sun.
Already amnesia is setting in, but the taste is still on your lips.
People smile and shake hands
and return to their own homes.

PETER O'BRIEN

nec, nate, tibi comes ire recuso: Classical Formation and Latin Verse at King's in the 19th Century

For TC: otia nos Almae Matris quaesivimus ambo / sperantes quam praebet ibi doctrina quietem.

In 2014, the University of King's College celebrated its 225th anniversary, simultaneously marking the quasquibicentennial of post-secondary Classics in English Canada. In addition to various forms of celebration, that milestone encouraged reflection on the character of classical studies at King's within four distinct centuries—from the end of the eighteenth to the beginning of the twenty-first. My own contribution[1] was a paper based on some forays into the College archives and to those of Dalhousie University as well as some reading in the history of higher learning in Nova Scotia.[2] I focused mostly on materials of the 19th century. It is not surprising that the official and collegiate documents I found showed Classics to be not simply a touchstone of curricular fashion, but an index of how universities understood their place

1 Peter O'Brien, "From *exemplum virtutis* to *instrumentum utilitatis*, or, 'those who can only conjugate will continue to decline': Classics at King's and Dalhousie from 1789-1950." http://cdn.dal.ca/content/dam/dalhousie/pdf/fass/Classics/225%20and%2070%20speeches/From%20Exemplum%20to%20Instrumentum.pdf.

2 In assisting with that research, I thank Janet Hathaway and Patricia Chalmers of the University of King's College Library.

in the wider polity. In this offering I want to specialize my earlier presentation, based on continued archival research. I will present a sampling of the pedagogical, religious, and political attitudes of teachers and students of King's in the 19th century on display in original Latin poetry by some of its most notable alumni and staff. By focusing on six poems, my paper seeks first to explore the extent to which 19th-century King's students and faculty thought and felt in the languages and idioms of Greece and Rome; and second, how that tradition could mediate the aspirations of both high-tory Loyalist conservatism and a more progress-minded liberalism in the contemporary world of Georgian and Victorian Nova Scotia. More broadly, I hope that the paper contributes a helpful perspective to our ongoing struggle to defend the "relevance" of the field by retrieving a tradition of classical studies that predates 20th century historicism. Succeeding in these goals, I believe I will have done something to evoke the spirit and character of the honoree of this collection, whose career at this university college has been devoted to the cultivation of perspectives in the humanities tradition that can look both backwards and forwards within it, the better to understand, and act within, the present.

I begin with a historical note on the founding of King's, for that is intimately connected with the character and scope of its classicism as well as its institutional identity in a colony of Great Britain. The most important thing to know is that the College came to be as a direct result of the American Revolution. In 1789, several individuals with oblique connections to King's College, New York (an institution soon after reconstituted "with the aggressively patriotic name of Columbia College" by its new republican masters)[3] began a fledgling new King's College in Windsor, N.S.,

3 Henry Roper, University of King's College, "King's Traditions: A Lecture," September 3, 2013. https://ukings.ca/news/kings-traditions-a-lecture-by-henry-roper (accessed May 26, 2019).

a small Annapolis Valley town about an hour's drive from Halifax today. These included the refugee Loyalist, Dr. Charles Inglis (formerly Rector of Trinity Church, Wall Street, and, briefly, interim president of King's, New York) who had been consecrated the first Anglican Bishop of Nova Scotia a couple of years earlier; and Dr. William Cochran, another clergyman. Cochran, a graduate of Trinity College Dublin, became the new College's first president and its first professor in Greek and Latin.[4] Despite early attempts to re-form it otherwise, King's for many years remained narrowly Anglican, not just in the sense that it served as a regional seminary for training clergy, but also because it effectively limited enrolment to members of the Established Church. Inglis had hoped not only to pack the pulpits with Kingsmen, but also "to create a cadre of leaders for the tory society [he] and his fellow Loyalists wished to create in Nova Scotia."[5] Since Anglicans never made up more than about 25% of the population, the College could not serve a broad cross-section of the province's inhabitants. In its reactive origins, support for hierarchical social structures, and staunch imperial affiliations, King's emulation of the mother country sometimes outdid the model in self-crippling ways. Internally, for example, a requirement imposed in 1803 limited the presidency to graduates of Oxford and Cambridge. This meant that Cochran had to be demoted permanently to Vice-President and supplanted by Dr. Charles Porter, pure English and pure Oxonian.[6] Such internal

4 The story is amply told in Fenwick Williams Vroom, *King's College : A Chronicle, 1789-1939: Collections and Recollections* (Halifax, N.S.: The Imperial publishing company limited, 1941), 1-13. It should be noted that received and long-standing traditions concerning direct institutional genealogies between King's College, New York, and King's College, Windsor, have been recently brought under withering scrutiny by Henry Roper in his contribution to the King's scholarly inquiry on slavery. See Henry Roper, University of King's College, "King's College, New York and King's College, Windsor: Their Connection in Fact and Legend." https://ukings.ca/wp-content/uploads/2019/02/20190204KingsandKingsNYbyHenryRoper-November2018.pdf (accessed May 26, 2019).

5 Roper, "King's Traditions."

6 Vroom, *King's College*, 47-52.

division did not escape the notice of external observers. On a visit to the College during his term as Lieutenant Governor, George Ramsey, ninth Earl of Dalhousie, remarked that the two Rev. gentlemen managed the College from their separate studies without ever speaking to each other! Ramsey's observation of King's inner workings could only have whetted his animus against its parochialism, in response to which he lay the foundations of the secular University that still bears the Dalhousie name.[7]

All of these developments ensured that King's remained small and elite—if only in its own self-important estimation—and entrenched in its somewhat shabby rural fiefdom throughout the 19th century. It gradually gained a local reputation for high-minded classicism. Like most liberal arts foundations of the day, the college's BA curriculum was from the beginning based squarely in mathematics and Classics—the latter quite broadly construed in the sense that both philology and composition in Greek and Latin were required, as well as the heavy reading in Greek and Roman authors that supplied authoritative texts in literature and history and formal rhetoric. A quick consultation of the curriculum in the mid-19th century College calendars available in the archives will substantiate this assessment. [8]

7 On the foundation of Dalhousie, see Peter B. Waite, *The Lives of Dalhousie University: Volume 1: 1818-1925: Lord Dalhousie's College* (Montreal: McGill-Queen's University Press, 1994), 3-26. In years to come, other denominations would respond to King's exclusivity in their own right, by establishing their own colleges. Most of these still exist, accounting for the remarkable plurality of universities today in such a small province.

8 The College's Matriculation (i.e. entrance) requirements in original-language reading would give an undergraduate of today pause, if not palpitations. The various changes and developments in the classical course through the 19th century were not drastic; for a representative conspectus of full curriculum at the beginning of the century at King's we see here how courses were divided between President Porter and Vice-President Cochran in 1814. Thomas B. Akins, *A Brief Account of the Origin, Endowment and Progress of the University of King's College, Windsor, Nova Scotia* (Halifax: N.S.: s.n., 1865), 73.

The pedagogy of this curriculum involved regurgitation of rote learning and translation from the original languages to English and back. While thus engaged, students were also thoroughly enculturated into a high tory political and religious ideology. The classics they learned were meant to underwrite the empire of which they were citizens; it helped Kingsmen distinguish themselves from their distant relatives in the "revolted colonies" (as the College's early documents insist on referring to the United States). Many (if not most) of the works of creative Latin verse composition in evidence in the archive are translations from exemplary texts in English or other modern languages—we find versions of hymns and patriotic efforts by the poet laureate Tennyson, for instance. While these may be more-or-less adept attempts to form the modern sentiments of others into Latin idiom, I want to focus attention today on really original works, since they provide a more sensitive gauge of the extent to which the poets' minds were shaped by ancient languages and ideals. I also have preferred poems set in contemporary reality rather than those that treat topics exclusively from the ancient world.

A useful *visual* emblem of what I have in mind is provided by the high-relief tableau of Aeneas, Anchises, Ascanius and Creusa now overlooking the Halifax quad.[9] An Alumni gift of 1861, it first decorated the old Convocation Hall in Windsor. The group evidently recalls the flight of Aeneas from Troy, and presents an exemplary hero who leaves all—including his wife—to a marauding enemy. Those who lived in the presence of this sculpture were no doubt expected to recall that Aeneas, with his elderly father on his shoulders and leading his young son by the hand, would go on to build a new and greater city in Italy. That city would stand at the centre of an empire that understood present strength in terms of reverence for the past and careful nurture for the future. In fact,

9 Photograph by P. O'Brien.

the Latin motto originally under the sculpture in Windsor and taken from *Aen.* 2.704, read *nec, nate, tibi comes ire recuso*, "My son, I am ready to go with you and be your companion." The panel was intended to evoke paternal, filial, and imperial *pietas* in the descendants of Loyalists who had fled their burned homes in Manhattan to build a new home, and new seat of learning, in Nova Scotia. What I find so affective in the sculpture's classicism is that it makes no concessions to historicist reconstruction according to ancient Roman or 18th century templates: *this* Aeneas teaches his lesson as a mustachioed 19th-century British Hussar; he might be fighting in the Crimea, as recent alumni at the time of its installation indeed had. Interestingly, Aeneas' *exemplum* has proved uncannily resilient with the passage of time and the relocation of the College in space. How could its donors have known that a fire would destroy the old King's in 1920, and that the College would be set on new foundations in Halifax? Like Anchises' *penates*, the sculpture would be preserved and translated to a new setting, where it continues to provoke edifying reflection in successive generations of students.[10]

10 Thomas Curran, "... Nec, Nate, Tibi Comes Ire Recuso," *Tidings*, Winter 2006/2007, 2007, 7, offers one timeless perspective on the sculpture from 2007: "Our College is a living inheritance, and the symbol of the Penates in our Quad are a constant reminder that we did not build this College but inherited it from others;

Two poems in the archives represent the creative adaptation of the Virgilian ethos of sacrificial service to empire in Latin elegiacs. Both are letters of former students (Alfred Gilpin and Joseph Clinch) addressed to presidents of the college; both were originally written in English, and then lovingly and elegantly translated—with amplifications, addenda, and "improvements"—by the now retired President Porter. They were printed in Halifax (with quaint pedantry dubbed "Olicana" on the title pages after an obscure Roman camp near the "real" Halifax in Yorkshire) and apparently read at Encaenias in 1861 and 1864.[11] Interestingly, the call to service is rendered more poignant by the fact that these authors develop it within a modified pastoral nostalgia that itself owes a debt to Virgil and Horace. The contrast here between the bucolic "groves of Academe" and the outside world of toil and strife strikes a leitmotif of subsequent King's verse from Windsor. Thus Gilpin:

O! loca grata mihi! Videor nunc cernere prata
Hortos florentes, silvas collesque remotos
Ecce Scholam Templumque Dei, Collegium et aedes
Hospes ubi convivas excipiebat amice.

Delightful scenes! my memory traces still
The verdant meads, the grove, the distant hill,
The Church, the College, and that friendly dome
Where hospitality had made her home.[12]

---

we move ahead, but never by turning our backs on our founders and benefactors, who have made us what we are."

11 See Vroom, *King's College*, 50–51 on the circumstances of the poems' composition, translation, and presentation, as well as brief details on their original authors. Joseph Hart Clinch, c.1806–1884, was a Newfoundlander who eventually served as Archdeacon in Boston (cf. *ibid*, 99) and published several volumes of original (English) poetry there.

12 Alfred Gilpin, *Epistola Poetica ad Amicum*. Halifax, N.S.: Jacob Bowes, 1863, 8–9.

The texture of Clinch's poem, written from the perspective of the 1850s, is a more complex and indeed more vivid Augustan counterpoise of bucolic/scholastic reminiscence and the pathos arising when youth is summoned from civilian pursuits to dangerous duty for a higher cause. Thus his poem passes from sweet memories of studious hours to this:

Accidit humano nulli sincera voluptas:
non raro dulces turbat Discordia cantus,
sol tegit interdum dense se splendidus umbra,
et rosa sub foliis spinam pulcherrimus celat.

But ah! Unmingled bliss to none belongs:
Some jarring discord mars our sweetest songs,
Some cloud across our brightest sunshine steals,
Some envious thorn our fairest rose conceals.[13]

He goes on to relate how many of his fellow-scholars have found graves far from the common "home" that "Alma Mater" gave them. He provides vignettes of several, including this one (note Porter's augmentations):

Quonam Musa modo lugens, fortissime Welsford,
Res a te gestas dicet? Quando ignifer imber
Faucibus evomitus ferri provolvit in auram
Flammas, flammarumque globos, tu scandere primus
Redani aggrederis muros; tu, sanguine sparso,
Inter saxa cadis lethali vulnere caesus.
Te multi aetatis meminerunt flore vigentem
Tempore quo magis apta toga est quam pluma vel ensis.

13 Joseph Hart Clinch, *Epistola Poetica ad Familiarem*, Halifax, N.S.: Jacob Bowes, 1863, 6–7.

Nec tunc viginti ante annis et quinque putabant
Vera tui exemplo fati fore verba poetae:
"Dulce et decorum est pro patria mori."

And thou, brave *Welsford*! When the battle's van
Rolled its red surges on the firm Redan,
Thou with the first upon the rampart stood,
And bathed its stones with thy devoted blood.
Well I recall thee in thy youthful bloom,
Ere cap and gown were changed for sword and plume,
Nor thought I then, ere *lustra* five, to see
The Poet's verse applied with truth to thee:
"*Dulce et decorum est*," runs the glowing line,
"*Pro patria mori*." Such a death was thine.[14]

Maj. Augustus F. Welsford, an alumnus since 1830, had had his head blown off by a cannon ball at the battle of the Great Redan during the Crimean war in 1855.[15] He is well known to Haligonians from the Welsford-Parker monument, patterned after a Roman triumphal arch, found in the Old Burial Grounds on Barrington Street. While the community at large honoured Welsford with the downtown monument, the University has honoured her alumnus since the 1850's with a prize first offered by Dr. William Almon for the best Latin composition on the subject of the martyr (or "another suitable topic") written by a first-year Latin student.[16]

---

14 *Ibid.*, 8-9.

15 Cameron W. Pulsifer, "WELSFORD, AUGUSTUS FREDERICK," in *Dictionary of Canadian Biography*, vol. 8, University of Toronto/Université Laval, 2003–, http://www.biographi.ca/en/bio/welsford_augustus_frederick_8E.html (accessed May 26, 2019).

16 While the "Almon-Welsford Testimonial Prize" is still awarded by the college, most of the stipulations, save that it go to an undergraduate Latin student, have fallen away. I was recently reminded of this monument's classical inspiration and important place in Halifax's architectural landscape by several student presentations in Dr. Emily Varto's class, "Ancient Art from the Pyramids to the Forum."

An early winner of this prize shows a noteworthy development of the pastoral theme while at the same time engaging in contemporary world politics. It incidentally illustrates just what sort of other topic the faculty juries could deem "suitable"! *In memoriam Jacsoni Ducis* was offered by in 1863 by Newman Wright Hoyles, son of a Newfoundland Premier and the future principal of Osgoode Hall law school in Toronto.[17] Here we have a specimen notable for the window it opens to Loyalist descendent views on the old revolted colonies at the height of the American Civil War. The subject of this *"Jacsoni Dux," "cui cognomen Saxeo-vallo fuit,"* was none other than Stonewall Jackson, the famed Confederate general, whose allegedly noble southern-agrarian virtues the author opposes to the brute industrial might of the Yankees:

Quis tamen ignorant bella moventes,
Nec tremit ut fratrum proelia caeca legit?
Sanguine cognato binas America gentes
Nutrit; at his socias distrahit ira domos.
Praevalidi numero Boreales agmina cogunt;
Seque Afro simulant indoluisse iugo.
Exacuunt Martem rabie fastuque tumentes;
Imperio tenat ut latus omne suo.
Attamen Australes claros egere triumphos,
Iustitia freti subsidioque Dei:
Nam patriae fines salvos retinere laborant,
Et gaudent pura ducere bella fide.
His dux Saxoval:—merito cognomina notus,
Instantes inhibens disiiciensque manus.

17 Hoyles (1844-1927; B.A. 1864) was the son of a premier of Newfoundland and went on to a distinguished legal career in Toronto, serving as Principal of Osgoode Hall Law School. Cf. Vroom, King's College, 99; Christopher Moore, "HOYLES, NEWMAN WRIGHT," in *Dictionary of Canadian Biography*, vol. 15, University of Toronto/Université Laval, 2003–, http://www.biographi.ca/en/bio/hoyles_newman_wright_1844_1927_15E.html (accessed May 26, 2019).

Ille Britannorum nulli virtue secundus
Ornaret fastos, Anglia clara, tuos.

Who has not heard of civil wars that rend
Confederates, Federals, severing friend from friend?
Two kindred races in the western world,
United once, Mars' banner have unfurled.
The Northern hordes contend with savage glee,
Pretending zeal the negro slave to free.
Fiercely they war, swelling with vengeful pride,
That nought henceforth their empire may divide.
The Southern champions brilliant triumphs gain,
And faith in God inflexibly maintain;
Homes of their sires their birthright they defend
Till chivalry prevail, and war shall end.
These *Stonewall* led: —and surnamed well was he,
The surging host withstanding steadily.
In valour yielding to no Briton born,
E'en England's annals he might well adorn.[18]

In case the reader wonder about Hoyle's true loyalties, he enthuses that Jackson "yields in valour to no Briton born," and that "E'en England's annals he might well adorn."

A more mainstream expression of Commonwealth patriotism comes from an anonymous work in the monthly College magazine in October, 1879, commemorating the obliteration of a British force by a Zulu army at Isandlwana, South Africa some months earlier. Its form is certainly more subtle: Horatian Alcaics with the nice conceit (another variation on the grove/battlefield-toga/helmet binaries) that the poet has been called from lyric love to sing an incongruously martial song:

18 N.W. Hoyles, *In Memoriam Jacsoni Ducis: Carmen Latinum*. Halifax: Jacob Bowes and Sons, 1863, 4–5.

Flores volentem nectere, et in nemus
Pulchra vagari cum Lalage mea,
Me classici clangor procacis
Excitat, et manibus trementi

Phoebus sonoram dat citharam mihi,
Alcaeus olim quam digitis ferox
Pulsabat: o flores aprici
Tuque comes zephyrorum hirundo

Fontesque dulces quos volui loqui,
Valete!

While desirous of plaiting garlands and
Strolling the groves with my lovely Lalage
The bugle's brash bray awakened me,
And to my timourous hands

Phoebus delivered the sounding cithara,
Which bold Alcaeus once strummed:
O sunloving blossoms,
And you, swallow, friend of the breezes,

And you, sweet streams, of whom I wished to speak,
Farewell![19]

Not all the Latin poetry from King' in the 19th century was as rooted in "timeless" conservative themes. The special collections also contain a MS volume of leather-bound Latin poems by Judge A.W. Savary,[20] an alumnus who exemplifies the King's tradition

19 Anon. "Isandula," *The Record*, University of King's College, October, 1879, 1.
20 Alfred W. Savary, *Latin Poetry and other College Exercises*, (MS, University of

of public life in the civil sphere. Savary was a lawyer, judge, Nova Scotian historian and patriot, a champion of the Acadians among whom he was raised, and staunch Anti-confederationist in Canada's first Dominion Parliament.[21] In the same typewritten preface in which he explains that he is gifting King's with his florilegium "in case of future publication," he rather pompously informs the reader that in his school days he was never known to mistake a quantity and that he was the only one ever to have caught out the legendary president McCawley on such a fault. It's true that the poems in this book are elegant and facile, but the majority are mere translation exercises. Even his original elegies on the death of the Duke of Wellington and on an Atlantic shipwreck seem to lack the allusive depth of Porter's earlier work. Yet two other poems strike out in quite a different direction. 1854's "Viae per Novam Scotiam Ferro Struendae" is a striking example of liberal progressivism blended with provincial patriotism and tender affection for Alma Mater. The occasion is the proposed first railway to be built in Nova Scotia; when this actually happened some four years later, one of the two lines running from Halifax went as far as Windsor, obviating the call from some even then that the College be moved to the city:

Intima nisi patriae, sylvasque per arva silentes
Ferreus ardet aequus fremitu stimulare secundo,
Par rapidis zephyris, volucri par fulminis igni
Nasibus elatis, glomeransque ad sidera fumum!—
Almaque tu mater laetos simul indue vultus:
Nam spatio cedente tuos prope sopspes alumnos
Mox eris.

King's College Archives, n.d.).

21 On the poems, see Vroom, *King's College*, 101.

> If only a smooth iron rail running through the fatherland's innermost fields and silent forests, seeking to disturb them with a propitious rumble, and rolling smoke to the skies while noses are raised—
> And you, Alma Mater, likewise put on a smiling face:
> For soon you will be near your alumni, your deliverers, as distance falls away. [22]

A companion piece, "Ad Scientiam" is another paean to Victorian positivism. Its Latin descriptions of mining and steamships conjure up a classicising steampunk world.[23]

I'll end with a mysterious specimen I've only just stumbled upon in a box of miscellaneous items related to Encaenia. An undated and unsigned manuscript on embossed letterhead, I suspect it comes from the period between1860 and 1867, when a pitched roof and cupola were added to the original flat-top building in Windsor.[24]

22 Savary, *Latin Poetry*, 29.

23 *Ibid.*, 31.

24 See the two plates, the first an engraving from an 1860 diploma showing the main building with a flat, unadorned roof, the other an engraving from the 1867 Librarian's report showing the main building with a cupola. I am indebted to Janet Hathaway, Interim University Librarian and Archivist, for these images.

The poem takes a stand against this innovation, but in a clearly tongue-in-cheek, mock invective style. The poem runs through several consequences of the prideful folly of adding weighty ornament to a building whose function and tradition eschews such trappings. What attracts me particularly is the poem's reliance, once again, on the Virgilian theme that seems to preside over King's institutional history. Under the title of this poem is the Virgilian tag *Antiquam exquirite matrem*, which ostensibly stands as a motto for holding to the old ways; the ironic tone of the poem itself, though, makes it seem just possible that the author was aware of the ambivalent prophecy it refers to at *Aeneid* 3.96, and the unfortunate misinterpretations that followed. This quotation, which follows a description of the "great pile's collapse" and imagines a stranger happening upon the ruins, gives a sense of the tone:

Vix tellure sonans clamabit, "siste viator,
Alma ego Mater eram quae nuper incolui
Has sacras sedes—heu novi gloria mundi!—
Dicatas litteris, artibus ingenuisque

Ut periere Troes, et qui sic Ilio everso,
Achaici terram repetiere suam.
Sic populi eversores qui altae moenia Romae
Ignarunt humo, mole ruere sua.

A voice will cry out, sounding from the earth: "Halt, Wayfarer!
I was the Alma Mater who lately dwelled in
This sacred site —alas a new world's glory!—
Consecrated to letters. And as by native wit
The Trojans perished, so also, with Illium overturned,
The Greeks sought out their own country.
So too those destroyers of a people forget that the walls
of high Rome, built on soil, would fall to ruin by their own weight.

I'd like to adapt the anonymous poet's Virgilian motto to a very brief closing reflection on what my exploration of the Latin tradition at one Canadian university has taught me as a teacher of classics in the same university today. That is that despite the sometimes unfamiliar, even to us odious, postures their classics encouraged the scholars of the past to adopt, and despite the fact that there are ways in which their readings of the ancients were clearly wrong, it seems to me that they may have *lived* their books and their languages with an intimacy that our generation has a hard time feeling. This alienation can only contribute to the creeping defeatism we are increasingly feeling in a discipline under siege. Perhaps, like Aeneas and the readers of the anonymous poet, we should be seeking our ancient mother where we least expect to find her. With guides like Virgil from antiquity, Dante in the Middle Ages, and—for this generation—Tom Curran himself, we can be confident that the quest may not be in vain.

References

Akins, Thomas Beamish. *A Brief Account of the Origin, Endowment and Progress of the University of King's College, Windsor, Nova Scotia*. Halifax, N.S.: s.n. 1865.

Anon. "Isandula." *The Record* (University of King's College), October, 1. 1879.

Clinch, Joseph Hart. *Epistola Poetica ad Familiarem*. Halifax, N.S.: Jacob Bowes. 1863.

Curran, Thomas. "... Nec, Nate, Tibi Comes Ire Recuso." *Tidings*, Winter, 7. 2006/2007.

Gilpin, Alfred. *Epistola Poetica ad Amicum*. Halifax, N.S.: Jacob Bowes. 1863.

Hoyles, N. W. *In Memoriam Jacsoni Ducis: Carmen Latinum*. Halifax: Jacob Bowes and Sons. 1863.

Moore, Christopher. "HOYLES, NEWMAN WRIGHT." *Dictionary of Canadian Biography*. Vol. 15. Toronto and Québec: University of Toronto/Université Laval. http://www.biographi.ca/en/bio/hoyles_newman_wright_1844_1927_15E.html (accessed May 26, 2019). 2003–.

O'Brien, Peter. "From *exemplum virtutis* to *instrumentum utilitatis*, or, 'those who can only conjugate will continue to decline': Classics at King's and Dalhousie from 1789-1950." http://www.dal.ca/content/dam/dalhousie/pdf/fass/Classics/225%20and%2070%20speeches/From%20Exemplum%20to%20Instrumentum.pdf (accessed May 26, 2019). 2014.

Pulsifer, Cameron W. "WELSFORD, AUGUSTUS FREDERICK." *Dictionary of Canadian Biography*. Vol. 8. Toronto and Québec: University of Toronto/Université Laval. http://www.biographi.ca/en/bio/welsford_augustus_frederick_8E.html (accessed May 26, 2019). 2003-.

Roper, Henry, University of King's College. "King's Traditions: September 3, 2013." https://www.ukings.ca/files/u42/Henry-Robers-Traditions-Lecture-11-Sept-2013.pdf (accessed May 26, 2019). 2013.

—. "King's College, New York and King's College, Windsor: Their Connection in Fact and Legend." https://ukings.ca/wp-content/uploads/2019/02/20190204KingsandKingsNYby-HenryRoper-November2018.pdf (accessed May 26, 2019). 2018.

Savary, A. W. "Latin Poems." MS, University of King's College Archives. n.d.

Vroom, Fenwick Williams. *King's College : A Chronicle, 1789-1939: Collections and Recollections.* Halifax, N.S.: The Imperial publishing company limited. 1941.

Waite, Peter B. *The Lives of Dalhousie University: Volume 1: 1818-1925: Lord Dalhousie's College.* Montreal: McGill-Queen's University Press, 1994.

CHRISTOPHER SNOOK

"... the final stroke of nine": *Reading* THE WASTE LAND *with Thomas Curran*

In his contribution to the Atlantic Theological Conference in 2018, Dr Thomas Curran guided the attendees through a careful consideration of T.S. Eliot's monumental 1922 poem, *The Waste Land.* A life-time student and teacher not only of Eliot's poem, but also of the rich world of literatures to which Eliot alludes explicitly and implicitly throughout the work, Dr Curran included in his analysis an observation that may well be entirely unique within the voluminous commentary that continues to be generated by Eliot's masterpiece. In section one of the poem, "The Burial of the Dead," Eliot writes:

> Unreal City
> Under a brown fog of a winter dawn,
> A crowd flowed over London Bridge, so many,
> I had not thought death had undone so many.
> Sighs, short and infrequent, were exhaled,
> And each man fixed his eyes before his feet.
> Flowed up the hill and down King William Street,
> To where Saint Mary Woolnoth kept the hours
> With a dead sound on the final stroke of nine.[1]

1 T.S. Eliot, *Collected Poems* (Faber and Faber, 1963), l.60-68.

The immediate historical context for this section of Eliot's poem is the burgeoning commuter culture of post-war London. As Eliot observed (himself a member of the city's office culture for the entirety of his career), following the exodus of residents from the downtown core of London, crowds of commuters made the morning rush into the business district. Directly referencing Dante's *Inferno*, Eliot compares the crowds crossing London Bridge into the city-centre with the hordes jostling to make their way into the underworld in the Divine Comedy: "I had not thought death had undone so many." The commuters become, then, the living dead and, as Dr Curran observed so poignantly and insightfully, their particular agony is related to Eliot's easily overlooked addition to the scene of the time of day: the bell of St Mary's tolls, as Eliot writes, on "the final stroke of nine." Though in the first instance the stroke of nine refers to the beginning of the business day, this initial reference is made deeper and more profound by Dr Curran's suggestion that the tolling of the Church bell alludes not only to nine in the morning, but (with Eliot's remarkable economy) to the hour of Christ's death as recorded in the Synoptic Gospels at the ninth hour:

> And about the ninth hour Jesus cried with a loud voice, saying, *Eli, Eli, lama sabachthani*? that is to say, My God, my God, why hast thou forsaken me? Some of them that stood there, when they heard that, said, This man calleth for Elias. And straightway one of them ran, and took a sponge, and filled it with vinegar, and put it on a reed, and gave him to drink. The rest said, Let be, let us see whether Elias will come to save him. Jesus, when he had cried again with a loud voice, yielded up the ghost. (Matthew 27:46-50)

Eliot's conflation of "nines" at this point in the poem collocates the beginning of the day with the end of life and in so doing produces an extraordinary intensification and proliferation of meanings. This gesture highlights, of course, the connection between the newly dead in Dante's *Inferno* and *The Waste Land*'s living dead in urban England, but now Eliot deepens the analogy by portraying London's office culture as a modern day underworld: going to the office is harrowing hell. In so doing, the poet makes an oblique reference to the unique importance of the Cumean Sybil for the poem as a whole. She appears in the epigraph of *The Waste Land* as both a prophetic figure and as the first image of the living death that characterizes the inhabitants of Eliot's poem, but these lines in the "Burial of Dead" insist that she also serves the poem in her classical role as gatekeeper of the underworld, uniting the action of the poem with the great epic narratives of underworld adventure, chiefly in Book Six of Virgil's *Aeneid* and, following Virgil, in Dante.

But the proliferation of meanings continues. Eliot's inclusion of St Mary Woolnoth's tolling the ninth hour connects this moment of the poem to the contemporary debate over the closure of city churches in downtown London following the city's post-war demographic shift—the proposed death-knell for some of the city's most significant architecture built immediately after the London fire of 1666. Writing in 1921 against the proposed closure of nineteen churches by the Diocese of London, Eliot conjured the mood that dominates the poem that he was crafting at precisely the same time. The city churches, he writes, possessed:

> a beauty which its hideous banks and commercial houses have not quite defaced [. . .] the least precious redeems some vulgar street, like the plain little church of All Hallows at the end of London Wall. Some, like St. Michael Paternoster Royal are of great beauty.[2]

More importantly, Eliot notes that urban churches have a purpose that exceeds their aesthetic beauty and even their parochial use:

2 Cited in Jacqueline Pollard, "TS Eliot's Wasted Churches," Jacqueline A. Pollard., https://japollard.wordpress.com/

> To one who, like the present writer, passes his days in this City of London (*quand'io sentii chiavar l'uscio di sotto*) the loss of these towers, to meet the eye down a grimy lane, and of these empty naves, to receive the solitary visitor at noon from the dust and tumult of Lombard Street, will be irreparable and unforgotten.[3]

The tolling of the ninth hour at St Mary Woolnoth's, then, connects the particular death of Christ (and his subsequent harrowing of hell) with the contemporary and metaphorical death of commercial life in London and with the larger narrative of decline described in the poem. Though this layering emphasizes the crisis of culture that characterizes the poem, it also includes the redemptive possibilities that belong to the quest narratives of the Arthurian and Dantean traditions, represented explicitly (if ironically) in the resurrection narrative which immediately follows the tolling of the bell.

And yet the connections with Dante illuminated by Dr Curran's observation are deeper and more subtle still. While making their way through the Malbowges in the lower regions of the Inferno, Virgil and Dante encounter a break in the bridges or arches leading them over the series of ditches or bowges that ring nether hell. A demon explains the cause of the rupture:

> … why, yesterday, five hours by the clock
> From now, 'twas just twelve hundred, sixty and six
> Years since the road was rent by earthquake shock.[4]

The specific reference in Dante's text is to nature's convulsion at the death of Christ on the ninth hour, amplifying yet again the significance of Dr Curran's observation and relating the 'action' of

3 *Ibid.*

4 Dante, *The Divine Comedy: Hell*, trans. Dorothy Sayers (Penguin, 1949), 21.112–114.

this canto with the larger narrative of *The Waste Land*. The bridge broken at the ninth hour conjures Eliot's reference a few lines earlier to the crowd flowing over London Bridge (the bridge itself is an evocation of the children's rhyme—"London bridge is falling ...") and the particular sins punished in this region of the Inferno are precisely those most closely identified with the commercial life of a city: fraud, in its various forms and iterations. (And this is to say nothing of the resonances between the first section of *The Waste Land* and Dante's vision of Beatrice in the *Vita Nuova*, which he tells us occurred at the ninth hour, thus establishing at least a sympathetic connection between Dante's *Vita*, the tolling of the bell in *The Waste Land*, and the mystical vision of the Hyacinth girl earlier in the poem: "I was neither / Living nor dead and I knew nothing / Looking into the heart of light, the silence.")

In his 1950 essay "What Dante Means to Me," T.S. Eliot's confirmed that his poetic vocation was nurtured by a sustained engagement with Dante. This engagement included a slow apprenticeship in the form and content of Dante's *Comedy* which resulted in the young Eliot's memorization of large parts of the text, a pocket version of which Eliot carried with him while composing *The Waste Land*.[5] As Eliot attests, this engagement reached its most explicit and imitative in the composition of "Little Gidding."

Eliot's life-long preoccupation with Dante will be well known to readers of his poetry, prose and dramas. But the specific ways in which the allusions or direct citations work in a poem like *The Waste Land* (as emphasized and underscored by a commentator such as Dr Curran) highlights the larger, ethical imperative at work in Eliot's *oeuvre*. As Eliot notes as early as 1919, artistic genius is not the fruit of an essentially romantic idea of radical and unique personal virtuosity, but arises out of the relationships cultivated

---

5 This according to his friend Conrad Aiken. See Dominic Manganiello, *TS Eliot and Dante* (Macmillan, 1989), 40.

with a network of other, older voices. Eliot calls these older voices the "tradition," and suggests that it is the difficult and costly appropriation of tradition that grounds the poetic endeavor:

> Tradition .... cannot be inherited, and if you want it you must obtain it by great labour. It involves, in the first place, the historical sense ... and the historical sense involves a perception, not only of the pastness of the past, but of its presence; the historical sense compels a man to write not merely with his own generation in his bones, but with a feel that the whole of the literature of Europe from Homer and with it the whole of the literature of his own country has a simultaneous existence .... This historical sense, which is a sense of the timeless as well as of the temporal, and the timeless and of the temporal together, is what makes a writer traditional.[6]

As Eliot writes more succinctly some twenty years late in the *Four Quartets*: "We are born with the dead: / See, they return, and bring us with them."[7]

Whatever else Eliot means by this discussion of tradition, it is most clearly demonstrated not in his essays but in the method of poetic composition revealed by close attention to the form and content of his poems. As Dr Curran's wonderful observation about the tolling of St Mary's bell on the stroke of nine indicates, Eliot's method is in large part the careful juxtaposition of literary fragments and allusions in order to generate meaning. So, for example, when the poet observes the living dead moving as a horde over London Bridge in *The Waste Land* ("I had not thought death had undone so many") we are given a kind of palimpsest of significant connections—there is, as noted above, the connection to Dante's *Inferno*, there is the nursery rhyme, "London Bridge is Falling Down" and the often contradictory accounts of that poem's origins (Viking invasion, child sacrifice, and perhaps even the fire

6 TS Eliot, "Tradition and the Individual Talent," *Selected Essays* (HBC, 1932), 4.

7 Eliot, *Collected Poems* 1909–1962, "Little Gidding," 5.17–18.

of London). And there is, through the tolling of St Mary's bell, the drawing of the action on the Bridge into proximity with Christ's sacrificial death at the ninth hour as well as other, additional resonances with Dante's *Comedy*.

All of these resonances add to the meaning of the poem but are also suggestive of the ethical dimension of Eliot's thought as it develops in his literary and cultural criticism. The "historical sense" required of the poet (and of the attentive critic) becomes for Eliot a way of being-in-the-world. This is made evident in a striking essay from 1934, "Personality and Demonic Possession." Published in the *Virginia Quarterly*, this essay is in fact a modified version of the third part of Eliot's *After Strange Gods*. In this essay, Eliot expands on his earlier understanding of tradition (memory) as a kind of collective consciousness cultivated by a readerly discipline and juxtaposes it with the importance of personality in contemporary writing. After prefacing the essay with a curious discussion of the impossibility of blasphemy in the 20th century, Eliot suggests that in lieu of blasphemy, evil seeks other avenues by which to exert its influence in the modern world. And it does so, he argues, through the romantic assumptions of the contemporary novelist which are largely concerned not with observing the world from within a received tradition of good and evil (no matter how tenuously affirmed) but in imposing a unique and personal moral vision on the reader. As Eliot argues elsewhere, his concern is that, for the first time in history, the reading public reads mostly if not exclusively works produced in its own time. This means, for Eliot, that the opportunity to be questioned about one's most common cultural assumptions is lost. Eliot writes:

> it seems to me that the eminent novelists who are more nearly contemporary to us, have been more concerned than their predecessors—consciously or not—to impose upon their readers their own *personal view of life*, and that this is

> merely part of the whole movement of several centuries towards the aggrandisment and exploitation of personality ...[8]

Eliot is concerned that personality cannot in fact bear the burden of a vulgar romanticism. He continues:

> The first requisite usually held up by the promoters of personality is that a man should "be himself"; and this "sincerity" is considered more important than that the self in question should, socially and spiritually, be a good or a bad one. ... the personality which fascinates us in the work of philosophy or art, tends naturally to be the *unregenerate* personality, partly self-deceived and partly irresponsible, and because of its freedom, terribly *limited* by prejudice and self-conceit, capable of much good or great mischief according to the natural goodness or impurity of the man: and we are all, naturally, impure.[9]

There is a great deal that might be said about Eliot's use of the term "unregenerate" as well as the larger set of theological convictions at work in this essay, but at one level Eliot's concern is simply to insist that the human is an embedded being rather than a buffered one—that the meaning of life, like the meaning of a poetic text, emerges from a network of relationships unconsciously or consciously affirmed. Indeed, it is the bringing to consciousness of those relationships in the form of dialogue, conversation, interrogation, or even (in the case of literature) criticism, that expands and amplifies a work and a person and thereby makes of the past a community of ancestors rather than a kind of haunting.

Dr Curran's insight with respect to "the final stroke of nine" in Eliot's masterpiece reveals the remarkable range of allusions that contribute to the texture of *The Waste Land*. This range of allusions, in turn, is an artistic realization of Eliot's convictions

---

8 T.S. Eliot. "Personality and Demonic Possession." *The Virginia Quarterly Review*, March 31 2010, https://www.vqronline.org/essay/personality-and-demonic-possession.

9 *Ibid.*

about the importance of tradition for the writer—tradition understood specifically as a series of hard won relationships with the dead that inform, shape and reform the poet's craft. This notion of tradition, in turn, contains within it an ethical exhortation about the fundamental embeddedness of the human within a network of relationships that may be consciously appropriated or unconsciously suffered.

This insight, finally, is not unconnected to Eliot's (and Dr Curran's) beloved Dante. As Dr Curran stresses in his teaching of the Comedy and its endlessly complex allusions to the worlds of classical and medieval culture, the text, though portrayed as a story about the next life, is in fact an allegory of the soul's passage from misery to bliss in this life. That passage is made possible not by Dante's romantic and heroic self-actualization, but in the very first instance by his surrender to the larger order of relationships in which he is situated—from Beatrice's condescension, which initiates his journey, to Virgil's friendship, to the many and various interlocutors on the way.

Dante conceives of life's misery poetically as the frozen loneliness of Satan in the pit of the *Comedy*'s Inferno; Eliot perceives it in the trudging crowd of commuters in post-war England and the series of broken relationships that populate the poem. The bliss is described by each in various ways, but it is in some sense chiefly a bliss characterized by the recovery of community. Dante represents this by his remarkable vision of the celestial rose at the end of the *Comedy*, which both stands in sharp contrast with the final image of the *Inferno* and is itself an *imago* of the more fundamental and primary vision of the Trinity. Eliot gestures towards this recovery in *The Waste Land* with more reserve and hesitation (but nonetheless truly) in the divine commands that conclude his poem, all of which relate to life in community: give, sympathize, control.

The widening circles of meaning and allusion that proceed from Dr Curran's unique insight into Eliot's poem make available to readers new voices and perspectives from the larger tradition that is, for a writer like Eliot, their inheritance and their community. Strikingly, the form of classical education to which Dr Curran has dedicated his career in many ways embodies the allusion-laden, relationship-building, poetic methods of both Dante and Eliot. His teaching continues to be an invitation for students (no doubt now too many to number!) to discover all their relations, from Plato to Eliot, and in so doing to take tentative steps on the journey from the experiences of isolation that the characters in Dante and Eliot's poem both suffer and will, into the bliss of a community limited neither by space or time.

SUSAN DODD

Communing with the Deep: Water as Reciprocity in the DIVINE COMEDY[1]

Deep calls to deep
in the roar of your waterfalls;
all your waves and breakers
have swept over me.
(Psalm 42:6–7)

Introduction: water and the poetics of reciprocity[2]

As Tom Curran and Robert Crouse emphasize, the *Divine Comedy* is a work of ethics: the poet's aim is to move his readers from misery to bliss in this life (as he famously wrote to his patron). In this "academic musing," I consider Dante's use of water to depict a deepening reciprocity between the pilgrim and God, as well as the poet and his readers.[3] In the *Inferno*, Dante fearfully closes himself off from "perilous waters" that confront him as a threatening abyss. When Dante finally comes to know "the great sea of being" ("*lo gran mar de l'essere*," *Paradiso* 1.113) as the unfathomable creativity of God, his heart overflows in a gift—the *Commedia*.

All waters in whatever state evoke this polysemous "great sea of being," and so always offer a promise, a threat, and an inspiration.[4] The great sea of being is the source from which all things spring and to which all things desire to return. It is the "Deep" over which the spirit moves in Genesis.[5] It is the flood, and the threat of the dissolution of all things into non-being.[6] Water's dynamic combinations with earth and air as smoke, mist, and rain, convey exchanges between what Dante calls the "lake of the heart" (*Inferno* 1.21) and the "great sea of being."[7]

For Dante, the principle of reciprocity that animates the poem is also the life-blood of all existence: the purging, life-giving, and baptising waters of heaven call us home as "deep calls to deep" (Psalm 42:6). But this home-coming will not be the dissolution of the person, nor will the metaphorical chains dissolve in a polysemous deluge. Paradise is an articulated unity-in-difference, exemplified in the Empyrean rose. As Fr. Crouse insisted, the *Commedia* is always about our lives in this world. Reciprocity is what King and Robertson elsewhere in this volume call "a conjoining of two movements: the ascent of the human into the divine with the descent of the divine into the human"; it is a friendship between lovers, and a continual greeting and answering between pilgrim and God, words and Truth, poet and verse, and, of course, heart and ocean.

Inferno: Slowly, slowly it swam…

In the first canto of the *Inferno*, the great sea of being confronts the pilgrim as an unfathomable and hostile void, poised to swallow him. By likening the pilgrim's heart to a lake (*nel lago del cor*), the poet deepens the sense of alienation first figured in his waking, lost and alone in the "dark wood" (*selva oscura*).[8] From the safety of his memory, the author recalls that when he was an anxious pilgrim brooding over his inability to reform, the gulf between him and Mount Purgatory was like "the dangerous sea" or perilous water (*l'acqua perigliosa*):

> And as a man with labored breathing drags
> his legs out of the water and, ashore,
> fixes his eyes upon the dangerous sea …
> (*Inferno* 1.22-24)

In his fascination with the gulf between himself and the first steps of reform, the pilgrim was like an exhausted swimmer, obsessed with danger instead of marvelling at his buoyancy. In this distorted judgment, integrity seemed to require protecting the interior vessel of his soul.

> So too my mind, while still a fugitive,
> turned back to gaze again upon that pass
> which never let a man escape alive.
> (*Inferno* 1.25-27)

The great sea of being confronts the pilgrim as a hostile otherness that holds him hostage with its unfathomability.

At one of the most dramatic points in the journey through Hell, the monster Geryon carries Dante and Virgil through the dark space that connects the sins of violence with active fraud. It is here that the poet, as poet, faces his gravest danger. Dante is protected, of course, by that greatest poet of stoicism, Virgil, who medieval thinkers saw as a kind of forerunner to Christianity.[9] Virgil and Dante are nearly deafened as they stand by the waterfall that plunges from the region of violence to the realm of deception, when Virgil tosses Dante's belt/girdle into the chasm. Dante wonders silently: Why would my guide throw my old belt/girdle over the brink? Virgil reads Dante's thoughts, and the author addresses us readers:

> Ah, men, beware!
> How watchful you must be when you are near
> one who not only sees the action but
> can peer beneath and read your very thoughts!
> (*Inferno* 16.117–120)

This uncanny perspicacity is shared by the true poet and the liar. The belt/girdle that Virgil pitches into the abyss is one that the pilgrim initially thought he might use to restrain the leopard that menaced him as he tried to climb Mount Purgatory: the apparent disciplines of his old life are the dissipated habits that led him to the dark wood. (Dante was susceptible to lust, to rage against corruption in church and state, and pride, as we learn over the course of the *Commedia*). Frivolous only in appearance (we recall Fr. Crouse's noting the "playful spots" and "dappled pelt" of the leopard), the pilgrim's old practices are habits that invite fraud.[10]

Virgil explains that the outcome of this mysterious pitching of the belt/girdle over the edge will be a revelation to Dante. The narrator names his poem "*Commedia*" here, and thus identifies poetry as the medium in which the passage from misery to happiness will be effected; he distinguishes right allegory from manipulative rhetoric:

> Knowing a truth whose face appears a lie,
> a man should always keep his lips shut tight
> as long as he can, lest he be tagged with shame
> Though he has told the truth; but I cannot
> keep silent here; and, Reader, by the notes
> of this my Comedy, I swear—and may
> They keep in favor long …
> (*Inferno* 16.124–130)

The revelation is a monster, who seems to swim through the darkness as a swimmer moves through water.

> …—through that thick air
> I saw a figure swimming in the night,
> such as would stun the surest heart with wonder
> Just as a diver surfacing, who's gone
> below to pry an anchor loose from rocks
> or something hidden in the sea will stretch
> His arms and tuck his legs to thrust again.
> (*Inferno* 16.130-136)

This is Geryon, "'the beast whose stench sickens the world'" (*Inferno* 17.3); he has the "features of an honest man," and the stinging tail of a serpent (*Inferno* 17.10 and 25). Moving as if darkness is a positive element, Geryon is a kind of Manichean. He creates the illusion that darkness is a positive element and that he can carry others through it. This is a moment of particular danger: there is something stunning, even wonderful, about a great liar. For the great liar, the mystery of the deep becomes a lure to draw the self-indulgent and tyrannical ever deeper into antagonism against God. This monster carries the dissipated and furious down into fraud because in our twisted desires, men mistake fraud for a free ride: we no longer fall, but swim into misery.

The image of the swimmer pulling himself out of the depths is repeated from *Inferno* 1, but here, the safe, if anxious, landing is only apparent:

> And that disgusting likeness of deceit
> arrived, and lugged his head and chest ashore
> but did not draw his tail onto the beach.
> (*Inferno* 17.7-9)

Of all the mythical characters who carry Dante across barriers in the *Inferno*, Geryon is the most literary: he personifies communication that is twisted by self-interest. The poet must safeguard his own, true allegory from Geryon's evil poetics. Dante nervously makes sure that Virgil has his back as they ride the great liar through the viscous dark.

> He swung his tail around to meet his chest,
> swerved and stretched out and darted like an eel,
> sweeping the air behind him with his paws.
> (*Inferno* 17.103-105)

The true poet is a good teacher who eschews the great liar's manipulation of his readers' temptations towards oblivion. He aims instead to draw us out, into the dangerous sea, self-confrontation and, ultimately fruitful exchange. To ride Geryon without Virgil protecting one's back is the delusion that the divine order can be twisted against itself, for one's own selfish gain.

Dante cannot see anything as the great liar swims them from violence down to fraud.

> Slowly, slowly it swam and took its course
> wheeling descending, as I could not tell
> but for the breeze below, and on my cheek.
> (*Inferno* 17.115-117)

Out of the darkness, Dante can now see flickering flames as the landscape of lower hell comes into view: "Now I saw what could not be seen before" (*Inferno* 17.124).

Purgatory: Smoke that Wrapped us All About

The cleansing and reviving powers of water are crucial in Purgatory, and not just in the famous rivers of Lethe and Eunoe. The pilgrim arrives in his "little ship of ingenuity" (*la navicella del mio ingregno*), out of what Cato[11] calls "the sea of that deep night / forever blackening the infernal pit" (*Purgatorio* 1.44-45). Initially borne up by the Deep but still separate from it, the pilgrim-poet must pass through the airborne water—smoke and mist—from wrath to sloth, so that his orientation changes from over-action to passivity, and from assertion to reception. Before this is possible, the pilgrim-poet must be purged of the most entrenched forms of selfishness that can masquerade as healthy social ambitions (pride and envy).

The very first task of Purgatory is a kind of mini-quest, assigned by Cato. At the austere Roman's command, Dante and Virgil replace the belt/girdle of his old life with one made of reeds that grow on the rough shore between the Deep and reform's mountain path. Dante's old girdle—the one Virgil pitched into the abyss to attract Geryon—was the false discipline that deployed words as rhetoric, sophistry, and seduction into idolatry. The new girdle binds the pilgrim-poet with the stuff of earth that draws the vital sea up into itself. The new reed-girdle is also the "bridle" of the poet's art: words will be governed now by a reciprocity in all creation; not in literalism, but in allegory that is faithful equally to the particular creatures that populate the metaphors, and the archetypal truths of the eternal Deep.[12] The pilgrim-poet thus begins his arduous and gradual purification. Virgil washes away the grime of hell in Purgatory's saltmarsh and then an angel writes the seven Ps (*peccatum* or sin) on the pilgrim's brow. This pilgrim's undifferentiated guilt is now articulated into specific wicked inclinations: general sinfulness is transformed into a project of reform, with distinct and achievable stages.

At the literal centre of the *Commedia*, Dante undergoes a crucial conversion: he passes from the blinding smoke that purifies wrath into the slow light of sloth, and into a creative openness in the process. First, the pilgrim-poet is rendered helpless by smoke, and this turns his critical eye inward.

Profoundest darkness of the realm below,
    or of the night under a starless vault
    when it's most shrouded by the glooming clouds,
Never spread for my eyes so thick a veil
    as did that smoke that wrapped us all about
(*Purgatorio* 16.1–5)

Dante's rage becomes discerning: he distinguishes his self-indulgence from true righteousness at the crimes against Florence, and community generally. Smoke becomes mist as the imagination turns from rage to wonder:

Remember, Reader, if you've ever been
    trapped in a fog so thick upon the hills
    you see as moles see, through a film of skin,
How, when the humid vapours gradually
    begin to thin away, the sun comes through,
    a ball glimmering faintly in the mist:
Then your imagination will be swift
    to join in seeing …
(*Purgatorio* 17.1–8)

Dante marvels at both the emerging sun and the mist, that mix of water and air that makes human spiritual life so dynamic in its reciprocity with nature and the divine. The mist of perception reveals in its concealment, as the natural world offers its divine heart in a play of clarity and obscurity that is proper to human embodiment and spiritual yearning. We readers are invited to marvel at the metaphorical truths that break open in the poet's heart.

> Imagination …
> Who moves you, if our senses give you no
> matter to mold your images?
> A light formed of its own from heaven, or sent below
> By divine will
> (*Purgatorio* 17.16-19)

As they climb the narrow stair from rage to sloth, images burst into the pilgrim-poet's imagination. The transformations speak to Dante as poet, the righteous anger and just punishments for political evil address him as pilgrim:

> And when this image vanished of its own,
> light as a bubble when it meets the air
> and lacks the water to maintain its form,
> Into my vision rose a girl who wept …
> (*Purgatorio* 17.31-33)

Here Dante begins the shift from radical activity to radical passivity, and beyond, towards an active receptivity that will be perfected in Paradise. To receive inspiration is to welcome the otherness that engenders creativity in us. Dante sees Lavinia from Virgil's *Aeneid* who will become mother to the Romans as she mourns her own mother's suicide. Amata's suicide is a rejection of reciprocity—despair over losing her daughter, as she sees it, to marriage with an outsider, the Trojan Aeneas.

In a sequence that will be repeated in Paradise, Dante moves from obstructed vision to Pauline bedazzlement. Light replaces the fog of wrath when, blinded, he is guided by the voice of one he cannot see, up the stair towards sloth. Again, the poet's blind vision generates a reflection on words, recalling the angel at the opening of John's Revelation, which Dante had evoked earlier, noting that imagination "snatch(es) a man / so far out of his senses he can't hear / a thousand trumpets blaring in his ear" (*Purgatorio* 17.13-15). The angel shows the way without being asked, and thus reciprocity deepens into empathy. The angel:

> treats us as a man would treat himself,
> for if you see a need yet wait for prayer,
> in ill will you've already set yourself,
> Poised to deny.
> (*Purgatorio* 17.58-61)

Here, on the verge of the centre of the whole *Divine Comedy*, reception becomes a kind of action.

The angel, like the revealed truth in the vision, and indeed all figurative language, and even the divine purpose in every accident, "conceals himself in his own light" (*Purgatorio* 17.57). The pilgrim-poet feels the brush of a wing on his face, a breeze, and affirmation of his own righteous anger at corruption: "How blessed are the peacemakers whose anger is no sin!" (*Purgatorio* 17.68-69). Now the pilgrim-poet again sees the mountain robed with sunlight, as he did in his loneliest moment in the dark wood (*Inferno* 1.16-17), but this time, "everywhere you turned, you saw a star" (*Purgatorio* 17.72). His gradually transforming will sees not only the rays that once stilled the fear in his heart's lake, but now also sees the sun's brother and sister stars. The poets have climbed out of selfish rage into righteous rage, and this through visions where the content is expressly ethical (righteous anger and good judgment) and made expressly poetical. The creative process is a work of grace: each figurative image that reveals/conceals is "as a bubble when it meets the air," surfacing out of the deep.

Having purged his impulse to over-act, the danger now is languor. Dante and Virgil are paused for the night; their ascent must wait until morning, but the time without advancing is not without "beneficial fruit." Virgil's speech on love and will introduces the circle or cornice of sloth, *acedia*. Virgil lays out the Platonic teaching that all desire seeks the Good.[15] Love seeks its source: mist moves as water and air seek their proper places, just as souls move to God when they keep "good measure in the second goods" (*Purgatorio* 17.98).

> But when it twists to evil, or does not
> race for a good with the appropriate care,
> the Potter finds rebellion in the pot.
> (*Purgatorio* 17.99-101)

Creation is likened to a pot, and this reminds us of the container of the heart and its fear-filled waters of *Inferno* 1. The repentant heart seeks rest in one particular good, such that it can "dimly see," and "struggles valiantly / To join with it" (*Purgatorio* 17.127-129).

Reciprocity opens between the pilgrim's heart and the Deep in upper Purgatory. Once Dante has been retrieved from the Siren who entices him towards oblivion in a dream (*Purgatorio* 19.7-33), images abound of enclosures opening up. The avaricious repent in an outpouring of tears and lamentations, and Dante responds with a receptive thirst (*Purgatorio* 20). Pulled away by Virgil, he takes his sponge unquenched from the water (*Purgatorio* 20.3). Inching along the winding stair, Dante recalls the she-wolf from *Inferno* 1: he is set upon with a recollection not simply of boundless appetite, but of an urge to cosmic mastery where lust and wrath combine in self-deluded pride (as in Satan's futile yearning to rule). The penitent praise Mary, crying out as if they themselves were giving birth; and they recall greedy rulers who sell their own children (*Purgatorio* 20.19-21; 79-84). Statius uses images of water in its various forms to depict the lack of movement in Purgatory; the changes are internal to the souls (*Purgatorio* 21.43-51). Virgil is surprised that greed "found a harbour" in Statius' noble heart (*Purgatorio* 22.22). The Secular poetry in the sweet new style is unfolded in the cornice of the Gluttons, "the fault that fills the throat" (*Purgatorio* 24.127). The fluid in the heart is "first blood," and that is reproductive: the fearful water of the first canto of the *Inferno* is now the blood of procreation (*Purgatorio* 25.37-49). Our response to the Deep is our life's work, offspring, and legacy.

In the Earthly Paradise, Dante learns that the mists on the mountain are part of the Purgatorial hydrology that, along with Lethe (release from memory) and Eunoe (recollection of particular life), spring from God's will (*Purgatorio* 28). The Deep is further presented in pageants of all prophesy at the end of time. Dante is fascinated by the pageants, enraptured by Beatrice, and ready for the supra-explicit reciprocity of Paradise.

Paradiso: Droplets of Sweet Distill into my Breast

The opening of our hearts in Purgatory made us thirsty for communion with the Deep. In *Paradiso* the receptive aspect of reciprocity is perfected. Dante's lust, rage and pride fuse into ecstatic magnanimity as he emulates God by generating a poetical cosmos *for us*: this overflow increases as his poetry strains to celebrate its source. As Beatrice explains when Dante marvels at the fact that he's flying:

"No more amazement should it bring to you
that you ascend, than if a mountain stream
should tumble rushing to the plains below."
(*Paradiso* 1.136-139)

The reader's receptivity is perfected, too, when we accept Dante's invitation into poetical pilgrimage. Receptivity is not passive, but exalting, and as King and Roberston emphasize, "trans-humanizing." In Canto 1 of *Paradiso*, the poet explains that the unity-in-difference on which reciprocity depends flows from the very source of heaven; the "One who moves all things / penetrates the universe with light" of varying radiance (*Paradiso* 1.1-4). In fact, no particular communion with the deep produces a universally communicable experience:

For as we near the One for whom we long,
our intellects so plunge into the deep,
memory cannot follow where we go.
(*Paradiso* 1.7-9)

Memory fails, but our integrity as particular persons is perfected because our souls are infused with the virtues of Christ and we are turned outward in charity.

Dante calls upon Apollo, the Greek god of the sun, music, and poetry: "Make me a fit vessel of your power" (*Paradiso* 1.14), and, more than a little dauntingly:

Then surge into my breast
and breathe your song, as when you drew the vain
Marsyas from the sheath of his own limbs.
(*Paradiso* 1.19-21)

Dante prays that he might be filled with divine music and skinned—both overfilled, and utterly released from self-enclosure: he is asking to be reborn. Yet he is not ready to receive the heavenly deep full blast: he must gradually "sustain the brilliant rays" of Beatrice's face as she gazes "into the everlasting wheels of light" (*Paradiso* 1.64). Again, he turns to a classical image of the heart's opening, saying that looking at Beatrice as she "gazed with silent constancy:"

> … had the same effect in me
> as did the plant that Glaucus tasted
> when it made him share the godhood of the sea.
> (*Paradiso* 1.67-69)

Whereas in *Purgatorio*, the plant that drew up water from the Deep served as a girdle, here, the fisherman eats the sea plant, and becomes a god. In this "trans-humanization" (*trasumanar*), Dante becomes divinely charitable; "reciprocity" now means to receive the other gratefully and to answer with overflowing generosity. The pilgrim's centre of gravity is completely shifted from worldly goods to God, and in water images, he no longer fears drowning. The Deep is now explicitly "the great sea of being" (*lo gran mar de l'essere*) and Dante is at home in it (*Paradiso* 1.113).[14]

Canto 2 opens with a warning: the "little ship of ingenuity" from the opening of *Purgatorio* dare not go it alone:

> O all you in your shallops (*piccioletta barca*) following
> my furrows as I sail across the sea,
> you who desire to listen as I sing,
> Don't try the open ocean—turn and see
> your own familiar shores, for you'd remain
> forever lost, should you lose sight of me.
> (*Paradiso* 2.1-6)

We will be enticed into the Deep, engulfed, skinned, struck by lightning, filled with song, drenched with rain, and overwhelmed in every way. Those without mystical preparation must open to Dante's siren song but stay tied to the mast of our particular lives. Gradually, in *Paradiso*, we become so infused with Dante's vision that we see God in all earthly things—we will be transhumanized in our experience of ordinary life.

The first souls Dante meets in the sphere of the Moon emerge as if from under water. Dante sees himself in the pool until Constanza floats into view. His narcissism is interrupted now by his heavenly openness to others.

A nun, forced to marry, who "never unbound the veil that robed her heart" (*Paradiso* 3.117) evokes Mary:

> So did she speak, then she began to sing,
> "Hail, Mary," and so singing she was gone,
> like a smooth heavy object vanishing
> into a shadowy pool…
> (*Paradiso* 3.121-123)

One of the ways that reciprocity works is that all souls get exactly what they will. The souls in the varied light of the Moon are attracted still to the goods of the world, and so they remain submerged, in a sense, in embodiment. The overflowing reciprocity of Paradise is shown in the pilgrim's acknowledgement of his own shallowness being expanded only by the flooding light.

> "O soul divine, beloved of the first Lover,"
> said I, "whose words wash over me and steep
> me in such warmth, I grow in life and youth,
> The ocean of my love is not so deep
> as to suffice to give you grace for grace;

> let Him who sees, and can give you your due.
> I see our intellects cannot be filled
> unless the one Truth floods them with its light,
> beyond which nothing true can find a place ..."
> (*Paradiso* 4.118–126)

Dante deploys increasingly complex metaphorical fusions of light, fire and water, as he passes beyond his urge to solve his vision, as if a puzzle, and into an enjoyment of the play of images.[15]

The principle of reciprocity is most explicit in the heaven of the Sun. Here, the "rebellion in the pot" from *Purgatorio* is revised: the enclosed container of the heart from the dark wood is now the "pail" of the entire cosmos, as if in Paradise, all hearts turn inside out:

> Water in a round pail will swirl about
> from centre to the ring, or the reverse,
> if the pail's jarred from inside, or without.
> (*Paradiso* 14.1–3)

The pilgrim sees the most influential and impassioned leaders of the church dancing in concentric circles as individual flames; when they speak to Dante, they present the stories and theological positions of their lifelong adversaries. Instead of guarding itself in fear, as in *Inferno* 1, the heart flows out into otherness and back to itself joyfully. The pilgrim-poet receives this image forcefully; it came "sweeping into my mind" (*Paradiso* 14.1–5).[16]

In the high theology of *Paradiso* righteous love is "like water shining clear" (*Paradiso* 15.2), in perfect transparency between souls: "in this life / all souls gaze into the reflecting lake / wherein, before you think your thoughts appear" (*Paradiso* 15.61–63). Integrity and openness coincide, as Dante exclaims to his Florentine forefather:

"So many rivers of exhilaration
now flood my heart that it's a joy for me
even to bear the gladness and not break"
(*Paradiso* 16.19-21)

During his examination in Faith, the pilgrim recalls that Saint Peter walked on the depths even as Beatrice gives him the nod, "that I should free the waters / and let the well within me overflow" (*Paradiso* 24.55). In his examination in Hope, Dante recalls his "baptismal spring" (*Paradiso* 25.9), and that grace both fell on him from Saint James and overflows from him: "then did you shed your rain upon me too / in your epistle, and my well's so full / for other men I spill the overflow" (*Paradiso* 25.78).[17] And, blinded again, first as a loss of vision and then by a blaze of light (repeating the sequence from the Cornice of wrath in *Purgatorio*), Dante faces Saint John in an examination in love, and so, from the Alpha to Omega. The pilgrim explains that he is grateful that:

... "All of the teeth, the spurs
that lead a man to turn to the Divine,
converge to call my heart to charity
...
[and they] have drawn me from the ocean that deceives [*del mar de l'amor torto*]
and set me on the shores of the true love.
I love the green and vine-adoring leaves
of the eternal Master of the vine,
according to the good each leaf receives."
(*Paradiso* 26.55-57, 62-66).

It is particular to Dante to write this allegory, and to each of us to read it as our own conversion.

Recalling the reciprocity between their journey and the mind of God (*Paradiso* 27.106–110), Beatrice combines all the images that I have tried to highlight: enclosures (heart's lake, rebellious pot, pail), plants (dark wood, reed, sea plant), mists (viscous abyss, smoke-fog of wrath, rains), and waves (destroying, chastening and buoying).

> And now to you it should be manifest,
>   time grips its roots into this vase, unseen,
>   while in the rest breaks into leaf and crown.
> Cupidity! You who drown mortal men,
>   so far beneath you, no one has the power
>   to lift his eyes out of your waves again!
> (*Paradiso* 27.118–124)

Beatrice concludes here with a figure of "rays" which "storm down the fortune you await" and return the wayward fleet to its proper course.

Dante's final preparation for seeing Christ, and thus the Trinity, is a vision of Mary (*Paradiso* 32.83-87). Before the angel Gabriel descends to lead an antiphonal singing of "Hail, Mary, virgin full of grace," Mary is showered with "a rain of … felicity" by angels, or "the holy minds / fashioned for crossing that exalted sea" (*Paradiso* 32.88-90). Dante is at the very limit of his literal descriptive capacity now, in describing Mary:

> In your womb was the flame of love reborn,
>   in the eternal peace of whose warm ray
>   this flower has sprung and is so richly grown.
> For us you are the torch of the noonday
>   of charity; below, you are the spring
>   of ever-living hope …
> (*Paradiso* 33.7–12)

The penitent poet has made his pilgrimage from "the lowest pool of the universe" through all human possibilities (*Paradiso* 33.22-25) and he gives thanks to Mary because, "by your prayers you melt the mist away / that clouds the intellects of mortal men" (*Paradiso* 33.31-32). Mary is the generating virgin, the holy vessel, the Star of the Sea, the seat of wisdom, and the mother of God: in all aspects, her prayers burn through the mists of temporal experience to give perfect, heavenly sight to created, earthly eyes (*Paradiso* 33.31-33).

Dante's singular vision evaporates—as it must:

> and yet, born from that vision, to this day,
> droplets of sweet distill into my breast.
> (*Paradiso* 33.62-63)

The waters of the great sea have seeped into the lake of the poet's heart, and inspired his poetical account of unity-in-difference, where:

> ...the scattered elements unite,
> bound all with love into one book of praise,
> in the deep ocean of the infinite;
> Substance and accident and all their ways
> as if breathed into one: and, understand,
> my words are a weak glimmer in the haze.
> (*Paradiso* 33.85-90)

Feeling "the bliss within my heart expand" (*Paradiso* 33.93) Dante revisits the Deep. This time, though, trans-humanized, he recognizes himself *as* that ocean. Grace overflowing through Mary, to Lucy, to Beatrice, via Virgil, has changed the alienated fear in his lake's heart into a generous outpouring: Deep calls, and Deep answers. He even joins Neptune in wonder at the first-ever ship, the

Argo, and every little human ship that crossed the ocean in search of the very Good that already buoys her up and drives her on. Now Dante, too, is a sea god, startled by human striving—in folly and in glory, that bravery which "made the sea god gape at *Argo*'s shade" (*Paradiso* 33.96). Dante is now both immersed in creation and transcended from it. He is ready to see the Trinity as light refracting in mist:

> three colors and one measure in their gleaming:
> As rainbow begets rainbow in the sky,
> so were the first two, and the third, a flame
> that from both rainbows breathed forth equally
> (*Paradiso* 33.117-120)

Conclusion: Communing with the Deep in THIS *Life*

Flowing, raining, evaporating, and immersing—water is the eternal, the ephemeral, and the mediation between them. From the bloody, burning rivers and frozen lake of the *Inferno*, through the cleansing and restoring mist and rivers of *Purgatorio*, and finally, to the river of light and overflowing fullness of *Paradiso*, water's transformations are human transformations. Dante's trans-humanization (*trasumanar*) is effectual in and through his reciprocity with us, his readers. The poet offers us his words, this "weak glimmer in the haze"; we greet the *Commedia*'s ethical claim on us; and together we commune with the Deep. The entire *Commedia* is a gift for each of us from the deepest fountain of charity as it flows through the figurative words of the poet.

From fear of being swallowed, to the demanding safety of Cato's "rocky shore," to the poetical remnants of the mystical vision, Dante's double persona—as pilgrim and as poet—draws us onto the long path of an ethical life. We move step-by-step as the weight of idolatrous loves draws us away from our source and—our desire excruciatingly clarified by absence—that same weight lifts us up, into Paradise. A crucial aspect of the poem, then, is the coming-to-self-consciousness that the poet's calling is ethical, not in the sense of hammering home an ideology onto his opponents, but rather in moving with the reader from misery to happiness (as he writes to Cangrande), and from selfishness to gratitude with all that entails.

The ethics of the *Divine Comedy* is a branch of practical philosophy, as King and Robertson argue following Crouse and Curran in their essay elsewhere in this volume. Embedded in this practical life is also a practical mysticism: through our continual flowing with the poet from natural images to divine presence and back again, readers are moved ever more deeply to realize that the divinity of nature—of plants, animals, water, and light—is also the divinity of other people.[18] The "ecstatic" vision of *Paradiso* is a vision of *this life*.

Dante's *Divine Comedy* is an allegory that invites us to move from misery to joy; it is a transformative work of charity. The greatest gift that we might offer Dante in thanks is to join him in a trans-humanizing community. For those of us fortunate enough to do FYP, this is our reciprocity with one another—our ongoing argument—around, about, in, and through our collective communing with the Deep.

Endnotes

1. Thank you to Dr. Victoria Goddard, Dr. Neil Robertson, Dr. Evan King, and Catherine Campbell for discussion and comments. This is a meditation in the King's-Crousian tradition of reading Dante.

2. One of the joys of the inordinate amounts of time we FYP colleagues spend together is when the Reverend Doctor Curran is triggered by a comment, and a meeting is punctuated with a Tom-intervention. Impossible to predict, yet always true-to-form, such Tom-moments remind one of a fundamental principle of Dante's *Divine Comedy*, as taught to many of us by Robert Crouse and emphasized in Dr. Curran's lectures. Dante explains in his letter to Cangrande that "reciprocity" is a fundamental principle in the *Commedia* and, it is particularly important between a poet and his patron because it valorizes friendship among people of different stations. It is most explicit in the heaven of the reverend doctors, where lifelong opponents dance as points of light, proclaiming each other's standpoints (*Paradiso* 14.131). I offer these musings in that spirit of exchange.

3. Hell is a spiral downwards for the living soul (the inhabitants of hell do not move; their wills are fixed). Purgatory is a steep mountain path, an inverted vortex that draws the pilgrim up with increasing speed as the weight of his love is released from the world and attached to God. Paradise is a nest of spheres where, again, only the still-earthly soul changes place, and as King and Robertson argue in this volume, the converted pilgrim gravitates to his proper place in the divine light. Dante's complex waterworks invites us to puzzle over the poem's hydrography. The rivers and lakes in the *Inferno* comprise a closed system that flows with human tears from our earthly realm—from The Old Man of Crete, trapped inside Mount Ida (*Inf.* 14.94–120). The rivers of Purgatory, Lethe (cleansing forgetfulness) and Eunoe (recovered particularity), spring gracefully from God. The water in *Paradiso* is a river of light that the pilgrim drinks with his eyes in a poetical fusion of elements that flow into and out of one another in Dante's final ecstatic cantos. I'm leaving the relatively well-mapped river- and lake-scape to more auguste commentators; for example, in "Ice, Fire, and Holy

Water," the concluding lecture in Cambridge's *Vertical Dante* series, Rowan Williams argues that reciprocity is rejected in the mute, frozen pit of *Inferno*, and erupts into the pilgrim-poet's heart in the fluid poetry of *Paradiso*. The turning-point, back into community, is a purgatorial melting of the pilgrim's self-enclosure under Beatrice's loving gaze: "Water—holy, baptismal water—flows again in Purgatory, rising simply at God's will, so that it is always flowing in the direction of our healing, so to speak, and its flowing becomes a potent metaphor for the renewal of speech" (Williams 2017, 224).

4. In Scripture, and especially the Psalms, profound waters are a danger and a salvation. The psalmist is drawn out of deep waters by the hand of the Lord (18:16), and he fears sinking (69:14). The Deep awakens gratitude at creation (107:22), and vigilance about God's righteousness and justice (36:6). The Lord gathers the waters in jars (33:7); and he unleashes them so that "deep calls to deep in the roar of your waterfalls," such that the psalmist is flooded with inspiration and wonder—"all your waves and breakers have swept over me" (42:7). The "Deep" is the unfathomable generosity of God's creativity, and the profound mysteries of His purpose.

5. "In the beginning God created the heaven and the earth. And the earth was without form, and void; and darkness was upon the face of the deep And the Spirit of God moved upon the face of the waters" (Genesis 1:1-3).

6. For writers, the great sea of being is a temptation to lie, to claim to be a meaning-giver in a cosmos of polysemous regress. For readers, it is a temptation to assert one's will, to be an organizing principle in an endless play of images. For each of us, in our particular responsibility and guilt, the great sea of being is a call to rest, and a temptation to oblivion. Epicurus and his followers, who believed in the soul's return to the vital energies of the cosmos upon the death of the individual, are each encased in a flaming tomb, in *Inferno* Canto 10.

7. Water's role as a mediating figure has been considered often with reference to the fictional landscape's river and lake systems. For instance, Rowan Williams highlights water as a metaphor for communication: from Satan's frozen silence, to the return of community in *Purgatorio*, and culminating in *Paradiso*'s flow of ecstatic words (Williams, 2017). As Rowan Williams puts it in the conclusion of his essay on the final cantos of each Canticle:

> Dante … lets us know, in both the intricacy of his metaphor and the acknowledged inadequacy of the 'fit' of his words to what has been shown, that he is making no claim to a comprehensive telling of the mysteries of grace. Words exhibit grace as they move: that is a part of what poetry of any sort is about. Words that have to do with the unimaginable divine have to move more than most, to move out of their own light, out of their own confidence. And in the echo chamber of the imagery of the *Commedia's* three movements, especially in these concluding passages, we have a trajectory of movement and speech released; a mobile and fragile enacting of how the stillness-in-motion of Heaven all at once inhabits, disturbs and 'fixes' human speech. (Williams 2017, 228)

The pilgrim's path follows progressive liquid swirls: Hell is a cesspool that can be traversed only with outside help; Purgatory is an inverted whirlpool—a water spout; and Paradise is an undulation out to the edges of the cosmic bowl and back into its centre. In the infernal cesspool, Geryon's "swimming" depicts the self-serving rhetoric of fraud: the dark mystery of the abyss only seems a positive element through which Geryon carries us. In *Purgatorio*, at the very centre of the poem, water mixed with air as smoke, mist, and cloud, veils and unveils, and the author marvels at the source of his artistic vision. In *Paradiso* "droplets of sweet distill" into the pilgrim's breast, and then evaporate, leaving an impression of unity-in-difference in a heart expanded by happiness.

8. Singleton notes Dante's direct reference to Virgil's *Aeneid* here, as the hero seeks the golden bough that will gain him entry to the underworld, "They pass into the forest primeval, the deep lairs of beasts.... And alone [Aeneas] ponders within his own sad heart, gazing on the boundless forest, and, as it chanced, thus prays: 'O if now that golden bough would show itself to us on the tree in the deep wood!'" Singleton also quotes a Latin gloss on the *selva oscura* from Bernard Sylvestris: "*In silvam* (in the woods), in the totality of the things of this world. *Umbrosam* (shadowy) and *immensam* (immense), because the shadows are everywhere. *Antiquam* (ancient), born at the beginning of time" (Singleton, *The Divine Comedy translated with a commentary, Inferno* Vol. 2. Commentary, note 2, Princeton: Princeton University Press, 1970), p. 4).

9. Virgil's ethics were taken by medieval thinkers to be a forerunner to Christianity. Writers pointed especially to Virgil's seeming prophesy of Christ in the Fourth *Ecologue*. We might emphasize also the exchange of the gift of renewal through poetry in Virgil's Fifth *Ecologue*:

So is thy song to me, poet divine,
As slumber on the grass to weary limbs,
Or to slake thirst from some sweet-bubbling rill
In summer's heat. Nor on the reeds alone,
But with thy voice art thou, thrice happy boy,
Ranked with thy master, second but to him.
Yet will I, too, in turn, as best I may,
Sing thee a song, and to the stars uplift
Thy Daphnis- Daphnis to the stars extol,
For me too Daphnis loved.
(Virgil, *Fifth Ecologue*, http://classics.mit.edu/Virgil/eclogue.5.v.html)

See also "The Messianic Prophecy in Vergil's Fourth Eclogue," Ella Bourne *The Classical Journal* Vol. 11, No. 7 (Apr, 1916), pp. 390-400

(11 pages). Bourne traces accounts of Virgil's *Fourth Ecologue* as a prophesy of Christ through Constantine, Augustine, Abelard, and of course Dante, as well as popular mystery plays and prayers up to the 15th century.

10. The Fraudulent are those who trade the true complexity of reciprocity for the false simplicity of asserting one's will upon others sneakily. The plunge from violence to fraud is from the self-interested use of open force into the self-interested manipulation of others' trust.

11. An upstanding, moral devotee of the Roman republic who chose to die rather than live under Caesar's tyranny, Cato is the guardian of the shores of Mount Purgatory.

12. Rather than what Harold Bloom will call the "anxiety of influence," Dante's 13th century relation to precursor texts, especially Scripture, is one of necessary repetition of the same truth in multiple modes: again, the principle of reciprocity means that the message is told and received in manifold ways. Beatrice will command Dante to tell what he has seen. He cannot: his vision exceeds his art, even as it exceeds the categories of his reason and earthly experience: it is a spiritual experience and as such can be conveyed even in part only through moving others to the form of mystical experience proper to them. In all, the universal aspect is to experience the reciprocity between each heart and the whole of creation, and then to carry that reciprocity in our hearts into our earthly relations with one another. Again, this is the poetical imperative in the ethical for the character Dante as pilgrim-poet: his gift is to move us, not to turn us into poets, but to calm the waters of our hearts, to feel the movement of reciprocity between our hearts and the Deep, and to bear that also into the sharing of our particular gifts with others. The ethical poet must meet his readers with the right combination of seeing earthly things as symbols for divine things, and vice versa. As Austin Farrer says:

> What we are talking about is an act of mind in which something finite serves as a symbol for the infinite. The mind which performs such an act will be bound to tip in one of two directions: it cannot hold the balance even. Either it will take itself to be thinking about the infinite being, or it will take itself to be thinking about the finite being. Suppose, for example, my own act of knowledge or will is the finite symbol to be employed. Then one of two things will happen: either I shall be saying, 'God's existence is the absolute expression of such knowledge and will as these of mine': or I shall be saying, 'This knowledge and this will of mine are but limited, cramped, adulterated expressions of sheer knowledge and sheer will, activities intrinsically infinite and divine.' In the first case I shall be thinking of God by the light of myself: in the second case I shall be thinking of myself as a partial ray which falls from the full brightness of God. (Farrer, 1948, 90-91)

13. Perhaps the angelic intervention in the transition from self-centred rage to righteous rage is needed because Virgil cannot fathom evil for its own sake. In any event, Virgil explains:

> Nor the Creator nor a single creature,
> as you know, ever existed without love,
> the soul's love, or just the love that comes by nature.
> The natural love is just and cannot rove.
> The soul's love strays if it desires what's wrong
> or loves with too much strength, or not enough.
> (*Purgatorio* 17.91-96)

14. The true interpenetration is between Dante's soul and the order of the cosmos, which is made in the likeness of God. All things tend to their Source, which is figured variously as the great sea of being, the prime mover, "world-ordaining providence, an immovable light in highest heaven," and still the pilgrim's soul is free (*Paradiso* 1.103-141): "what is happening is love moving itself

eternally and moving creatures in their proper motions of harmony. The poem ends with just this evocation of the love that moves the heavenly bodies in perfection, a love with which the *disio* and *velle* (l.143) of the creature are at last perfectly aligned — both fixed and free." (Williams 2017, p. 226)

15. Austin Farrer distinguishes the "puzzles" internal to philosophical systems from metaphysical mysteries: "The believer in God must suppose that the mystery of God's existence is no mere puzzle, but a genuine mystery, presented to us by the stuff of our own existence: whether we describe it well or ill, whether we speak of it or ignore it, it is still there. For God appears in our thoughts as the name of a real being we attempt to describe, not as a convenient analogical term used by us in describing something else, in describing the moral conscience, for example" (1948, p. 80).

16. Barolini explains of the water-infused images of exchange in the Heaven of the Doctors: "If we listen to the sound and the rhythm of "*Ciò che non more e ciò che può morire*"—if we say the verse out loud—we hear the vibration of being and creation as presented by Dante in *Paradiso* 13: we hear the sound and the rhythm of the waves crashing on the shore of the great sea of being itself." https://digitaldante.columbia.edu/dante/divine-comedy/paradiso/paradiso-13/ (The verse here, in Esolen's translation: "What has to die and what can never die" continues "are nothing but the glimmerings of that Word / our Father has begotten by His love…" (*Paradiso* 13.52-54).

17. in Mandlebaum's rendering the reciprocal "raining", and the overflowing from God, to Saint James, and from Saint James to us, via Dante's poem, comes through most clearly:

I said: "Hope is the certain expectation
   of future glory; it is the result
   of God's grace and of merit we have earned.
This light has come to me from many stars;

but he who first instilled it in my heart
was the chief singer of the Sovereign Guide.
'May those'—he says within his theody—
'who know Your name, put hope in You'; and if
one has my faith, can he not know God's name?
And just as he instilled, you then instilled
with your Epistle, so that I am full
and rain again your rain on other souls."
(*Paradiso* 25.67-78)

18. The ethical in Dante is the movement out of self-enclosure into general wonder. The poet seeks to engage readers in a transformation like the one Evelyn Underhill describes:

> The tendency of all worship to decline from adoration to demand, and from the supernatural to the ethical, shows how strong a pull is needed to neutralize the anthropocentric trend of the human mind; its intense preoccupation with the world of succession, and its own here-and-now desires and needs. And only in so far as it is released from this petty subjectivism, can it hope to grow up into any knowledge of the massive realities of that spiritual universe in which we live and move. It is the mood of deep admiration, the meek acknowledgement of mystery, the humble and adoring gaze, which makes us capable of this revelation. (Underhill, 2003, p.107)

Bibliography

Bloom, Harold. *The Anxiety of Influence.* Oxford: Oxford University Press, 1973.

Crouse, Robert. *Images of Pilgrimage: Paradise and Wilderness in Christian Spirituality.* Charlottetown: St Peter's Press, 1986.

—. Lectures in the Foundation Year Programme, 1998-2005. (Susan Dodd notes).

Di Scipio, Giuseppe C. "Dante and St. Paul: The Blinding Light and Water." *Dante Studies, with the Annual Report of the Dante Society,* No. 98, 1980 (pp. 151-157).

Donno, Daniel J. "Moral Hydrography: Dante's Rivers," *MLN,* Vol. 92, No. 1, Italian Issue, January, 1977 (130-139).

Dante. *Inferno.* Trans. Anthony Esolen. New York: Modern Library, 2004.

Dante. *Purgatory.* Trans. Anthony Esolen. New York: Modern Library, 2004.

Dante. *Paradise.* Trans. Anthony Esolen. New York: Modern Library, 2004.

Farrer, Austin. *The Glass of Vision.* Glasgow: Robert MacLehose and Company, The University Press 1948.

Freccero, John. "Dante's Prologue Scene." *Dante Studies, with the Annual Report of the Dante Society*, No. 118, 2000 (189-216).

King, Evan, and Neil Robertson, "The Structure of Ascent in Dante's "Paradiso," in this volume, 2019.

Singleton, Charles S. "Dante's Allegory," *Speculum*, Vol. 25, No. 1, The University of Chicago Press on behalf of the Medieval Academy of America, January 1950 (78-86).

Singleton, Charles S. *The Divine Comedy translated with a commentary, Inferno* Vol. 2. Commentary. Princeton: Princeton University Press, 1970.

Singleton, Charles S. *The Divine Comedy translated with a commentary, Purgatorio* Vol. 2. Commentary. Princeton: Princeton University Press, 1973.

Singleton, Charles S. *The Divine Comedy translated with a commentary, Paradiso* Vol. 2. Commentary. Princeton: Princeton University Press, 1975.

Praycar, Rudy S. "Dante's 'lago del cor'." *Dante Studies, with the Annual Report of the Dante Society*, No. 96, 1978 (1-19).

Underhill, Evelyn. *Essential Writings Selected with an introduction by Emilie Griffin*. New York: Orbis, 2003.

Williams, Rowan. "Ice, Fire, and Holy Water." In *Vertical Readings in Dante's Comedy*, Volume 3, eds. Corbett and Webb. Cambridge: Open Book Publishers, 2017 (217-228).

EVAN KING AND NEIL ROBERTSON

The Structure of Ascent in Dante's PARADISO

> For now we see through a glass, darkly; but then face to face: now I know in part; but then shall I know even as also I am known. And now abideth faith, hope, charity, these three; but the greatest of these is charity.
>
> —1 Corinthians 13:12-13

This academic year (2018-19) Dr. Thomas Curran described the journey of the soul in Dante's *Divine Comedy* as a movement from the pusillanimous soul portrayed in the opening cantos as cowardly, suffering a smallness of soul such that he, Dante, shrinks back from the prospect of the journey necessary to his release from the "Dark Wood" (*la selva oscura*), in which he finds himself midway through the journey of his life, to a final greatness of soul, the perfection of human personality figured in the poetry, and failure of that poetry, in the final canto of the poem. In this paper, we intend to focus on the final stage of that attainment of magnanimity, the *Paradiso*. We want to revisit this canticle to consider for a moment the structure and logic of the ascent recounted there and in doing so we will be led by the guidance of Robert

Crouse, whose lectures and writings on Dante have been so formative for all of us who have studied, whether as students or faculty, in the Foundation Year Program.[1]

Readers of the *Paradiso* often assume that its cosmological structure is primary, but this turns out to come at the expense of the *Commedia's* deeper continuity. The structures of the *Inferno* and *Purgatorio* are clearly defined by vices and virtues (*Inferno* XI; *Purgatorio* XVII). Each circle of Hell and terrace of Purgatory corresponds to a particular form of love, whether ordered or disordered, or love's opposite, despair. And this reflects what Dante himself explains in his letter to his patron, Cangrande, the importance of which has been a hallmark of Dr. Curran's teaching: the *Commedia* belongs to the branch of practical philosophy called ethics, and ethics is about how to live well and achieve happiness or bliss in this life. The letter to Cangrande is principally concerned with explaining the background to the *Paradiso*. A reading of the canticle in terms of ethics, in continuity with the rest of the poem, should seek out a structure that is shaped by the virtues.

The second way our reading is indebted to Dr. Crouse is by our making fundamental the concept captured by Dante in his neologism, *trasumanar*, which appears in the first canto of *Paradiso*:

> In watching her, within me I was changed as Glau-
> cus changed, tasting the herb that made
> him a companion of the other sea gods.
> Passing beyond the human cannot be
> worded; let Glaucus serve as simile—
> until grace grant you the experience.
> (*Paradiso* 1.67–72)[2]

---

1 E.g., Robert D. Crouse, "Dante as Philosopher: Christian Aristotelianism," *Dionysius* 14 (1998), 141–156.

2 Translations of the *Divine Comedy* are those of Allen Mandelbaum, unless otherwise noted.

This is the wonderful moment when Dante experiences the shifting of his *pondus*, his weight, so that it is no longer drawn to the Earth's centre, but to a heavenly centre, and he finds himself rising from the Earthly into the Celestial Paradise by gazing into Beatrice's eyes. One way to gloss Dante's word *trasumanar* is, as Fr. Crouse argues, with reference to Aquinas's dictum: "Grace does not destroy nature, but perfects it."[3] This activity of grace perfecting nature, above all human nature—by taking it beyond itself, while preserving it—is the whole work of the *Paradiso*: the transformation, transhumanization of nature effected by grace to its perfection. Indeed, the basic structure of the *Paradiso*, we shall argue, is the thoroughly neoplatonic and thoroughly medieval one of Purgation (as Dante travels through the planets under the shadow of the Earth), Illumination (through the upper planets) and finally Perfection or deification (attained through the post-planetary spheres). This is a way of articulating this whole movement of transhumanization.

However, let us pause for a moment. Dante uses a metaphor taken from the ancient world when he introduces the term *trasumanar*: that of Glaucus, who eats a plant or herb and is transfigured from mortal to immortal, from Earthly to divine. This process of transhumanization we can describe as "the infinitization of the finite." This process of infinitization is what characterizes the *Paradiso* as a whole: in and through it there is a crucial transmogrification of ancient virtues that has both elements of preserving those virtues but also translating them.

It is crucial to see in this principle of *transumanar*, if read through Aquinas's tag, that the nature—the finite, if you will—is not destroyed, but presupposed and taken up into its perfection. It is also important to see in this the difference between Aquinas's account of nature and that of the ancients; the presence of Limbo

3 Thomas Aquinas, *ST* Ia.1.8.

in *Inferno* testifies to this: there is an instability to nature taken in and for itself, in the relation of human happiness to nature as end.[4] So the truth of *Paradiso* is the fulfillment of this perfection: the Empyrean Rose sustained and infused through union with the incarnational Trinity imaged in Canto XXXIII. But, as Beatrice suggests, what we need, what Dante needs, is the mediation of stages of transhumanization to attain to this truth—which is itself still an allegory of the end of ethical or practical life in this world. The whole movement between Canto I and Canto XXXIII is this mediation, which by stages more fully unites nature and grace, and so brings our ethical/human nature, our personality as Augustine understood this—an activity of memory, intellect, and will—to its fulfillment in a Divine charity that moves in all things, but above all in our perfected personality. The specific movement of this transhumanization is through a mediation of human ethical life, the life of the virtues as it is transfigured step by step.

This way of conceiving the movement and structure of the *Divine Comedy* is to suggest that it is at every point, as Robert Crouse has made fundamental for all who have learned and taught in the Foundation Year Program, a journey whose most basic subject matter is the odyssey of Augustinian trinitarian

---

4 There is a certain tension between *De Monarchia* and the *Divine Comedy* in the way of conceiving the distinction between earthly and celestial paradises. For the *De Monarchia* III.xvi: "The providence which cannot err has set before man two ends to be pursued. A blessedness, namely, of this life which consists in the operation of his own virtues and is represented by the Earthly Paradise. And a beatitude of eternal life which consists of the fruition of the divine aspect and which he cannot attain to by his own virtue unless aided by divine light which is given—to be understood in the Celestial Paradise. To these beatitudes as to different ends, different conclusions, it is appropriate to arrive by different means. For, to the first we arrive through philosophical teachings when we follow them according to the moral and intellectual virtues. To the second, through spiritual teachings which transcend human reason—spiritual teachings which we follow according to the theological virtues—namely, faith, hope, and charity." This clear separation of earthly and heavenly, natural and theological, is not in fact displayed in the *Divine Comedy*. Most fundamentally, while variously symbolized, we do not see there any sphere or circle dedicated to the cardinal virtues in their natural form.

personality. What Dante effects in the mediation of this personality is a kind of joining together, especially in the *Paradiso*, of a Thomistic principle of "grace perfecting and not destroying nature," with a Bonaventurian (Dionysian) structure of purgation, illumination, and perfection. At its foundation, however, the *Paradiso* is Pauline.[5] As *Paradiso* I, XXVIII, and the *Epistle to Cangrande* make clear, the pilgrim in this journey becomes a new Paul. Dante reads Paul through his convert Dionysius the Areopagite (*Paradiso* 28.136-139), who is interpreted through his major 13th-century exponents Thomas Aquinas and Bonaventure, the two conducting doctors in the Heaven of the Sun.[6] Dante's synthesis of Thomistic content and Bonaventurian structure forms the ladder in the *Paradiso* that brings that trinitarian personality to its journey's end.

In terms of that structure, it is important to reiterate Beatrice's clarification of Dante's more substantial confusion in the Heaven of the Moon: the souls that appear to Dante in his journey do not actually dwell in those particular spheres. Their presence is gratuitous, an act of grace comparable to the condescension of Scripture, providing signs suited to the condition of his mind (*Paradiso* 4.37-45). They appear in order to prepare him for his final vision and the fulfillment of his desire. So while there are stages to this journey, they must be seen as stages of a preparation, an initiation or, in other words, a hierarchy, comprising stages in a journey that transforms the pilgrim, with Beatrice, "the lady who imparadises/ my mind" (*Paradiso* 28.3), acting as hierarch, at least until they reach the Empyrean. This Dionysian logic is taken up by Dante insofar as he structures the *Paradiso* according to the stages of purgation (Moon-Venus), illumination (Sun-Saturn), and

5 1 Cor. 13; 2 Cor. 3 (transformed into the same image from glory to glory); 2 Cor. 12 (rapture into third heaven).

6 For Dante, as for Dionysius, the work of "purgation" is not exclusively moral, but can also be applied to the intellectual purgation and ascent of angels (*On the Ecclesiastical Hierarchy* c. 6, 537AB; *On the Celestial Hierarchy* c. 7, 208AD).

perfection or union (Fixed Stars-Empyrean).[7] This structure emerges only if one reads the Moon to the Fixed Stars in terms of the virtues.

Robert Crouse has argued that the basic logic of this transhumanization is found in a reflection on the theological virtues of faith, hope, and charity. In fact many commentators have understood the three planets under the shadow of the Earth as representing defective forms of the three theological virtues: the Moon (defective faith), Mercury (defective hope) and Venus (defective love or charity).[8] What is unusual is Dr. Crouse's claim that the next group of planets, the planets outside the shadow of the Earth, also represent the theological virtues, but now free of defect: the Sun (Faith), Mars (Hope), Jupiter (Charity as Love of Neighbour), and Saturn (Charity as Love of God). Dr. Crouse is reading these planetary spheres in contrast to a more conventional account of understanding them in terms of the four cardinal virtues of Wisdom (Sun), Courage (Mars), Justice (Jupiter), and Temperance (Saturn).[9]

---

7 Bonaventure, *Itinerarium mentis in Deum*, trans. P. Boehner (Saint Bonaventure, N.Y.: Franciscan Institute, 1956), IV.2-4: "Therefore, if we wish to enter again into the enjoyment of Truth as into Paradise, we must go in through faith and hope in, and love for the Mediator between God and man, Jesus Christ, Who is like the Tree of life in the midst of Paradise. The image of our soul, therefore, must be clothed over with the three theological virtues, by which the soul is purified, enlightened, and perfected. In this way the image is reformed and made conformable to the heavenly Jerusalem, and part of the Church Militant, which, according to the Apostle, is the offspring of the heavenly Jerusalem [...]. These things attained, our spirit, inasmuch as it is in conformity with the heavenly Jerusalem, is made hierarchic [*efficitur spiritus noster hierarchicus*] in order to mount upward. For into this heavenly Jerusalem no one enters unless it first comes down into his heart by grace, as St. John beheld in the Apocalypse. It comes down into our heart when, by the reformation of the image, the theological virtues, the delights of the spiritual senses, and uplifting transports, our spirit becomes hierarchic, that is, purified, enlightened, and perfected."

8 Frank Ordiway, "In the Earth's Shadow: The Theological Virtues Marred", *Dante Studies* 100 (1982), 78-92. Ordiway also reads the first three spheres in terms of a purgation: "Now that the penance of Purgatory and the moral character has been completed, Dante finds himself on the threshold of a sort of theological penance" (89).

9 See, for example, the schema provided in the classic Reynolds and Sayers translation of *Paradiso*.

In a Dantean spirit, we want to argue that both readings are in a way right—that these planets are best understood as being about the transhumanization of the cardinal virtues. A little-recognized aspect of Thomas Aquinas's ethical thought captures this standpoint by speaking of "infused cardinal virtues."[10] The infinitization of finite human nature and personality is precisely what Dante is figuring here in these unshadowed planets—they show us the logic of this infinitization or transhumaniziation, at least as this appears in human ethical personality. The work of the post-planetary sphere (a realm which does not present planets but forms of "motionless motion"), the Fixed Stars, the Primum Mobile, and the Empyrean heaven, allow an apprehension of the principles of this infinitization. So it is here that our whole standpoint will be reversed and we can come to see that the true operation of the cosmos—our ethical cosmos—is not primarily through our ascent, but by Divine creative-redemptive love, both as creative will and emanation acting through the whole hierarchical and angelic orders but seen in and through human personality—through Beatrice, through Bernard, through Mary, through Christ in the life of the Trinity. This reversal is at once our perfection and our divinization; it is simultaneously an "*excessus mentis*" and a fulfillment of that *mens*, that human personality, perfected, not destroyed, in God.

Before attending to these structural matters, we need to be clear about the actual character of the "transhumanization" that this structure mediates. This is best brought out in thinking through Dante's first encounter in his ascent and one that is perhaps especially disturbing to ordinary human sensibilities: his encounter with Piccarda. This encounter can seem to be simply an instance of the Moon as the sphere of defective faith. Beatrice explains the

10 Odon Lottin, *Psychologie et morale aux XIIe et XIIIe siècles*, t.II: *Problèmes de morale*, deuxième partie (Gembloux: J. Duculot, 1949), 459–535.

deficiency of Piccarda's faith in terms of the violent assault she and Constanza suffered in relation to their covenantal vows. The issue is that Piccarda and Constanza give in to the force that, against their absolute will, they nonetheless—if only conditionally—submit to. The radicality of Beatrice's argument is that, in so conceding, Piccarda and Constanza actually contribute to the force that violated their wills: in modern parlance this can appear to be blaming the victim. Beatrice in fact argues that the claim made here will be seen by mortal justice to be unjust (*Paradiso* 4.67-9). But, the text continues, from the standpoint of divine justice, the Beatrician judgment is true. Here we see a crucial break between mortal or finite justice and infinite or divine justice. From the latter point of view the will is properly infinite and moved out of its own freedom, unconstrained by any conditionality or contingency in the world. Here St. Lawrence and his rather extreme behaviour at his own conflagration is evoked. The point being made at this moment of initiation into transhumanization, at this moment of intellectual purgation, is that transhumanization is precisely the shift from a finite to an infinite or divine context in will and knowledge.

A way to consider this point is in contrast with Aristotle's ethical thought. For Aristotle it is fundamental to and constitutive of ethics that it takes place in a context, above all a set of changeable contingencies: all virtues internalize this and are in fact constituted by this contingency. This is why, for Aristotle, virtues are means between extremes: there is a "too much" and a "too little" that the virtue is relative to and which is constitutive of that virtue, even as its truth is to order this context to its end in human nature.[11] Thus, for courage, there is a deficient form in cowardice, but an excessive

11 Aristotle, *Nicomachean Ethics* II, 6-7. See the discussion of the question of the mean in virtues in Aquinas, *ST* Ia-IIae.64.1-4. While virtues in general observe a mean, Aquinas notes that in themselves the theological virtues do not have a mean: "Accordingly the good of such virtues does not consist in a mean, but increases the more we approach to the summit" (*ST* Ia-IIae.64.4).

form in recklessness. *Phronesis* or the capacity to judge context is then internal to all the practical virtues in Aristotle. So there is an inherent finitude to the cardinal virtues and an otherness internal to them. The problematic of this standpoint is brought out in the Earthly Paradise, where the limitation of merely natural virtues is shown in various ways, but especially in the emptiness of this realm: its proper inhabitants, virtuous pagans (*Purgatorio* 28.139-141), in fact belong to Limbo.

The four cardinal virtues—prudence, courage, justice, and moderation—begin to feature in the poem as soon as we enter into Purgatory, when Dante and Vergil encounter Cato on the shores of the mountain:

> Then I turned to the right, setting my mind
> upon the other pole, and saw four stars
> not seen before except by the first people.
> Heaven appeared to revel in their flames:
> o northern hemisphere, because you were
> denied that sight, you are a widower! [...]
> The rays of the four holy stars so framed
> [Cato's] face with light that in my sight he seemed
> like one who is confronted by the sun.
> (*Purgatorio* 1.22-39)

As interpreters usually observe, these stars are an allegory for the cardinal virtues. However, they cannot be identical to the cardinal virtues known, for example, to the denizens of Limbo. The inherently finite form of the natural virtues means that they cannot be found in a perfected form on Earth—the Earthly Paradise remains empty. By having these heavenly cardinal virtues illuminate Cato's face, Dante is suggesting that the Roman's suicide, motivated by the affirmation of liberty rather than by despair, displays the same hope that animates every love ascending the mountain (*Purgatorio* 1.73–75). The substantial connection between the perfected cardinal virtues and the theological virtues is asserted here, but in its most attenuated form.

The connection between the perfected cardinal virtues and the theological virtues is brought out more clearly in the Earthly Paradise, and in a way that directly anticipates the *Paradiso*. After Dante has completed a sort of moral purgation, being cleansed in the river Lethe, he is received by the cardinal virtues, appearing as four ladies dancing around Beatrice, who identify themselves as stars in heaven that serve as her handmaidens (*Purgatorio* 31.106–111). They bring him to her eyes, through which he marvels at the oscillating natures of the griffin, but it falls to the three theological virtues to persuade her to reveal her face (*Purgatorio* 31.133–145). The journey of the *Paradiso* is the unfolding and realization of this intuition.

The seven virtues are hinted at the opening of the *Paradiso* under the image of the four circles and three crosses (*Paradiso* 1.37–45). One can summarize their presence in the canticle as follows. First, it is clear that Dante groups the first three stages of his journey together: the Moon, Mercury, and Venus all fall in the "shadow of the Earth," insofar as the theological virtues are seen imperfectly because of an Earthly deficiency. These appearances are adequate to the pilgrim's own excessively Earthly way of knowing, and serve to lead him nearer to the truth. This deficiency or Earthly shadow is poetically displayed even in the way that souls appear to him; the individuality of each soul emerges from undifferentiated, somewhat chaotic groups.

In the next four stages, souls appear as members of highly orchestrated collectives. In each sphere, one of the cardinal virtues predominates. It is here that we finally understand why Dante has the four dancers identify themselves as stars, and why they are intrinsically connected to the other three virtues. These are the virtues of Earthly human life in heavenly form. Dante is almost certainly inspired by the Thomistic doctrine of the infused cardinal virtues, according to which each of the virtues is transformed and perfected by charity. The whole movement of the *Paradiso* is to move ethics, the virtues, from an Earthly or worldly finite standpoint to an infinite or divine one. This is what each of the planets beyond the shadow of the Earth especially displays where a specific cardinal virtue is "infused," raised up to an infinite standpoint and in doing so implicitly changed (transhumanized) into a theological virtue. This result is then taken up in the examination of the theological virtues in the sphere of the Fixed Stars. So, in the Sun wisdom is infused and is implicitly faith, the standpoint of the theologians; in Mars, courage is infused and is implicitly hope, the standpoint of the warrior martyrs; in Jupiter, justice is infused and is implicitly love of neighbour, the standpoint of providential, predestinal rulers; and in Saturn temperance is infused and is implicitly love of God, the standpoint of contemplative monks.

In each of these spheres we see displayed the transformation to an infinite logic. For example, oppositions which seem absolute from a natural or Earthly perspective are resolved in a heavenly inclusive perspective where the opposition is not negated, but rather is brought into the service of a more comprehensive truth and so becomes reciprocal. The monophony of the *Purgatorio* becomes the polyphonic harmony of the *Paradiso*, in which a whole, a *civitas*, is articulated that includes but also unites the parts that comprise it. This sense of a virtue that is inherently communitarian is figured by the symbols in each of these planets, which are the work of the inhabitants of that sphere constituting a symbol of which they are a member and so part of a larger whole. The part becomes more concrete the more it is integrated into this *civitas*. In Dante's poetry, this is figured by the increasing focus on the human face in the ascent.

In what follows, we assume the account of the first three spheres within the shadow of the Earth as expounded by Robert Crouse, and pass directly to the more novel points of emphasis in our interpretation, beginning with the sphere of the Sun.

The Virtues Beyond the Shadow: the Sun to Saturn

Interpretively the challenge of the four planets beyond the shadow of the Earth is that they appear on their surface to portray cardinal virtues and yet they cannot and should not belong to the celestial paradise according to Dante's explicit account in *De Monarchia.* Nor does it make sense, theologically or poetically, to move from the theological virtues, even if in defective form in the three lowest planets, to these natural virtues; surely this would be a descent. So Dr. Crouse's account is a most welcome resolution. Yet, to state simply that these upper planets figure the theological virtues leaves somewhat unexplained the initial impression: why does Dante so clearly image the cardinal virtues, even if christianized in various ways? Here the under-appreciated Thomistic doctrine of "infused cardinal virtues" is crucial. What is being imaged are these cardinal virtues infused by the principle of charity, by their infinite end.

But more than this: insofar as the appearance of souls in the planets is an appearance for Dante, these planets are not simply fixed portrayals but function as steps in a movement of adequation to the vision in the Empyrean. This is where Dr. Crouse's account becomes so compelling: these planets are about the theological virtues. We would only add this clarification: that what is in fact figured as an infused cardinal virtue is in Dante, the pilgrim, transhumanized into a theological virtue: so wisdom becomes faith, courage becomes hope, justice becomes love of neighbour, and temperance becomes love of God. This reading is confirmed when

Dante's illumination effected in and through these upper planets results in his capacity to articulate what he has internalized in his examination in the Fixed Stars concerning the definitions of faith, hope, and charity. In short, the work of these upper planets is to portray the very perfecting of nature into grace at the level of the virtues. As Dr. Crouse himself beautifully put it: "[Paradise] is not however a matter of discarding the natural virtues or leaving them behind; rather they are taken up and perfected in the celestial virtues. Grace does not destroy Nature but perfects it."[12]

What is figured in these upper planets are representations that largely accord with Aquinas's account of the infused cardinal virtues: that is to say, cardinal virtues that have been taken up or infused in the light of charity.[13] So the sphere of the Sun culminates in the figure of Solomon. Solomon was wise, to be sure, but his wisdom did not consist in knowing philosophical subtleties, such as the number of angels or the relation of necessity and contingency. Rather, Solomon asked God for "a mind to govern [God's] people," and for the power "to discern between good and evil" (1 Kings 3:9). Dante's inclusion of Solomon among the theologians shows how the cardinal virtue of prudence is taken up and transhumanized in heaven. Prudence deals with human affairs and actions—how best to realize a given end. Prudence is taken up into heaven insofar as it acts within a new realm of possibilities. Its ends are not devised by human beings but are divinely given. The theologians and Solomon are examples of how human beings reason from divinely given principles.[14] This is how theology was

12 Robert D. Crouse, "Lecture on *Paradiso*" (unpubl., King's Seminar).

13 For Aquinas on the infused cardinal virtues see: *ST* Ia-IIae.63.4 and 65.2. The status of the infused cardinal virtues is a matter of debate in the scholarship. Indeed for some scholars, especially Servais Pinckaers and his students, the whole account of the virtues in the *Summa theologiae* is concerned with the virtues as infused, because only as infused are they perfect virtue.

14 Cf. *ST* Ia-IIae.65.2. In the Earthly Paradise, the dancer who represents prudence has three eyes, perhaps referring to the past, present, and future, or to the

understood by Thomas Aquinas and it is why Solomon, on a more practical level, asked for God's illumination to give him the standards for his rule.[15] Therefore, in the Sun, we have seen the way that charity transhumanizes prudence.[16]

This pattern continues in the next three spheres: with martyrs (infused courage),[17] rulers (infused justice),[18] and monks (infused temperance).[19] In this section, Dante glimpses the perfect forms of faith, hope, and charity, but always through the lens of an infused cardinal virtue.[20] What Robert Crouse's reading suggests and the logic of the ascent implies is that these images of infused cardinal virtues belong to a further transhumanization as they are converted into theological ones: so that prudence or wisdom becomes implicitly faith, courage is implicitly hope, justice is implicitly love of neighbour and temperance is implicitly love of God. The structure of Augustinian personality is thereby being

---

fact that it keeps watch over the other three dancers. Prudence comes first among the cardinal virtues, even in heaven. Prudence relates to means, and this aspect may be present here in both a theoretical and practical way, in sacred doctrine and in kingship. Both are operating under ends and principles supplied by a higher light.

15 Since human reason or prudence depends on this higher power, Dante ends Canto XIII with Aquinas's warning to always be patient and self-critical in our judgements (*Par.*13.133–135).

16 In Solomon's speech we have the clearest articulation of how faith, hope, and charity are implicitly present. Faith apprehends the Trinity and Incarnation (*Par.*14.25–30), Hope awaits the day of Resurrection (*Par.*14.61–66), which will lead to an increase in vision and, accordingly, an increase in Love (*Par.*14.40–57).

17 See the very interesting account of the relation of acquired and infused aspects of the cardinal virtues in Rudi te Velde, "The Hybrid Character of the Infused Moral Virtue According to Thomas Aquinas," H. Goris (ed.), *Faith, Hope and Love: Thomas Aquinas on Living by the Theological Virtues* (Leuven: Peeters, 2015), 25–44, and particularly on the relation between infused courage and martyrdom.

18 Infused justice: *ST* Ia-IIae.63.4: "men behave well in respect of their being *fellow-citizens with the saints, and of the household of God* [Eph. 2:19]"; Ia-IIae.100.12.

19 Infused temperance: *ST* Ia-IIae.63.4: "whereas, according to the Divine rule, it behooves man to *chastise* his *body, and bring it into subjection* [1 Cor. 9:27], by abstinence in food, drink and the like". Cf. *Par.*22.88–90: "Peter began with neither gold nor silver,/ and I with prayer and fasting, and when Francis/ began his fellowship, he did it humbly."

20 The individuals he meets are meant to serve as examples for the pilgrim in his ascent and, by extension, for the readers (*Par.*17.136–142).

perfected in this transhumanizing, this infusing of nature by grace. Two movements are conjoined in this: the ascent of the human into the divine with the descent of the divine into the human. The crucial reversal of perspective in the Empyrean will correct the apparent primacy of the first, showing the whole work to be a work of divine Love that "moves the Sun and the other stars" (*Paradiso* 33.145).

So what characterizes these four planets when viewed as Robert Crouse viewed them is that they begin from a divine revelation that exceeds and completes nature: one that places nature in an infinite context that is both in excess of it and yet without which it remains incomplete. So the premise of the theologians is faith: the circle of the Sun is filled with those who assent to a truth beyond natural knowledge, a truth that to the world is foolishness. Mars present us with warriors who assume in their wills an accomplished end that cannot be willed by nature: their individual eternal salvation, an end that to the world presents their actions as recklessness.[21] Jupiter presents us with Biblical or Christian rulers who bring about in their judgement a mercy and equity that from a worldly appearance looks arbitrary and relies on a divine justice and a friendship with God that appears impossible. Saturn presents us with monks whose self-denial is premised on a contemplative love of, toward and in God, that to the world looks like excessive self-denial and negation.[22]

21 Another work that Dr. Curran has lectured on with great insight and ardor, *The Song of Roland*, displays beautifully the transhumanizing work of grace where Roland is viewed by Oliver as "reckless" in his hope in refusing to blow his horn. Oliver presents an example of Aristotelian prudence, but it is Roland whose excess is judged the most complete embodiment of Christian fealty.

22 An example: the sphere of Jupiter is explicitly about justice, but as infused by charity so that its end is not a worldly determination of appropriate merit and proportion, but an eternal end and good. But in turn this infused justice is implicitly charity: willing the known good as effected in and by the divine charity that exceeds, without destroying, justice as a cardinal virtue. So the subject matter of the illumination (Beatrice's speech) is predestinal salvation, which exceeds all human natural merit or expectation ("a life too high for man," as Aristotle claims). This love

In each of these spheres we find present the premise of an inclusive infinite activity in the soul—a theological virtue—that is assumed in the infused cardinal virtue explicitly figured in that sphere. This sense of inner movement at work in the transhumanizing of nature by grace is also, as Dr. Crouse so beautifully illustrated in his lectures of the *Paradiso*, what is at work in the argument both within each sphere and between each sphere. The argument of the Sun leads to Mars as its fuller realization, and so Jupiter and Saturn arise from what went before and more fully accomplish what is implicit at the earlier stage, a more and more complete fulfillment of human trinitarian-incarnational personality. This is all to say that each sphere is not a set piece, a "tableau vivant" of each virtue, but is more fundamentally a mediating of transhumanization and, in the case of these upper planets, of moments of illumination: hence the vital role of seeing Beatrice's eyes is as fundamental as her arguments for the upward movement. The natural outcome—or perhaps better, supernatural outcome—of this ascent is the examination of the theological virtues in the sphere of the Fixed Stars where Dante is found able to articulate what he has internalized in his ascent through the upper planets.

The Heavenly City: the Fixed Stars to the Empyrean

At the end of Canto XXII, Dante and Beatrice ascend to the Fixed Stars, which marks the final transition point in Paradise. Dante draws this boundary to our attention in several ways. After they leave Saturn behind, Beatrice tells him that he is "so near the final blessedness" that he will now require "vision clear and keen,"

---

of neighbour is, as through a worldly institution or mediation, incomplete in itself, and so points to Saturn as representing the charity that is love of or friendship with God found in contemplative monasticism. In this latter form of charity is completed the transhumanizing of the cardinal virtues into theological virtues and so too the illumination of Dante by the upper planetary spheres.

and for this he must look back at the Earth and the seven planetary spheres traversed so far (*Paradiso* 22.124-129). Looking ahead, she describes the next stage of Dante's initiation by coining the verb *t'inleiare*, "in-it yourself," signaling that "the final blessedness" is a divine-human union.

The most adequate metaphor Dante finds to describe the perfection and deification of the human is face-to-face vision, which brings out the deeper unity of these final Cantos. Dante will set this image apart from every other metaphor in the poem when he describes how, after uniting his vision with the incorporeal light, the masks of allegory fall away (*Paradiso* 30.91-96). In this section, we can merely note how Dante repeatedly describes the highest realization of one's deepest desire, union with God, in terms of face-to-face vision, both with the God-man and with the saints. "Face" can be readily understood as a metaphor for "personality". This establishes clearly that the fulfillment of concrete personality is the goal of the transhumanization and hierarchical initiation of the *Paradiso*. This conclusion is anticipated by some of the most important lines of the poem, found at the end of the pilgrim's conversation with St. Benedict before he ascends the Ladder to the Fixed Stars. In response to Benedict's affectionate and courteous greeting, Dante likens the increase of his confidence to a rose opening in sunlight (*Paradiso* 22.52-57). The simile is proleptic, and is perhaps the only adequate image to prepare for the request that arises from it, which Benedict acknowledges as the profoundest of human desires:

> "Therefore I pray you, father—and may you
> assure me that I can receive such grace—
> to let me see, unveiled, your human face."
> (*Paradiso* 22,58-60)

Benedict's reply brings us to the heart of the remainder of the poem:

> "Brother, your high desire will be
>   fulfilled within the final sphere, as all
>   the other souls' and my own longing will.
> There, each desire is perfect, ripe, intact;
>   and only there, within that final sphere,
>   is every part where it has always been."
> (*Paradiso* 22.61–66)

So far, the souls Dante encountered have been veiled from his vision in their own light. The deficiency was in his sight, whose weakness was accommodated by Beatrice's hierarchical activity through the spheres. He is about to leave that deficiency behind. But we must note the essential point here: Benedict is saying that the deepest desire of the pilgrim and, indeed, of every individual, is face-to-face vision, to see the human face entirely infused with divine virtue. In other words, his ultimate desire is a vision of how the divine and the human can be united without confusion—that is, he longs for a vision of the human face of God.

Already upon his entry into the Fixed Stars, this desire finds a kind of satisfaction. Here he reaches the summit of the human hierarchy, so that the work of purgation and illumination is in one sense complete: Dante sees before him the Church and the saints in triumph, and the Sun of divine grace shining upon it, "the Potency/ that opened roads between the Earth and Heaven." This incarnational vision, as at the end of the poem, overwhelms his mind, which enters an ecstasy beyond memory (*di sé stessa uscìo, / e che si fesse rimembrar non sape*). He is recalled to himself with the inviting words of his beloved guide:

"Open your eyes and see me as I am [*riguarda qual son io*].
The things that you have witnessed
have given you the strength to bear my smile."
(*Paradiso* 23.46-48; trans. Hollander)

With the Fixed Stars we come back to the theological virtues, but no longer glimpsed under the shadow of the Earth or as informing the infused cardinal virtues. The virtues have mediated Dante's relationship to Beatrice from the beginning, and now a trajectory sketched in the Earthly Paradise has reached its perfection: the infused cardinal virtues bring him to Beatrice's eyes, but it falls to Dante's explicit articulation of the theological virtues to persuade her to reveal her face (*Purgatorio* 31.106-145).[23] Though all the Muses may sing, says the poet, that would be inadequate for describing the holy smile of Beatrice, whose face itself is Paradise (*Paradiso* 23.55-63).[24] The elaborate simile Dante constructs at the beginning of the Canto, which compares Beatrice to a bird, awaiting the dawn, suspended in attentive contemplation (*Paradiso* 23.1-15), displays striking lexical similarities with his account of his own contemplative fixity in Empyrean (*Paradiso* 33.97-99). For her, the Fixed Stars are in a sense already the Empyrean.

Beatrice immediately tells Dante to look back at the garden before them, and especially at "the Rose in which the Word of God became/ flesh," who descends with the saints to appear to the

23 The entire journey of the *Paradiso*, from the Moon to the Fixed Stars, is an explication of what is given here in miniature, in the command, "*Guardaci ben!*" (*Purg*.30.73). In the spheres where the infused cardinal virtues preside, Dante draws attention in particular to Beatrice's eyes: *Par*.10.61-63 (Sun), 14.127-139 (Mars), 18.7-21 (Jupiter), 21.1-24 (Saturn). Her smile raises him to the Primum Mobile (27.91-105).

24 The imagery of the garden, and the presence of Adam in the Fixed Stars, is telling. Dante spends six hours in the Earthly Paradise and six hours in the Fixed Stars, just as Adam spent six hours in Eden before the Fall (see Hollander comment to *Par*.26.139-142).

pilgrim (*Paradiso* 23.70-111).[25] For the rest of the poem, Beatrice gradually withdraws and Mary enters more into focus, until the Virgin, through the intercession of her troubadour Bernard, raises Dante to the vision of and union with the Trinity and the Incarnation. This refocusing of mediators characterizes the remainder of the poem. Faith, hope, and charity now found within him, the pilgrim has attained the fulness of human life in the sanctifying habit of the virtues, and is surrounded by the saints in triumph. What remains is to enter more deeply into that perfection, to become united to the conditions of possibility of transhumanization, until Dante, for a moment, is welcomed by the Rose into itself (*Paradiso* 30.52-54), passing from time to eternity (*Paradiso* 31.38), and finally is united in love with God as incarnational Trinity in an excess of the mind (*excessus mentis*) which simultaneously perfects and fulfills the mind or human personality.[26]

This gradual deepening of perfection into union is already underway in the Fixed Stars, when Dante is examined on faith, hope, and charity. Beatrice invites St. Peter to "test" Dante on his faith, not so that Peter would discover something new, but so that Dante can offer his praise along with all the others in this place (*Paradiso* 24.34-45; 24.112-114). The pilgrim is no longer asking the questions. He answers them from within himself, but always with the mediation of Beatrice. This is the first time in the *Paradiso* that Dante has actively participated in the spectacle of praise that he witnesses (*Paradiso* 24.55-56; 25.76-78). Dante compares the

---

25 This turning away from Beatrice repeats the movement at *Purg.*32.7-18. The parallel invites a comparison between the earthly dividedness of the Church Militant with the heavenly unity of the Church Triumphant. The promise that Beatrice bears and is, which cannot change, connects the two scenes.

26 The concluding vision of God in the *Divine Comedy* is complex both in itself and, following the letter to Cangrande, as allegory for bliss in this life. The breaking off of poetry and the incapacity of memory in this latter sense become allegorical for the limits of what is comprehensible or fully knowable in this life: namely, the mysteries of the Trinity, Incarnation, and predestined, eternal, redeemed life in God.

presence of the theological virtues within him to seeds and sparks, since they are the sanctifying gifts of grace. He has nurtured them such that now he is said to be all aflame or blossoming with them (*Paradiso* 24.145-147; 25.46-48). He participates the harvest represented in the Fixed Stars.

The celestial hierarchy of the Primum Mobile is a principle and ground for the journey thus far: "These orders all direct—ecstatically—/ their eyes on high; and downward, they exert/ such force that all are drawn and draw to God" (*Paradiso* 28.127-129). In these cantos, the limitations of human knowing and activity are brought out repeatedly. Even Beatrice's beauty displays more of God's joy than something recognizably human (*Paradiso* 27.104-106).

The passage through the Primum Mobile is framed by the "mad course" of Ulysses' wanderings and the excessive subtleties and digressions of the schools (*Paradiso* 27.76-84; 29.70-129). These wayward linear trajectories are juxtaposed with the inclusive circularity of angelic life. The structure of the visible cosmos, glimpsed from the angelic perspective, appears to be turned inside out. God is no longer imagined to be outside the order but is known as the infinite centre around whom the angels move. Against the overdetermined speculations of the schoolmen, Beatrice states that the angels have no need of memory, since they see everything in a single present moment in the face of God (*Paradiso* 29.76-81). Therefore, degrees of penetration or vision into the actuality of God give rise to degrees of active love and movement. This vision of angelic life provides the final instruction necessary to prepare Dante for the passage from images to reality. This encounter with a perfectly ordered diversity in unity, in which each rank of the hierarchy enters with vision and love into principle of the order, is the closest approximation to the Rose thus far. Each stage of the ascent has been a more concrete realization of the principles articulated by Piccarda (*Paradiso* 3.70-90) and Beatrice in the Heaven of the Moon:

> But all those souls grace the Empyrean;
> and each of them has gentle life–though some
> sense the Eternal Spirit more, some less.
> They showed themselves to you here not because
> this is there sphere, but as a sign for you
> that in the Empyrean their place is lowest.
> Such signs are suited to your mind, since from
> the senses only can it apprehend
> what then becomes fit for the intellect.
> (*Paradiso* 4.34-42)

As Dante's mind is corrected and instructed by Beatrice, it becomes more adequate to this reality. The final and most crucial element of that instruction is the encounter with the inclusive, eternal, circular vision of the angels, whose sense of their own limits and their longing made them fit to receive the Good (*Paradiso* 29.57-66).

The passage from image to reality is accomplished in Canto XXX, and the pilgrim's entry into the Empyrean Rose is described in Pauline terms.[27] It is anticipated in the poet's final attempt to describe Beatrice's appearance: "The loveliness I saw surpassed

27 At first, he is compelled to look at Beatrice by "seeing nothing" (*Par.*30.13-15). This, alongside the light encircling him as he enters the Empyrean (*Par.*30.49: *circunfulse*), makes it clear that Dante has in mind Acts 9:8-9 ("Surrexit autem Saulus de terra, *apertisque oculis nihil videbat.* Ad manus autem illum trahentes, introduxerunt Damascum. Et erat ibi tribus diebus non videns, et non manducavit, neque bibit." ["And Saul arose from the Earth; and when his eyes were opened, he saw no man: but they led him by the hand, and brought him into Damascus. And he was three days without sight, and neither did eat nor drink."]) and 22:6 ("Factum est autem, eunte me, et appropinquante Damasco media die, subito de caelo *circumfulsit* me lux copiosa." ["And it came to pass, that, as I made my journey, and was come nigh unto Damascus about noon, suddenly there shone from heaven a great light round about me."]) Dante would perhaps connect this episode with the rapture into the third heaven described in 2 Cor. 12:2.

not only/ our human measure—and I think that, surely,/ only its Maker can enjoy it fully." The reality of her "sweet smile," still retained in memory, is beyond his poetic powers (*Paradiso* 30.19-27). The refocusing and expansion of mediators is being accomplished here, as Dante lets Beatrice go, since she has brought him to see her place within the larger order that grounds and sustains her, to know her as she is known. As was signaled in the Fixed Stars, the remainder of the journey consists in becoming united with the light grounding the heavenly City.

The final stage of the initiation, the final likeness before the reversal of the Empyrean is accomplished, is a tribute to Vergil:[28]

> And I saw light that took a river's form—
> light flashing, reddish-gold, between two banks
> painted with wonderful spring flowerings.
> Out of that stream there issued living sparks,
> which settled on the flowers on all sides,
> like rubies set in gold; and then, as if
> intoxicated with the odors, they
> again plunged into the amazing flood:
> as one spark sank, another spark emerged.
> (*Paradiso* 30.61-69)

The passage from perfection to deification or union is accomplished as Dante's eyes "drink" of that river. Immediately everything is transformed: the field of flowers becomes one flower with the source of light at its centre. In a sense, each flower on the riverside has expanded to become the whole:

---

28 Hollander (comment to *Par.*30.64-66) notes the echo of the Elysian Fields in *Aeneid* VI.703-709. Just as the ancient sages dreamt of the Earthly Paradise in their visions of the Golden Age, so here those visions are "shadowy prefaces" of the truth of Heaven.

But as my eyelids' eaves drank of that wave,
  it seemed to me that it had changed its shape:
  no longer straight, that flow now formed a round.
Then, just as maskers, when they set aside
  the borrowed likeness in which they hide,
  seem to be other than they were before,
So were the flowers and the sparks transformed.
(*Paradiso* 30.88-94)

This is the central pivot point of the *Paradiso*. The simile of the masque carries the Pauline imagery to its completion; the realities themselves are the faces of intellectual beings. With his powers elevated by the light of glory, the pilgrim sees the dual ranks of angels and the saints, the latter emphatically with the same concreteness they will display on Judgement Day (*Paradiso* 30.43-45).

The poet can only rhyme the verb "I saw" (*vidi*) with itself (*Paradiso* 30.95-99) because this seeing inherently defies comparison. The most important element in this account of the transformation through the light of glory is the shift from the linearity of the simile—a river passing between banks, with only the angelic "sparks" in cyclical motion—to the circularity of the reality in itself (*Paradiso* 30.103-120). His vision was linear; it has become circular. Linear vision is inherently exclusive, passing from one thing to the next. Circular vision, however, includes a diversity of individuals in its gaze: "Within that breadth and height I did not find/ my vision gone astray, for it took in/ that joy in all its quality and kind" (*Paradiso* 30.118-120). He sees every face in the Rose as vividly as if it were immediately present before him (*Paradiso* 30.121-123; 31.19-27). At times he observes how each face looks toward the single source of light (*Paradiso* 31.27) and, at others, how certain individuals gaze at another across the Rose, as Anna looks to Mary and "does not move her eyes" (*Paradiso* 32.133-135).

This apparent contradiction is in fact a deliberate paradox. Dante is describing what the world looks like from the standpoint of charity. To look into the light is to embrace other individuals in their particularity: "There I saw faces given up to love—/ graced with Another's light and their own smile—/ and movements graced with every dignity" (*Paradiso* 31.49-51).

The centrality of face-to-face vision is reinforced when Dante turns in wonder to ask Beatrice about what he sees. She has left his side to return to her place in the Rose. Bernard of Clairvaux, with "gracious gladness" filling his face, stands in her place. After Dante's extraordinary parting request to Beatrice, "guard your magnificence in me," to which we will return, Bernard introduces himself. The pilgrim's reaction confirms the essential motif of the Empyrean:

> Just as one
> who, from Croatia perhaps, has come
> to visit our Veronica—one whose
> old hunger is not sated, who, as long
> as it is shown, repeats these words in thought:
> "O my Lord Jesus Christ, true God, was then
> Your image like the image I see now?"—
> such was I as I watched the living love
> of him who, in this world, in contemplation,
> tasted that peace.
> (*Paradiso* 31.102-111)

The sight of the Veronica, the "true icon" (*vera eikon*), was a site of pilgrimage. What is most striking is that Dante uses this simile of the Veronica to describe his reaction to seeing Bernard's face. The face of Jesus the God-man and the face of the saint are brought together more explicitly than before, from the astonishing entrance of Beatrice in the chariot pulled by the Griffon to the identification of her appearance with Paradise in the Fixed Stars.

The final mediator, the condition and ground, before the total coincidence of human and divine is the Virgin Mary. She is the measure and mediator of Christ to the City and, with John the Baptist opposite her, makes the seating plan of the Rose intelligible. Bernard describes her in terms of her resemblance to Christ: "Look now upon the face that is most like/ the face of Christ, for only through its brightness/ can you prepare for your vision to see Him" (*Paradiso* 32.85-87). The desire that Benedict had identified in Dante is now to be fulfilled, but only after Bernard beseeches Mary to raise Dante to that final end, to "disperse/ all of the clouds of his morality" in order to enjoy, for a moment, a vision beyond the limits of speech and memory (*Paradiso* 33.22-57).

The vision is beyond memory because it is beyond the capacities of the human mind, at least of this life (*Paradiso* 1.7-9).[29] Dante can only recall the vision when divine grace assists him in pursuing the traces of the joy that are the imprint and proof of the experience (*Paradiso* 33.55-75). He joins his gaze (*l'aspetto mio*) to the Infinite Good, and sees the entire universe brought together like a book, "bound by love into one single volume," upheld in the creative divine light (*Paradiso* 33.86). Suspended in a state of attentive wonder, his mind is strengthened more and more as it gazes into that light, so that a vision of the divine unity passes into the Trinity (*Paradiso* 33.109-123). And then his vision rises even higher, to its final end:

29 Dante writes in his letter to Cangrande: "To understand this, know that the human intellect, when it is exalted in this life, because of its being co-natural and having affinity with some separate intellectual substance, is so far exalted that after its return memory fails it, because it has transcended the measure of humanity" ("Letter to Cangrande della Scala," trans. A. Esolen, *Paradise* [New York: Modern Library, 2007], Appendix A, 370).

That circle—which, begotten so, appeared
in You as light reflected—when my eyes
had watched it with attention for some time,
within itself and colored like itself,
to me seemed painted with our effigy,
so that my sight was set on it completely.
(*Paradiso* 33.127–132)

The human form appears within the divine, but the mind is entirely overcome as it tries to fathom *how* the human face finds its place within the divine circle.

As the geometer intently seeks
to square the circle, but he cannot reach,
through thought on thought, the principle he needs,
so I searched that strange sight: I wished to see
the way in which our human effigy
suited the circle and found place in it—
and my own wings were far too weak for that.
(*Paradiso* 33.133–139)

His intellect fails, but in that very failing, he is given the fulfillment of his desire.

But then my mind was struck by light that flashed
and, with this light, received what it had asked.
Here force failed my high fantasy; but my
desire and will were moved already—like
a wheel revolving uniformly—by
the Love that moves the sun and the other stars.
(*Paradiso* 33.140–145)

The unity of human and divine is somehow known, in a moment of sheer receptivity, in which Dante finds himself already responding actively under God's impulse: "my/ desire and will were moved already." Love brings him into that unity of the divine and human; he is moved with the same love that moves the sun and the other stars which, in other words, means that his love has expanded to the inclusive circularity that characterizes the heavenly City. The culmination of Dante's poem is the contemplation and the activity of the divine-human: an adoration or *admiratio* that is at once active and contemplative and so unites the division of Leah and Rachel, the practical and the theoretical.

All of this, as Dante tells us in an early work, arises out of his desire to honour Beatrice:

> There came to me a miraculous vision in which I saw things that made me resolve to say no more about this blessèd one until I would be capable of writing about her in a nobler way.
>
> To achieve this I am striving as hard as I can, and this she truly knows. Accordingly, if it be the pleasure of Him through whom all things live that my life continue for a few more years, I hope to write of her that which has never been written of any other woman.
>
> (*Vita nuova*, XLII.1-2, trans. Musa)

The *Divine Comedy* fulfills this project because it sets out to include all possible forms of love. For Dante, these are ultimately all the ways that the divine-human can be despaired of (Limbo), betrayed (Judas), sought for (Purgatory) and enjoyed (Paradise). In other words, in the revelation that was Beatrice, the God-bearing image, all potentialities of human love are somehow contained. The conclusion of the poem, with its admiration and wonder at the possibility of a divine-human union is a return to the beginning and to the love that first spoke to him.

For Dante, the *Comedy* aims to lead readers from a state of misery to a state of bliss, in this life. At the beginning of the *Paradiso*, the poet promises the dedicated reader a wonder like that experienced by Jason's companions (*s'ammiraron*) when he, with the assistance of Medea's magic, tamed fire-breathing oxen (*Paradiso* 2.10-18). Indeed, with Neptune's marveling at the *Argo* (*ammirar*), the final classical reference in the poem (*Paradiso* 33.93-96), it could be said that the reader is invited to marvel at the fulfillment of the journey, the arrival of Dante's "little bark" to the home of the God of the sea of being (*Paradiso* 1.112-114) and, in so doing, is pursuing the traces of joy in the spirit of hope that animates the *Comedy* from beginning to end. Therefore, the bliss in this life promised by the poet comes down to a renewed hope or, as Dr. Curran has maintained in his lectures on the *Comedy*, to following the pilgrim from cowardice to becoming magnanimous, generous, great-souled enough to carry on. This is all captured in Dante's final words to Beatrice, after she resumes her place in the Rose, which show him to be the new Jason that avoids the offence against Medea:

"O lady, you in whom my hope gains strength,
    you who, for my salvation, have allowed
    your footsteps to be left in Hell, in all
the things that I have seen, I recognize
    the grace and benefit that I, depending
    upon your power and goodness, have received.
You drew me out from slavery to freedom
    by all those paths, by all those means that were
    within your power. Do, in me, preserve
your generosity [*magnificenza*], so that my soul,
    which you have healed, when it is set loose from
    my body, be a soul that you will welcome."
(*Paradiso* 31.79-90)

As Beatrice herself says of Dante, there is no child of the Church Militant so filled with hope; therefore he has been granted a vision of the heavenly Jerusalem before the time of his warring ends (*Paradiso* 25.52–57). Indeed, as with Augustine's *Confessions*, the restlessness of the heart has been transformed into its pilgrimage. All of earthly life is now seen under the banner of a journey to or from the heavenly City, where all earthly divisions are brought into concord and the fragments gathered up.

HANS-GÜNTHER SCHWARZ

"Art only begins where Imitation ends"
Oscar Wilde on Art

Oscar Wilde's pronouncement in *De Profundis*[1] might be seen as another paradoxical remark among many. It runs counter to the Aristotelian concept of "mimesis," normally translated as "imitation." We speak of the imitative arts and consider imitation as the basis of all artistic activity. By making imitation the cornerstone of art we confirm the experience of reality as the core of our existence.

In contrast to Western art, the "symbolic arts of the East," as Hegel calls them, do not depict anything existing in reality. They do not fulfill the Aristotelian notion of verisimilitude. Yet the oriental arts, especially the carpets, became the inspiration of modern painting (Cézanne, Van Gogh, Matisse)[2] and literature. Oriental art does not concentrate on the fate of man, his actions or his character and the circumstances of his existence. It offers an abstract concept of order expressed by pattern and colour. There is no connection to anything verifiable in nature. The flowers it depicts are otherworldly, abstract and defy identification. They follow an ornamental logic that is older than any of the imitative arts of the West.

Anti-imitative Oriental art was the great inspiration for Oscar Wilde. Of equal importance were the German Romantics at the threshold of the 19th century. They provided Wilde with a theory that rejected imitation and saw the East as the alternative to Western thinking. The anti-imitative movement which began around 1798 in Germany spread all over Europe in the second half of the 19th century. Its origin can be traced to the meeting of three students at the University of Jena, Novalis (Friedrich von Hardenberg), Ludwig Tieck and Friedrich Schlegel. They became the founders of German Romanticism, a movement quite different from its English namesake. German Romanticism did away with all representational restrictions and laid the foundations for modern art and literature. These are regarded as anti-imitative and symbolic. Romanticism claimed the East as its inspiration.[3] Novalis, in his novel *Heinrich von Ofterdingen* (1801), has merchants ("Kaufleute") discuss art in the presence of young Heinrich. His curiosity about poets instigates a broad discussion about the arts. The differences between poets ("Dichter"), painters ("Maler") and creators of music ("Tonkünstler")[4], are fundamental. Music and painting can be more easily understood than poetry ("lassen sich weit eher begreifen" (26). There are no secrets to how they work, and with industry and patience both can be mastered ("Bei Malern und Tonkünstlern kann man leicht einsehen, wie es zugeht, und mit Fleiß und Geduld läßt sich beides lernen" (26)). The sounds produced by music have their origin in the instruments, the "Saiten," the chords being touched.

Painting benefits from nature as the most magnificent of all teachers ("die herrlichste Lehrmeisterin" (26)). The beauty of nature makes its imitation by the artist irresistible: "so mag uns auch die künstliche Nachahmung der Natur gefallen" (26). The imitation of nature by art is not the realism advocated by Lenz and the young Goethe during the Sturm und Drang period 30 years earlier. As was the case with Greek painting the artist selects the most beautiful elements of an object and combines those into an ideal painting: "das Angenehme und Liebliche von den Dingen absondert" (26). Thus the beauty of art is ensured. Life and art stay separate.

Both music and painting rely on an external impetus. For the Romantics poetry is quite different: "Dagegen ist von der Dichtkunst sonst nirgends äußerlich etwas anzutreffen" (26). There is no connection to the outer world: "Es ist alles innerlich" (27). In contrast to music and painting no instruments or hands are needed to create poetry: "Auch schafft sie nichts mit Werkzeugen und Händen" (26). Poetry is independent of the senses: "das Auge und das Ohr vernehmen nichts davon." It is a secret art; it is not its primary intention nor intended effect that words can be heard or things seen. Musicians and painters fill the senses with pleasant sentiments ("die äußeren Sinne mit angenehmen Empfindungen erfüllen"), the poet fills the inner sanctum of our soul ("das inwendige Heiligtum des Gemüts") with new, wonderful and agreeable thoughts ("mit neuen, wunderbaren und gefälligen Gedanken"). Wordsworth's famous definition of poetry as "emotions recollected in tranquility" is challenged by the German notion of poetry as a vehicle of thought. Poetry is the result of thought and provokes thought.

The Romantic notion of "Gemüt" is taken over by French Symbolists as "état de l'âme." The "Gemüt" is responsible for the creation and reception of poetry. From the Greeks to the Romantics, from the "eikos" to the realism of 18th century drama the congruence with a given reality (homoiosis, verisimilitude) was the touchstone of the art work. The Romantic poet, however, creates non-existing and unreal worlds: "gibt uns durch Worte eine unbekannte herrliche Welt zu vernehmen." This world of art cannot be verified by the senses or experience. It is "that beautiful unreal world of Art" (Wilde 909) which Oscar Wilde has made the aim of his work.

Oscar Wilde had encountered the ideas of Novalis in lectures by Walter Pater at Oxford. We can also assume that he had read Carlyle's essay on Novalis which was translated by Théodore de Banville and appeared in the *Revue de Deux Mondes*. This translation laid the foundation for the Novalis cult in France and the movement of Symbolism. In consonance with this movement Wilde states in *De Profundis* "Art is a symbol, because man is a symbol" (Wilde 922).

Walter Pater, in his Winckelmann essay, distinguishes Greek sculpture ("That is in no sense a symbol, a suggestion, of anything beyond its own victorious fairness," Pater 199)[5] from the symbolic arts of the East. He follows Hegel's fundamental distinction between the early arts of the Orient and Greek sculpture. The latter plays no role in Wilde's ruminations on art; the Orient does. Walter Pater's description, "In oriental thought there is a vague conception of life everywhere …," is contrasted with the Greek "lordship of the soul" (Pater 200). The Greek soul is in balance with idea and form, the spiritual and the visible world. This balance is missing in the Orient. It is not interested in the senses, what they perceive and verify. Oriental art is purely symbolic. Its meaning attests to an invisible world beyond the senses. Wilde combines Orient and Occident. Spirit and eye are of equal importance to him.

Wilde's assertion, "Like Gautier I have always been one of those *pour qui le monde visible existe*" (955), is counterbalanced by, "there is some Spirit hidden of which the painted forms and shapes are but modes of manifestation, and it is with this Spirit that I desire to become in harmony" (955). The spirit is invisible, only the visible world can be imitated. German Romanticism discovers the spirit ("Geist"), finds it in the Orient ("Im Orient müssen wir das höchste Romantische suchen" (F. Schlegel)). Geist is the manifestation of the "Inneres." It combines thought and imagination with the "Gemüt."

The search for the invisible spirit, the inner substance, the essence Wilde calls "The Mystical in Art, the Mystical in Life, the Mystical in Nature—this is what I am looking for …" (955). This cohesive, unifying view of Life, Art and Nature is reached in *De Profundis*.

Earlier writings by Wilde posit a contrast between art and nature, mind and nature. This contrast is evident in *The Decay of Lying*. Art is superior to nature: "Art is our spirited protest, our gallant attempt to teach Nature her proper place" (970). When it comes to "the infinite variety of Nature," "It is not to be found in Nature herself. It resides in the imagination, or fancy, or cultivated blindness of man who looks at her" (970). The cultivated blindness is one of the key elements of German Romanticism. The main character of Jean Paul's novel *Der Titan* covers his eyes before encountering the natural beauties of the *isola bella*. His imaginative powers create a more beautiful world than nature ever will. Man's imaginative powers no longer need nature as their guide thus provoking nature's reaction: "Nothing is more evident than that Nature hates Mind" (971). The imaginative power is the mark of the artist. He never imitates, he creates. Wilde's anti-realism becomes clear when he writes about Balzac: "But Balzac is no more realist than Holbein was. He created life, he did not copy it" (976). The interdiction of copying defines modern painting.[6] Wilde distinguishes between a naturalist novel, like Zola's *L'Assommoir*, and Balzac's *Illusions perdues*. The latter is more symbolic than naturalistic.

Friedrich Schlegel's notion that art has to be the most artificial of all artworks ("das künstlichste aller Kunstwerke") is enlarged by Wilde: "The only real people are the people who never existed, and if a poet is base enough to go to life for his personages he should at least pretend they are creations, and not boast of them as copies" (975). The copying of life, its realistic rendition in art, imitation as the principle of Western Art, is a deviation from its beginnings. Art in the East as in the West, e.g. the Book of Kells, had no connection with existing reality: "Art begins with abstract decoration, with purely imaginative and pleasurable work dealing with what is unreal and non-existent" (978). Art began with ornamental patterns; it knew no depiction of reality.

Wilde distinguishes between art as an "imaginative medium" (979) and art "using life as an artistic method" (979). The latter is introduced by Elizabethan and Jacobean artists. He refers to passages in Shakespeare as "language uncouth." These "are entirely due to Life calling for an echo of her own voice and rejecting the intervention of beautiful style through which alone should life be suffered to find expression" (979). Beautiful style is the true expression of art: it transcends the effects of life, it obliterates imitation. The things shown in drama "are taken directly from life and reproduce its vulgarity down to the smallest detail ..." (979). The differentiation between imitation and style in art was first made by Goethe in his essay *Einfache Nachahmung, Manier, Stil.*

Wilde sees the antinomy between life and art as a characteristic of Western art. It is particularly noticeable in the history of decorative arts: "The whole history of these arts in Europe is the record of the struggle between Orientalism, with its frank rejection of imitation, its love of artistic convention, its dislike to the actual representation of any object in Nature, and our own imitative spirit" (979). The latter always turns to life for inspiration. As a consequence the West does not create "beautiful and imaginative work in which the visible things of life are transmuted into artistic conventions, and the things that Life has not invented and fashioned for her delight" (979). Oriental art knows no imitation. We should follow its course: " But whenever we have returned to

Life and Nature, our work has always become vulgar, common and uninteresting" (979).

Realism has been the foundation of Western art since the Greeks. Art historians (but not literary historians) call the phenomenon "Naturalism" and see Greek sculpture as its first and most perfect appearance. The Aristotelian "mimesis" is often translated as "imitation," although modern interpretations prefer "presentation." Both translations imply the conformity with something which a human being may encounter. The Greeks called it "homoiosis," the Romans "verisimilitudo." As verisimilitude (German "Wahrscheinlichkeit") it defined French Classicism. German Romanticism breaks with the idea of existence as a prerequisite for art. Its model is the oriental fairy tale and its purely imaginative world. German examples are Novalis' *Heinrich von Ofterdingen* and E.T.A. Hoffmann's *Prinzessin Brambilla*. Both give a poetics of literary art based on the unreal and non-existent.[7] The latter was enjoyed by Baudelaire as the bible of modern aesthetics. Familiar with *Mille et une nuits* and convinced of the superiority of Art to Life, Oscar Wilde states, "As a method, realism is a complete failure" (979).

Wilde is fully aware that he contradicts Shakespeare's much quoted passage in *Hamlet* that "Art holds the mirror up to Nature." (981). This is taken as proof that art has an imitative, realistic basis. Wilde interprets this passage differently. These words, he maintains, are "deliberately said by Hamlet in order to convince the bystanders of his absolute insanity in all art-matters" (981). Wilde does not see Nature, "the world around us" (J.M.R. Lenz) as an inspiration for art: "Art finds her own perfection within, and not outside of, herself. She is not to be judged by any external standard of resemblance. She has flowers that no forests know of, birds that no woodland possesses" (982). Neither "homoiosis" nor "verisimilitude," as traditional aesthetics believe, motivate art; it has no mimetic function: "The highest art rejects the burden of the human spirit. She develops purely on her own lines. She is not symbolic of any age. It is the ages that are her symbols" (987). Art is not a transformation of what the eye sees or what the human mind thinks or worries about. It is unaffected by Life, is independent of it. It does not accept the constrictions of age, time and place. Art is as A.E. Poe says in his poem *Dreamland*: "Out of Space, Out of Time." It is not the expression or symbol of anything. As Heidegger states in the *Ursprung des Kunstwerkes*, art is characterised by its initiating role, the Ursprung. Therefore it is "Stiftung des Seyns" (95),[8] the very foundation of what is. As "real" art ("wirkliche Kunst"), it is never an imitation but a beginning.

In the dialogue, Cyril makes a last stand for the "arts of imitation": "for the visible aspect of an age, for its look, as the phrase goes, we must of course go to the arts of imitation" (988). Cyril poses an argument that had already been refuted: "Even those who hold that Art is representative of time and place and people cannot help admitting that the more imitative an art is the less it represents to us the spirit of its age" (987). Art is by definition distinct from Nature and Life. As Wilde points out: "No great artist ever sees things as they really are. If he did he would cease to be an artist" (988). The Western realist tradition is not the model for Wilde. The Oriental carpet and Japanese art are his inspirations. Both show an imaginative manner of vision and are independent of existing realities. Their study leads modern Western art to the adoption of anti-imitative methods in painting. "Surface, ligne, couleur" instead of Western three dimensionality and perspective became the ideal for painters like Cézanne, Van Gogh, Matisse etc. Earlier on Japanese painters Hiroshige and Hokusai had confirmed by their practice that imagination was the essence of painting. Wilde had absorbed the tendencies of Symbolism, its German Romantic basis, and was aware of the new tendencies in art.

His essay *The Critic as Artist* is the most anti-imitative of the works we have studied so far. Gilbert, one of the characters in the dialogue, affirms that criticism, a work of art, "is no more to be judged by any low standard of imitation or resemblance than is the work of poet or sculptor" (1026). The classicist concept of "verisimilitude," based on Aristotle's *Poetics*, and its general nature are here not distinguished from the particular, individualistic and characteristic observation of realism. Both are for Wilde "that cowardly concession to the tedious repetitions of domestic or public life" (1027). Art and criticism are "never trammelled by any shackles of verisimilitude. No ignoble considerations of probability" (1027). Both are dethroned by Beauty: "Beauty is the symbol of symbols" (1030).

The connection of beauty and symbol takes beauty out of the realm of the senses. Appropriately the discussion started with "Homer's blindness" (1017). Beauty is created by the artist "seeing less with the eyes of the body than he does with the eyes of the soul" (1017). The inward, as the German Romantics demanded, has replaced the outward. Their achievement was "striving to render, by visible form or colour, the marvel of what is invisible, the splendour of what is not seen" (1031). Instead of imitative art the German Romantics created symbolic art and thus laid the foundation for modern art.[9] Wilde is conscious of the problems caused by this shift from art which reflects common experience and perception to art which needs interpretation: "their imaginative beauty make all interpretations true; and no interpretation final" (1031). Wilde chooses the Oriental carpet to illustrate the difference between imitative and symbolic art: "Just as on the flowerless carpets of Persia, tulip and rose blossom indeed and are lovely to look on, though they are not reproduced in visible shape or line, [...] so the critic reproduces the work that he criticises in a mode that is never imitative, and part of whose charm may really consist in the rejection of resemblance ..." (1032). The "flowerless carpets of Persia" realize the aim of modern art. They are not copies of nature but suggest, "suggerer, déréaliser, déformer, produire" being the tenets of Symbolism. As Lord Hallward in *The Picture of Dorian Gray* states: "I should like to write a novel certainly; a novel that would be as lovely as a Persian carpet and as unreal" (Wilde, 45).

Artists "who merely paint what they see" (1051) miss out on the ornamental world of the East, "the imaginative beauty of design and the loveliness of fair colour" (1051). The abstract patterns of the Orient anticipate "surface, ligne, couleur," the ideals of modern painting: "Mere colour unspoiled by meaning, and unallied with definite form, can speak to the soul in a thousand different ways. The repetitions of patterns give us rest" (1051). Ornament is the ideal art: "By its deliberate rejection of Nature as the ideal of beauty, as well as the imitative method of the ordinary painter" (1052).

I should like to thank my friend Dr. Norman Diffey, Windsor, for his painstaking scrutiny of the text.

Notes

1 Oscar Wilde, *Complete Works*, intr. Vyvyan Holland, London, Glasgow: Collins, 1967, p. 936.

2 Hans-Günther Schwarz, *Der Orient und die Ästhetik der Moderne*, München: judicium, 2003, pp. 249-268.

3 Friedrich Schlegel, *Rede über die neue Mythologie, in: Athenaeum II*, ed. Curt Grützmacher, Hamburg: Rowohlt, 1969. "Im Orient müssen wir das höchste Romantische suchen" (We have to search for the highest form of Romanticism in the Orient) p. 179.

4 Novalis, *Heinrich von Ofterdingen*, ed. Wolfgang Frühwald, Stuttgart: Reclam 1987, p. 26.

5 Walter Pater, *The Renaissance*, London: Collins, 1967.

6 Maurice Denis, *Pour l'art français* (1916). "Ce qu'il y avait de nouveau et de caractéristique dans le système symboliste, c'était de tout refuser à l'objectivité. Nous renonçions au réel."

7 Novalis in his *Kunstgespräch der Kaufleute*, p. 26 ff. of his novel, and E.T.A. Hoffmann at the beginning of chapters 2 and 4.

8 Martin Heidegger, *Der Ursprung des Kunstwerkes*, Frankfurt: Klostermann, 2012.9

9. This shift was illustrated by the exhibition *Unwirklichkeiten. Das Imaginative von Caspar David Friedrich bis Picasso* initiated and co-curated by the author. Catalogue with the same title published by Wunderhorn, Heidelberg, 2018.

PASSION

MARTIN CURRAN

Afterword

One of my most cherished memories of my father is a recitation he gave of Percy Bysshe Shelley's "To a Skylark". The event was the second annual Pythian Games event held at the Dalhousie department of Classics. My mother had participated the first year. My father didn't attend and later regretted his decision because she had had such a good time.

My mother passed away before the second time the Games were held. As a tribute to her, my father memorized "To a Skylark" and recited it perfectly the next year.

I'm not going to try to describe the event or discuss the poem itself; but it was, of course, very moving. For me, the moment captured a lot of the different themes that the essays in this volume discuss.

The memory sticks out for me I think because it is very emblematic of his approach. He does not always separate out the different categories of his work. The recitation, for example, ties into the themes Performance and Poetry obviously. But his deciding to learn it was a part of his larger interest in Habit and Repetition. Through Presence of mind and a kind of self-Pedagogy he made the learning and recitation of the poem a spiritual practice or exercise. He likes to operate on different levels at once and this comes through in his work. Anyone familiar with his Preaching would agree he is not interested in keeping his scholarly work, or his own interests, separate from his sermons.

Another "P" word that might have fit with themes of this book is "Passion." This is what binds the different areas of his life together. And it is a part of the reason he is so popular with his students. His lectures and tutorials are passionate both about the subject but, also, about his desire for the subject to be understood by the students. If he has ever recommended a book or movie or TV show or piece of music to you, you have experienced the same passion that is put into his scholarly and clerical work as well.

He brings passion to the things that he reads and writes and thinks about. He brings it to preaching and lecturing and reciting poems. His passions are not confined to one discreet area of his life. He finds a way to bring them together.

This collection of essays was a labour of love from its contributors and what could be more appropriate? Serious scholarly work paired with love. The two cannot be separated out.

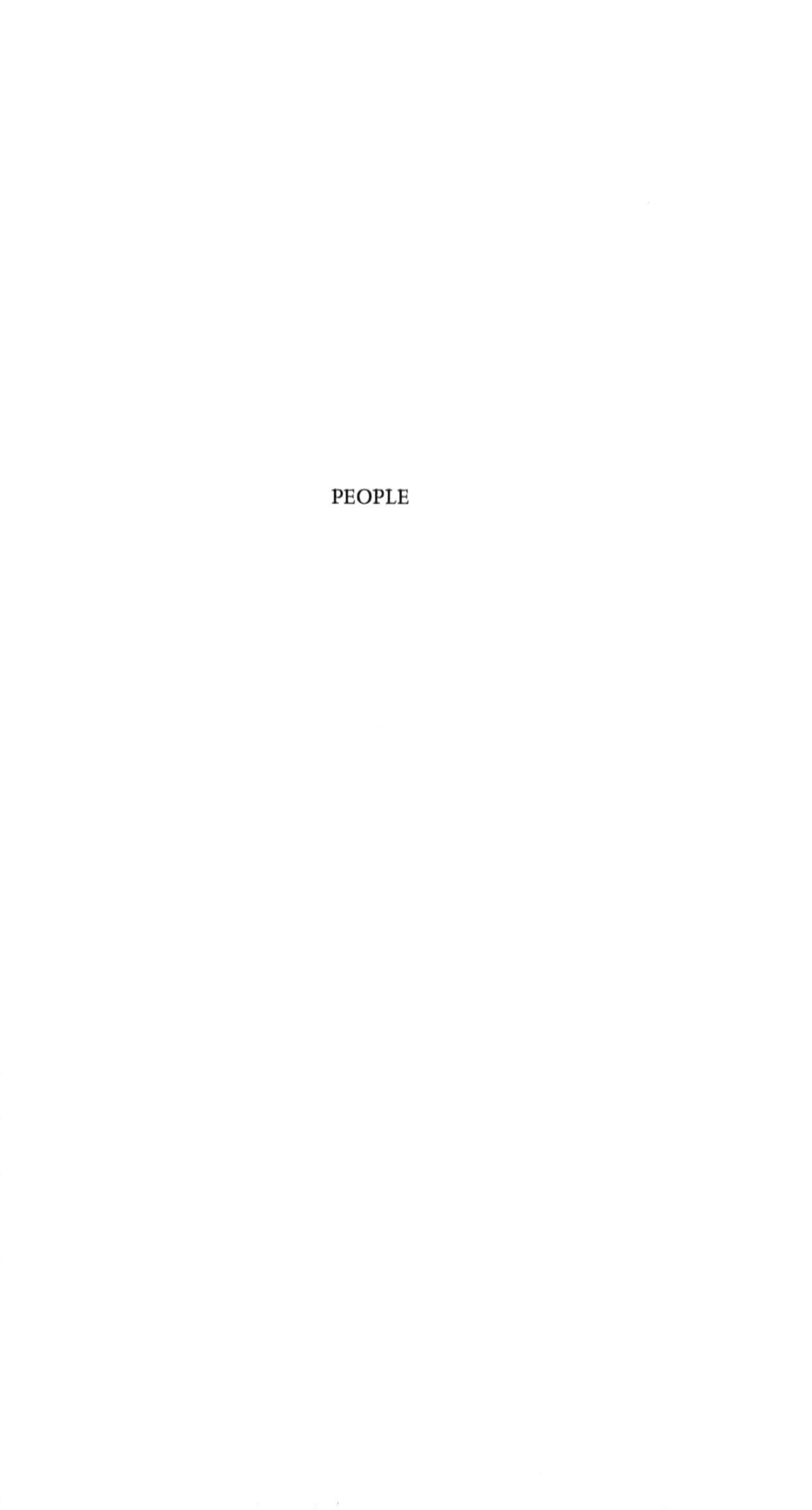

PEOPLE

Contributors

LAWRIN ARMSTRONG is a veteran of FYP (1976-77). He went on to complete a BA and MA in Classics at King's-Dalhousie, an MDiv at Trinity College, Toronto, and an MA and PhD in Medieval Studies at the University of Toronto. He was Associate Professor of History and Humanities at Simon Fraser University until 2002, and has just retired as Professor of Medieval Studies and History at the University of Toronto. He studies the history of economic ethics.

ROBERTA BARKER is Associate Professor of Theatre and Associate Dean Academic in the Faculty of Arts and Social Sciences at Dalhousie University. She is a member of the joint faculty at the University of King's College, where she has taught in the Foundation Year Program and the Early Modern Studies Program. Her research interests include early modern and modern drama, theatre history, gender studies, and medical humanities. She is also a working director of theatre and opera.

WILLIAM BARKER, Inglis Professor at King's and Emeritus Professor of English at Dalhousie and a scholar of Renaissance literature, has known Tom Curran for sixteen years.

Tom was WILL BARTON's main tutor in the FYP year 2009/2010. Will worked as Tom's student assistant for 3 years after that. Tom baptized Will in the King's Chapel in Epiphanytide 2012.

DANIEL BRANDES completed his doctorate at Northwestern University in Philosophy. His research focuses on political theory and modern Jewish thought. He has been teaching at King's since 2003, having served during that time as Director of FYP and Director of CSP. (Tom served, indispensably, as Associate Director during the stretch of his tenure as Director.) Daniel's current research is on a constellation of German-Jewish thinkers—Arendt, Scholem, and Benjamin—and he plans eventually to turn the essays published on these thinkers into a manuscript.

PETER BULLERWELL completed his BA at King's in 2009. He is currently a PhD candidate in Religious Studies at McGill. Peter's contribution marks his first attempt at creative writing in over a decade!

PETER BRYSON is a Justice of the Nova Scotia Court of Appeal and has been Tom's friend since they were Classics students together, 46 years ago.

STEVEN BURNS has Philosophy degrees from Acadia University, the University of Alberta, and the University of London. He taught in the Dalhousie Department of Philosophy and the King's Contemporary Studies Programme for a combined total of 44 years. He is now retired.

Since leaving Kings, JAMIE CARROLL (BA 2000) has worked at the highest levels of Canadian politics, advised the CEOs of Fortune 500 companies and started a number of his own businesses, all the while writing and speaking on issues of political interest. In other words, he has fulfilled the ambition of every FYP student and become a professional cocktail party guest.

GEORGE COOPER is a lawyer by profession, but with strong ties to King's. He has been a friend of Tom Curran for a quarter century, first through attendance at chapel, then as Chair of the King's Board, and finally as "Accidental President" from 2012–2016. He and Tom played together in the King's sandbox throughout, with Tom as Assistant Chaplain, Clerk of Convocation and Master of Ceremonies at Encaenia, Chair of Faculty—and finally as Teacher and Guide when George in retirement audited the Foundation Year Programme.

MARTIN CURRAN has an MA in Classics from Dalhousie University. He currently lives in British Columbia.

VERONICA CURRAN holds a B.A. Honours (2012) in German and Early Modern Studies from the University of King's College and an M.A. (2015) in German from Dalhousie University. She is currently a PhD Candidate at the Department of Germanic Languages & Literatures at the University of Toronto. Her research interest involves the development of German theatre. She is particularly interested in the *Sturm und Drang* period writers in the 1770s and the developments leading up to Georg Büchner's career in the 1830s. Within the area of theatre studies and German literature, she focuses on the development of discussions of morality and questions of genre, such as the classic distinctions of 'comedy' and 'tragedy'.

DAVID CURRY holds degrees in Classics and Theology from King's College, Dalhousie, Harvard, and Trinity College, Toronto and is currently the Chaplain, English and Theory of Knowledge Teacher at King's-Edgehill School, Windsor, and Rector of Christ Church, Windsor, NS.

SUSAN DODD is associate professor of humanities at the University of King's College.

STEVE DOWDEN teaches German language and European literature at Brandeis University in Waltham, Massachusetts. His main areas of research are modernism across the various arts—fiction, music, painting and poetry—and the novel as a form of consciousness.

ELIZABETH B. EDWARDS is jointly appointed to the Contemporary Studies and Foundation Year programs. She obtained her BA and MA degrees at Dalhousie University, and completed her PhD at Cambridge University in 1997. She has been teaching in in the Foundation Year Program since 1990, is a founding faculty member and past Director of the Contemporary Studies Program, and held the position of Vice President of the University from July 2001–June 2006. Dr. Edwards is appointed as adjunct Professor to the Dalhousie Department of English.

CHRISTOPHER ELSON is a King's Carnegie Professor of French and Canadian Studies in the Joint Faculty. He is currently Chair of the French Department. Forthcoming publications include no. 114 of *Dalhousie French Studies*: "Michel Deguy *Honoris Causa*" which includes papers from the May 2016 Study Day devoted to the work of the French writer and King's honorary doctorate recipient, including an essay from Thomas Curran.

WILL ENGLISH graduated in 2007 from King's with a BAH (EMSP/History). In the course of his time at King's he held several elected positions on campus including president of the KSU. At King's Will met his future wife Jennifer Adams (BJH 2008). In 2014 English completed a Master's in school counseling at Salem State University. Will lives in Beverly, Massachusetts with Jenn and two-year-old redhead Evan. Will is a school counselor currently working with 360 six graders.

ZACHARY FLORENCE (BAH 2005) is a theatre creator and producer.

CHRISTOPHE FRICKER did his M.A. in German at Dalhousie in 2002/03. He went on to do a doctorate at Oxford and a Post-doc at Duke before setting up a research and consultancy firm, which he has since sold. Christophe lives in Bristol and works as a discourse analyst. His latest book presents 111 reasons to love England. He could come up with just as many for Tom, and for Jane.

VICTORIA GODDARD (B.Humanities Carleton, M.A. and PhD. Toronto) is a former FYP Teaching Fellow and current novelist, cheesemonger, and gardener in Prince Edward Island. She owns Underhill Books, publisher of literary fantasy and occasional nonfiction. Her most recent novel is *The Hands of the Emperor* (Underhill Books, 2019).

RON HAFLIDSON is a faculty member in the great books program at St. John's College in Annapolis, Maryland and the author of *On Solitude, Conscience, Love and our Inner and Outer Lives* (Bloomsbury). He is a proud alumnus of King's and a former Teaching Fellow and Senior Fellow in FYP.

ALAN HALL was a student at King's in the mid-nineties and then again a tutor in Contemporary Studies, History of Science and FYP in the oughts. For the last decade or so he has been living in Fredericton NB and lecturing at St. Thomas University.

KARA HOLM was the Advancement Director at the University of King's College from 2004-2008. During her time at King's she became good friends with Tom Curran. She appreciates his carefully curated suggestions for books and articles; however, she finds his film and television recommendations mostly mystifying. Kara operates a technology start-up called TerraProForma built on a Tom Curran insight. She lives in Halifax with her daughter.

RANALL INGALLS is Chaplain at the University of King's College. Before moving to Halifax, he served a number of parishes in New Brunswick. For several years he taught in the Philosophy Department at St Thomas University in Fredericton. He is married to Sherry, who works at Halifax Grammar School as a Speech Language Pathologist. The Ingalls have three adult sons.

KIM KIERANS was a FYP student in 1979-80. She is a professor and former director of the School of Journalism, and former Vice-President of the University of King's College. She continues to be grateful to Tom for his friendship, and for continuing to ignite a love of learning at King's.

EVAN KING is a researcher in the ERC-funded project, "Neoplatonism and the Abrahamic Traditions," hosted at the School of Philosophy in University College Dublin. He graduated from the University of King's College in 2010 and taught in the Foundation Year Program from 2017 to 2019. Fr. Curran officiated at the wedding of Evan and Elizabeth, née Curry, at St. George's Round Church in 2013.

TORRANCE KIRBY, BA (Vind), DPhil (Oxon) is Professor of Ecclesiastical History and sometime Director of the Centre for Research on Religion, McGill University, Fellow of the Royal Historical Society, and life member of Corpus Christi College, Cambridge. He is author of *Richard Hooker, Reformer and Platonist* (2005).

SIMON KOW is an Associate Professor in the Early Modern Studies Program at the University of King's College, occasional FYP lecturer, and fellow film buff with Tom Curran.

WILLIAM LAHEY has been President and Vice-Chancellor at University of King's College since 2016; faculty member at the Schulich School of Law since 2001; Deputy Minister of Nova Scotia Department of Environment and Labour, 2004-2007; Chair of the Board of Directors of Efficiency NS since 2010. Public service highlights include the Environmental Goals and Sustainable Prosperity Act (2007) and the Independent Review of Forestry Practices in Nova Scotia (2018).

PETER MACLEOD (FYP 1997/98) is principal of MASS LBP and one of Canada's leading experts in deliberative democracy. He frequently writes about the citizen's experience of the state, the importance of public imagination and the future of responsible government.

GARTH MACPHEE is the Director of Music at St George's Round Church in Halifax. A graduate of the Schulich School of Music at McGill University (M.Mus 2006), Garth has been active as a church musician since the age of twelve. In addition to his work at the Round Church, he is the Resident Musician for the Anglican Formation Class at the Atlantic School of Theology. Garth is also the conductor of Seton Conservatory Choir at the Maritime Conservatory for the Performing Arts. His contribution, a gift of music, can be found at www.tomcurranfyp.com.

PETER O'BRIEN is Carnegie Assistant Professor of Classics at King's and Dalhousie. At King's he currently serves as Vice-President and Public Orator. The latter role brings him not infrequently into the world of Neo-Latin, which has become an area of research interest and publication, alongside Late Antique historiography and Latin poetry. He co-edits *Mouseion: a Journal of the Classical Association of Canada*. He is profoundly grateful for the warm friendship and support of Tom Curran for nearly two decades.

NEIL G. ROBERTSON is Associate Professor of the Humanities and Social Sciences at the University of King's College in Halifax, Canada and Director of its Foundation Year Program. He was also the founding Director of the Early Modern Studies Programme at King's. His publications include co-editing *Hegel and Canada* (2018), *Descartes and the Modern* (2008) and *Philosophy and Freedom: The Legacy of James Doull* (2003). He is currently writing an introductory volume on the thought and intellectual development of Leo Strauss.

HENRY ROPER is a retired professor of humanities, University of King's College, which awarded him an honorary D.Cn.L. in 2009. A fellow and former president of the Royal Nova Scotia Historical Society, he has published many articles and reviews, most recently biographies of Archbishop Clarendon Worrell and the Reverend Robert Norwood in volume 16 of the *Dictionary of Canadian Biography*. He is the co-editor of volumes 3 and 4 of *The Collected Works of George Grant* (University of Toronto Press, 2005 and 2009).

HANS-GÜNTHER SCHWARZ is a professor of German at Dalhousie University. He also has privileges at the University of Heidelberg where he is faculty member at the Institute of German as a Foreign Language Philology. Dr. Schwarz's research interests include: Art and Literature; the influence of Oriental Art and Literature on the West, and Ornament and Realism.

CHRISTOPHER SNOOK is a Senior Faculty Fellow in the Humanities at the University of King's College. A priest in the Anglican Church of Canada, he served parishes in Saskatchewan and Nova Scotia before returning to teaching.

ELISABETH STONES can't remember a time when she did not sing. While completing her undergraduate degree at the University of King's College she joined the King's Chapel Choir and the parish choir at St. George's Anglican Church, which inspired her to pursue interests in oratorio and chamber music. When she is not singing (and sometimes even when she is!), Elisabeth is usually knitting. Her contribution, a gift of music, can be found at www.tomcurranfyp.com.

GARY THORNE has a B.A. (Philosophy) from Acadia University and Aberdeen University, two Master's (Philosophy and Classics) from Dalhousie University, an M.Div. from the Atlantic School of Theology, and a Ph.D. (Theology) from Durham University. He has been ordained an Anglican priest for 38 years and in 2013 he retired as a reservist military chaplain after 23 years. He is married to Sandra with two adult children: Chelsea and Andrew.

ERIN WAGNER graduated from King's with a BA in English. She enjoys reading and writing poetry when she is not too busy caring for her two-year-old son. Erin has benefited greatly from Sunday mornings at the King's Chapel.

JERRY WHITE is Professor of English at the University of Saskatchewan. He was Canada Research Chair in European Studies at Dalhousie University from 2011–2019, which is how he came to know Tom Curran. His most recent book is *Stan Brakhage in Rolling Stock: 1980–1990* (Wilfrid Laurier University Press, 2018).

www.ingramcontent.com/pod-product-compliance
Lightning Source LLC
Chambersburg PA
CBHW030333310726
48979CB00001B/9

* 9 7 8 1 9 8 8 9 0 8 1 6 8 *